TASK DESIGN
An
Integrative Approach

The Scott, Foresman Series in Management and Organizations

Lyman W. Porter, Editor

Published:

Hall *Careers in Organizations*

Lawler / Rhode *Information and Control in Organizations*

Schneider *Staffing Organizations*

Steers *Organizational Effectiveness: A Behavioral View*

Stone *Research Methods in Organizational Behavior*

Baskin / Aronoff *Interpersonal Communication in Organizations*

Wexley / Latham *Developing and Training Human Resources in Organizations*

Carroll / Schneier *Performance Appraisal and Review Systems*

TASK DESIGN
An
Integrative Approach

Ricky W. Griffin
Texas A & M University

Scott, Foresman and Company
Glenview, Illinois
Dallas, Tex.   Oakland, N.J.   Palo Alto, Cal.   Tucker, Ga.   London, England

For Glenda,
Dustin, and Ashley

Library of Congress Cataloging in Publication Data

Griffin, Ricky W.
    Task design.

    (Scott, Foresman series in management and organiza-
tions)
    Bibliography: p. 228
    Includes indexes.
    1. Division of labor.   2. Work design.   3. Organiza-
tion.   I. Title.   II. Series.
HD51.G73   658.3′128   81–18316
ISBN 0–673–16544–2   AACR2

ISBN: 0–673–16544–2

THE SCOTT, FORESMAN SERIES IN MANAGEMENT AND ORGANIZATIONS

Copyright © 1982 Scott, Foresman and Company.

Printed in the United States of America.

1 2 3 4 5 6 7 8–KPF–88 87 86 85 84 83 82

CONTENTS

FOREWORD TO THE SERIES

The Scott, Foresman Series in Management and Organizations embodies concise and lively treatments of specific topics within the broad area indicated by the series title. These books are for supplemental reading in basic management, organizational behavior, or personnel courses in which the instructor highlights particular topics in the larger course. However, the books, either alone or in combination, can also form the nucleus for specialized courses that follow introductory courses.

Each book stresses the *key issues* relevant to the given topic. Thus, each author or set of authors has made a particular effort to "highlight figure from ground"—that is, to keep the major issues in the foreground and the small explanatory details in the background. These books are, by design, relatively brief treatments of their topic areas, so the authors have had to be carefully *selective* in what they have chosen to retain and to omit. Because the authors were chosen for their expertise and their judgment, the series provides valuable summary treatments of the subject areas.

In focusing on the major issues, the series' authors present a balanced content coverage. They have also aimed at breadth by the unified presentation of different types of material: major conceptual or theoretical approaches, interesting and critical empirical findings, and applications to "real life" management and organizational problems. Each author deals with this body of material, but the combination varies according to the subject matter. Thus, each book is distinctive in the particular way in which a topic is addressed.

A final word is in order about the audience for this series: Although the primary audience is the student, each book in the series concerns a topic of importance to the practicing manager. Managers and supervisors can rely on these books as authoritative summaries of the basic knowledge in each area covered by the series.

The topics included in the series to date have been chosen on the basis of their importance and relevance for those interested in management and organizations. As new appropriate topics emerge on the scene, additional books will be added. This is a dynamic series both in content and direction.

Lyman W. Porter
Series Editor

PREFACE

The topic of task design has emerged as a major area of interest to researchers and managers during the last several years. To a certain extent, many commonly heard phrases such as worker alienation, the blue-collar blues, quality of working life, and job enrichment are all related to task design. Further, innovative managerial approaches to task design such as job specialization and the assembly line have had significant (both positive and negative) consequences for contemporary American society. Perhaps of more immediate importance to most people are the simple facts that a large portion of us work and that the work we do is prescribed by someone else. This "prescription," as we shall see, is a basic component of task design. Therefore, everybody that works is directly influenced by one or more aspects of task design.

The approach taken here to the study of task design has a dual level of analysis. In the first five chapters, we focus on issues and topics central to a micro approach to task design. Specifically, we provide a historical overview and a summary of dominant theoretical frameworks for task design, a discussion of the consequences of properly designed tasks, and a description of major approaches to task measurement. In the remaining chapters, a more macro approach is taken. The emphasis here is on integrating task design processes with other major organizational systems such as technology, organization design, leader behavior, and group and social processes.

The book is aimed at two audiences. First, the student reader. The book can be used as a supplement in advanced undergraduate and graduate courses in organizational behavior, organization theory, industrial/organizational psychology, management, administration, and so forth. The integrative chapters, in particular, should blend well with most textbooks appropriate for such courses. The book could also be used in topics courses such as those found in many MBA programs.

The second audience, and one no less important, consists of practicing managers. Throughout the book, theory is related to practice and concept to reality. We have tried to go beyond the "why" of task design and describe the "how" of task design. Chapter 10, especially, should prove useful to the manager.

As in all projects such as this, a debt is owed to many individuals. Andrew Szilagyi introduced me to the topic of task design and, as my advisor, designed my task so as to afford me ample opportunity to satisfy my intellectual curiosity. At the University of Missouri, Columbia, where most of the writing was done, Ronald Ebert, Robert Monroe, and E. Allen Slusher were instrumental in creating the appropriate environment for this type of work. During the latter stages of the project, William Mobley and David Van Fleet at Texas A & M University also provided valuable assistance.

Charles O'Reilly, Jay Kim, and Lyman Porter reviewed the entire manuscript. Many parts of the book bear their positive imprint; of course, any and all errors of omission, interpretation, and emphasis remain the responsibility of the author. Lyman Porter deserves special recognition for his dual role as reviewer and editor. Valuable substantive contributions were also made by Arthur Jago, Gregory Moorhead, Bruce Johnson, Thomas Dougherty, and E. Allen Slusher. Essential research and administrative assistance was provided by Diane Whallon, Ann Welsh, Carla Dennis, and Ann Current, while clerical duties were ably handled by Diana Perl, Lynn Epstein, and Erin O'Flaherty. At Scott, Foresman and Company, Roger Holloway, Kathy Talley-Jones, and Don Dean played key roles.

At this point in most prefaces, the author's family is acknowledged. It is my sincere hope that these authors take a moment to explain to their families that the order of their inclusion in these things is by convention rather than by importance. The contributions made by my reviewers, colleagues, and editors can be pinpointed in specific passages throughout the book. The contributions of my family, however, transcend words, sentences, and paragraphs. They help keep my life in focus, build me up when I'm down, and, I must admit, occasionally reduce my hat size when it gets too large. When I submitted my doctoral dissertation three years ago, it was dedicated to "Glenda, for whom the sun rises, and Dustin, for whom the stars shine." Those words are even more true today than then, although I must also add ". . . and Ashley, who doesn't yet know the sun or stars, but who loves Barbapapa and Doctor Doo."

INTRODUCTION 1

Every morning at 6:30, Bill Thomas leaves home and drives ten miles to the automobile assembly plant where he has worked for the past 17 years. He parks his car, walks through the "Employees Only" gate, gets some coffee from a vending machine, and punches his time card. At 7:00, he takes his place on the assembly line. Bill's job is to attach body side mouldings to automobiles as they move past his work station. Every 60 seconds, one car moves down the line. The job involves inserting ten clips into pre-drilled holes along the side of the car, positioning the moulding against the clips, and applying pressure until the moulding snaps into place. The job has been engineered to take 55 seconds. If he drops a clip, or if a hole has not been properly drilled, or if the moulding strip is bent, the job simply doesn't get done. No one ever says anything about the mistakes; Bill knows that the quality control people generally take care of the slipups. Actually, Bill has figured out several shortcuts and could do the job in around 40 seconds, but the engineers have told him that he should follow standard procedures and do as he's told.

By 11:00, Bill has attached body side mouldings to 240 sedans. He usually has lunch with Art Smith, who works across the line, and Henry Patterson, who works beside him. Lunch is the only time they can talk, because the line is so noisy. Actually, the three men aren't particularly close friends. They occasionally go to a local bar for a beer after work, but Bill tries to get home pretty early every evening. He views any contact with the auto plant after quitting time as an infringement on his personal life. Art and Henry feel much the same way and use the lunch hour to "escape" the plant by talking about the weather, local politics, and sports. At 12:00, Bill heads back to his work station and another 240 body side mouldings before he leaves the plant at 4:00. Of course, the line keeps moving as first shift is replaced by second.

When Bill talks about his job, he says, "I guess it's about like any other job. I do what I'm told, put in my eight hours, and draw my check. Sometimes the work does get a little boring, though. Ten clips and a moulding, ten clips and a moulding, 480 times a day. The only time anything changes is when the line goes down. Boy, when that happens, all the engineers in the world crawl out of wherever it is they hide and run around with their clipboards under their arms acting important until some maintenance man fixes the damn thing. Then, it's back to the grind. I guess I really shouldn't complain, though, because I do make good money. Last week, I brought home $384.66. Anyway, when things get too bad, I can take a couple of sick days. I usually take one, at least, every month just to break up the monotony of work.

"Work is just one of those things you've got to do, you know? My father worked in a coal mine for 40 years. I can remember, when I was a kid, listening to him getting ready for work every morning. He had to get up at 5:00, so I was supposed to still be asleep. Generally, though, I would wake up when he and my mother would start talking during breakfast. Almost every morning, he would complain about his job, about the never-ending drudgery and about how much he hated doing the same thing day in and day out. The times I remember best, though, are the times he and I would talk about work. He used to tell me that he wanted something better for me. You know, college and an office job. Yeah, and I ended up a lot different, too; no coal mine, no company store, no poverty wages for me. Instead of that, I have my little work station on the line and 480 body side mouldings every day, 5 days a week, 50 weeks a year, for the past 17 years and probably for the next 25 to 30 years, too. No, you can't get away from it: like it or not, a person has to work, and work *stinks.*"

At about the same time Bill leaves for work every morning, his neighbor, Hal Williamson, is also leaving. Hal works at a machine shop which supplies parts to the auto plant. Hal arrives at the shop, stops by the coffee lounge, and then goes down to the shop floor. Everyone else in his unit is already there. Hal's work unit is composed of ten men and eight milling machines. One man coordinates the inflow of materials from other work units, another man is responsible for the outflow of milled parts to other units, and the remaining eight men handle the machines. On a daily basis, the men coordinate their own work activities and decide which two members get a "day off" of the machines. They also decide when to take coffee breaks, when to have lunch, and, during the summer, schedule their own vacations. The company has installed special mufflers on the machines to hold down the noise. If a problem arises, the group members try to solve it themselves before calling their supervisor. If the company needs someone to work overtime, the group decides who has to stay. Every

Monday morning, their supervisor comes by and discusses the previous week's production figures with them. She compliments them when they exceed quota, and asks for suggestions when they don't.

When Hal is asked about his job, he says, "You know, I really like my work. I work with a great bunch of guys. We don't always have a boss breathing down our necks, either. We get to make our own decisions and we have control over what's going on. If I need to make a phone call or want an extra cup of coffee, I don't need to ask anybody. Our supervisor keeps us posted on how we're doing, but leaves us alone and lets us work. Oh sure, things get hectic now and then. It's a challenge, though, when a big rush order comes in and we all have to work together to get the work out. And, when the order's done, you really feel like you've done something. The pay is good, but I think I'd take a cut before I'd work someplace like the auto plant.

"When I was in high school, I worked at the plant during the summers. The funny thing is, though, that it didn't seem so bad back then. I guess that's because I didn't really know there was anything better. The job down at the shop opened up kind of by accident, and I happened to be in the right place at the right time. Boy, I'm sure glad it happened, too. Those guys over at the plant sure have it bad, and don't even know it. Work doesn't have to be all that unpleasant; the machine shop has proved that to me. I really like my job. All it takes is for someone to treat you like a human being and to let you know that you're an important asset to the company."

Bill Thomas and Hal Williamson have many things in common. They are both middle-aged, married; both own homes and earn a respectable income. There is, however, at least one major difference between the two men: their attitudes toward their work. Hal is very satisfied with his work and feels that he is an important part of the organization. Bill, on the other hand, does not have a favorable attitude about his job and does not feel any noticeable degree of attachment or commitment to his work. A variety of factors could account for these differences, including differences in aspirations, experiences, motivation, and socio-economic variables. One additional factor which should also be considered is the nature of the work itself. One man performs a fairly simple, routine task with little variation and no control over how the job is done, while the other performs a relatively complex task which he can modify himself and over which he has considerable control. Hence, the nature of Bill's job is substantially different from the nature of Hal's job.

In recent years, managers and behavioral scientists have come to realize that the relationships between individuals and their jobs are among the most crucial linkages in formal organizations. The job that any particular individual performs may range from connecting wires in a toaster to making policy decisions affecting thousands of people. These activities are, to some degree, structured and defined by the organization. This structure takes the form of a formal job description and/or formal and informal role **3** prescriptions by the individual's supervisor and co-workers. More precisely, the way the task is to be performed is specified by some factor or set of factors other than the job incumbent. For example, some aspects of the job are constrained by the technological conversion process utilized by the particular organization, while other aspects of work define the basic interface between individuals and the work they do. The manner in which the organization formalizes this interface is referred to as the design of work, or task design.

A DEFINITION OF TASK DESIGN

For purposes of this book, task design will be defined as follows:

Task design is the formal and informal specification of an employee's task-related activities, including both structural and interpersonal aspects of the job, with considerations for the needs and requirements of both the organization and the individual.

This definition is necessarily broad, but it recognizes a number of important elements in the task design process. These elements are:

Most task-related activities are formalized for the majority of jobs. That is, there exist standard methods and procedures which are to be followed; few organizations could exist without prescribing at least some behaviors for their members.

Other task-related activities may be informal, but still a crucial part of the job. For example, in many organizations, it is common and accepted practice for the junior member to perform some relatively unattractive chores, such as making coffee or unlocking doors every morning. Failure to comply generally results in unpleasant sanctions.

Task design describes how the job is to be performed in terms of specific activities involving physical and/or intellectual processes.

Social facets of work must also be taken into consideration. To varying degrees, most jobs require at least some minimal degree of interaction among job holders. Further, social factors may influence how employees perceive and react to their tasks.

The final components of the definition indicate that jobs should be designed to optimize organizational goals such as efficiency and productivity in conjunction with individual goals such as personal growth, development, and well-being.

One additional point of clarification about our definition of task design is also needed before proceeding with the discussion. Writers in the task design area have used a variety of labels for the concept, terms which are sometimes interchangeable and other times distinct. We will use the term *task design* to indicate the general set of activities performed by an individual in a manner consistent with our definition. When appropriate (i.e., to be consistent with a particular theoretical orientation), we will use *job design* to refer to the same set of activities. That is, we will use the terms interchangeably, with a preference for task design. Other commonly used phrases, however, such as job rotation, job enlargement, job enrichment, and work redesign have unique meanings that should not be confused with the more general terms task or job design.

Job rotation involves the systematic movement of employees from one job to another. Job enlargement is an attempt to alleviate employee boredom by giving the employee more things to do (i.e., horizontal job expansion). Job enrichment involves giving the employee more things to do while also providing more autonomy with respect to how to do them (i.e., horizontal *and* vertical job expansion). Finally, work redesign is a more general label for an organizational attempt at improving the nature of employees' tasks. Each of these concepts will be described in later chapters.

WHY STUDY TASK DESIGN?

Before describing the contents and format of the book, we must answer one fundamental question: why bother? That is, why should managers, students, and behavioral scientists be concerned about a topic such as task design? Actually, in contrast to some areas of scientific inquiry, the importance of research in the task design area is fairly easy to demonstrate. An adequate understanding of the design of jobs and their impact on individuals is important to the employees themselves, the organizations in which they work, and society in general.

Importance to Employees

A phrase which is heard quite frequently these days is "quality of work life." While the phrase is sufficiently nebulous so as to avoid precise definition, Richard Walton (1974) has proposed eight criteria for assessing the quality of work life in organizations:

1. *Adequate and fair compensation.* Does pay received meet socially determined standards of sufficiency or the recipient's subjective standard? Does pay received for certain work bear an appropriate relationship to pay received for other work?
2. *Safe and healthy environment.* That employees should not be exposed to physical conditions or work arrangements that are unduly hazardous or unhealthy is widely accepted. In the future, when health will be less the issue than comfort, more stringent standards than today's will possibly be imposed. These may include minimizing odors, noise, or visual annoyances.
3. *Development of human capacities.* To varying degrees work has become fractionated, deskilled, and tightly controlled; planning the work is often separated from implementing it. So jobs differ in how much they enable the worker to use and develop his skills and knowledge, which affects his involvement, self-esteem, and the challenge obtained from the work itself.
4. *Growth and security.* Attention needs to be given to (a) the extent to which the worker's assignments contribute to maintaining and expanding his capabilities, rather than leading to his obsolescence; (b) the degree to which expanded or newly acquired knowledge and skills can be utilized in future work assignments; and (c) the availability of opportunities to advance in organizational or career terms that peers, family members or associates recognize.
5. *Social integration.* Whether the employee achieves personal identity and self-esteem is influenced by such attributes in the climate of his workplace as freedom from prejudice, a sense of community, interpersonal openness, the absence of stratification in the organization, and the existence of upward mobility.

6. *Constitutionalism.* What rights does the worker have and how can he or she protect these rights? Wide variations exist in the extent to which the organizational culture respects personal privacy, tolerates dissent, adheres to high standards of equity in distributing rewards, and provides for due process in all work-related matters.
7. *Total life space.* A person's work should have a balanced role in his life. This role encompasses schedules, career demands, and travel requirements that take a limited portion of the person's leisure and family time, as well as advancement and promotion that do not require repeated geographical moves.
8. *Social relevance.* Organizations acting in a socially irresponsible manner cause increasing numbers of their employees to depreciate the value of their work and careers. For example, does the worker perceive the organization to be socially responsible in its products, waste disposal, marketing techniques, employment practices, and participation in political campaigns?

Certainly, task design considerations would be related to Criteria 3 and 4 for the vast majority of organizational jobs. If jobs are properly designed and the requirements of the task matched with the needs of the individual, it follows that the individual's capacities and capabilities will be enhanced and developed. Further, Criteria 1, 2, and 5 would be influenced by task design variables in many settings. Social integration, especially, is becoming more of a concern as more organizations begin to utilize groups and teams as a basis for task accomplishment. Criteria 6, 7, and 8 are less immediately relevant to task design factors, but may become more important as time passes.

At a somewhat more basic level, the study of task design is also important to the individual because of its impact on satisfaction. Most working adults spend over 50% of their waking hours in work-related activities. If the assumption is made that these people have a basic human right to enjoy and be satisfied with their work, it follows that task design research is certainly justified to the extent that task design is related to individual satisfaction. That is, if people are more satisfied with some task design configurations than with others, we should attempt to determine what the desired configurations are, how and why they influence individual satisfaction, and how they can be made more prevalent.

Task design factors may also be related to the individual's mental and physical health. For example, one researcher interviewed 655 industrial employees and found that individuals performing simple, short-cycle jobs answered questions in such a way as to indicate poor mental health (Kornhauser, 1965). It has also been suggested that task design variables may be related to employee stress, which in turn may result in such physical problems as cardiovascular disease (Ivancevich and Matteson, 1978). Of course, these relationships among task design variables and health factors are stated tentatively at best. It has been suggested, for example, that results from these studies could be attributed to pre-existing conditions just as easily as to task design considerations (Hulin and Blood, 1968). However, the mere possibility that employee health could be affected by task design variables certainly justifies additional study.

Importance to Organizations

The study of task design is also important for reasons of immediate interest to managers. These reasons primarily relate to economic factors. Either directly or indirectly, task design may be related, in some settings, to productivity, turnover, and absenteeism.

Richard Hackman (Hackman and Oldham, 1976; Hackman, 1977), for example, has suggested that properly designed jobs should have a positive impact on an individual's productivity and/or quality of output. In the Hackman and Oldham study, results indicated that job design variables were positively correlated with work effectiveness (a summary measure of effort, quantity of output, and quality of output) for 658 employees on 62 different jobs in seven organizations. A positive relationship between task design variables and performance for individuals with a high need for achievement has also been documented (Steers and Spencer, 1977).

At Texas Instruments, job enrichment was used to improve the nature of janitorial jobs within the organization. The results of the program included a substantially improved level of cleanliness, a marked decrease in turnover, and estimated annual cost savings of $103,000 (Weed, 1971). Bankers Trust Company of New York reports that job enrichment had a dramatic impact on measurable performance variables such as productivity and turnover, resulting in savings of around $60,000 in replacement costs and another $97,000 in improved productivity. Success stories have also been reported by American Telephone and Telegraph and IBM. Of course, it is reasonable to assume that a large number of both successful and unsuccessful task redesign efforts go unreported. Further, task redesign aimed at improving productivity may be difficult, if not impossible, in some instances.

As suggested in the previous section, task design may also be related to individual satisfaction. Satisfaction, in turn, may be related to turn-over and absenteeism. Specifically, Hamner and Organ (1978, p. 228) conclude that "empirical studies have pretty well established that the satisfied worker is less likely than his dissatisfied counterpart to quit the job over a given period of time." Further, they note that job attitudes such as satisfaction are fairly good predictors of the frequency of employee absences. In the study conducted by Hackman and Oldham (1976), a significant relationship was found between perceptions of task design variables and the total number of days absent from work during the previous year. Finally, one organization found that a moderate improvement in job satisfaction (defined as a .5 standard deviation increase) resulted in direct-cost savings of $17,664 in turnover, absenteeism, and performance (Mirvis and Lawler, 1977). Obviously, many more variables besides task design influence turnover, absenteeism, and satisfaction, including the level of unemployment, job mobility, and age. However, proper attention to task design does offer opportunity for the organization to influence the level of satisfaction among **7** its members, and perhaps simultaneously to reduce training and replacement costs resulting from turnover and absence.

At a somewhat different level of analysis, employee productivity and satisfaction are both important for reasons pertaining to organizational effectiveness. A recent review of 17 models of organizational effectiveness found that productivity and satisfaction were suggested as appropriate evaluation criteria in six and five models, respectively (Steers, 1975). These were also the second and third most frequently suggested criteria (behind adaptability-flexibility). If an organization, then, is to be evaluated on the productivity and satisfaction of its members, it follows that attention should be directed toward enhancing these outcomes. Since task design variables have been shown to be related in some cases to productivity and satisfaction, organizations should be interested in the study of task design for reasons pertaining to overall organizational effectiveness.

Importance to Society

The study of task design is also important to society in general. The reasons for this relate back to employee productivity and job satisfaction. The concern here, though, is for a macro perspective of the two variables. That is, productivity and satisfaction are important not only to individual employees and organizations but also to the overall well-being of our society.

A recent article in the *Chicago Tribune* indicates that the productivity growth rate in the United States has fallen considerably behind other industrialized countries such as Japan and West Germany. For example, in the United States, the value of goods produced by each worker has increased by 62% from 1950 to 1977. However, the corresponding increases in Japan and West Germany for the same time period have been 531% and 256%, respectively. Productivity growth is an important factor in stabilizing our economy via improved living standards, higher wages, an increase in goods available for consumption, and so forth. Hence, if task design variables influence employee productivity, either directly or indirectly, then society may benefit from additional research in the area.

The societal manifestation of employee dissatisfaction is generally called alienation. There is basic disagreement among experts in the field as to whether worker alienation in the United States is a significant problem or not. Those who feel that alienation is not a societal problem usually use the Gallup polls for support. Gallup (1972) asks people a direct question about whether they are, in general, satisfied or dissatisfied with their present jobs. Since the late 1940s, the majority of American workers have indicated that they are satisfied; since the early 1960s, the percentage of satisfied workers has consistently exceeded 80%. Union officials, while not denying that alienation may exist, attribute dissatisfaction to factors other than task design. For example, William W. Winpisinger (1973) has argued that whatever problems the American worker has could be solved by higher wages, shorter working hours, better working conditions, and promotion based on seniority.

On the other hand, there is equally strong sentiment that alienation is a very real problem. In 1973, a Special Task Force chaired by James O'Toole presented a report entitled "Work in America" to the United States Secretary of Health, Education, and Welfare. A primary purpose of the Task Force was to investigate the functions of work in society, the expectations and attitudes of working people, the degree of alienation in society, and special problems of white-collar, blue-collar, and young workers. The Task Force feels that dissatisfaction, and therefore alienation, is a very significant problem, especially among blue-collar workers. They partially base their position on methodological weaknesses in surveys such as the Gallup polls and additional data from other sources.

Senator Edward Kennedy also holds the opinion that worker alienation is a significant problem. As quoted by Aldag and Brief (1979, p. 35), Kennedy (1972) has stated that "millions of Americans are alienated because they see their jobs as dead ends, monotonous and depressing and without value." Overall, then, it seems that there is basic disagreement as to the extent of alienation in the United States. Even those who do not feel that most workers are dissatisfied, however, acknowledge that a sizable minority of around 8 to 16 million people may be alienated. Whether these figures are an accurate representation or a significant understatement, many American workers would evidently change the nature of their work if they could.

Importance to the Reader

At a somewhat more personal level, task design processes in general, and this book in particular, may also be important to the individual reader from at least two perspectives. First, many of you are or will soon be working in an organization. Hence, you will be performing a task created for you by a complex set of factors and elements in the workplace. Perhaps this book will help you understand why you occasionally feel particularly bored or stimulated with your work, why others around you react the same way (or differently), and how your job may compare with other jobs that may or may not be available to you.

Second, from a managerial viewpoint, many of you are or soon will be in a position to influence the design of a number of jobs in your organization. Perhaps this book will help you in understanding the role that properly designed jobs play in enhancing the quality of work life for employees and overall organizational effectiveness. Further, it will, it is hoped, assist you in determining when work redesign will or will not result in favorable outcomes and what kind of task design changes are and are not feasible.

In summary, then, it appears that the study of task design and its impact on employees is an area worthy of study and discussion for reasons **9** of importance to individuals, organizations, and society in general. While task design certainly is not a panacea for all of the problems outlined in the previous sections, it may be one key among several which will broaden and enhance the knowledge base of organizational science.

OVERVIEW OF THE BOOK

This book has four basic objectives: (1) to take stock of current research and thinking in the task design area, (2) to describe ways in which the study of task design is being integrated with research in other areas, (3) to outline and suggest avenues for future research, and (4) to assist the reader in determining when task redesign is appropriate and in understanding other organizational factors which must be considered. The book is organized around the integrative model of task design presented in Figure 1–1.

The model is composed of three basic components. The center of the model represents the task itself. Of specific interest here is the objective task, the perceived task, and factors which may account for differences between the two. The left portion of the model depicts organizational factors which may influence and be influenced by the design of jobs. Finally, the right portion of the model specifies outcome variables that may be influenced by task design factors and possible moderating variables which may intervene between the task design and outcome variables.

Chapters 2, 3, 4, and 5 are concerned with the present state of task design research. Chapter 2 ("Historical Perspectives") is an overview and summary of past, and in some instances, current perspectives on task design, including scientific management, job enlargement, and job rotation. Chapter 3 ("Contemporary Perspectives") discusses approaches to task design that are more recent in origin, such as job enrichment, the job characteristics theory and the social information processing perspective. Also included in Chapter 3 is a discussion of how individual differences may influence task design processes, task design in other countries, and a brief summary of peripheral task design considerations such as flexi-time. Chapter 4 ("Work-Related Outcomes") describes what factors might logically be affected by task design variables. Included in this chapter is a conceptual model of how these variables interact. Chapter 5 focuses on measurement issues. The measurement of perceived task variables through diagnostic instruments and the assessment of objective variables by personnel and industrial engineering techniques are described.

Chapters 6, 7, 8, and 9 describe approaches to relating task design variables to other organizational variables. Chapter 6 relates task design to an organization's technology. Included in the chapter is a discussion of the socio-technical systems approach, which is concerned with interactions among technological and social factors. Task design and organization design are the topics of Chapter 7. Relationships among various organi-

FIGURE 1–1   An Integrative Model of Task Design

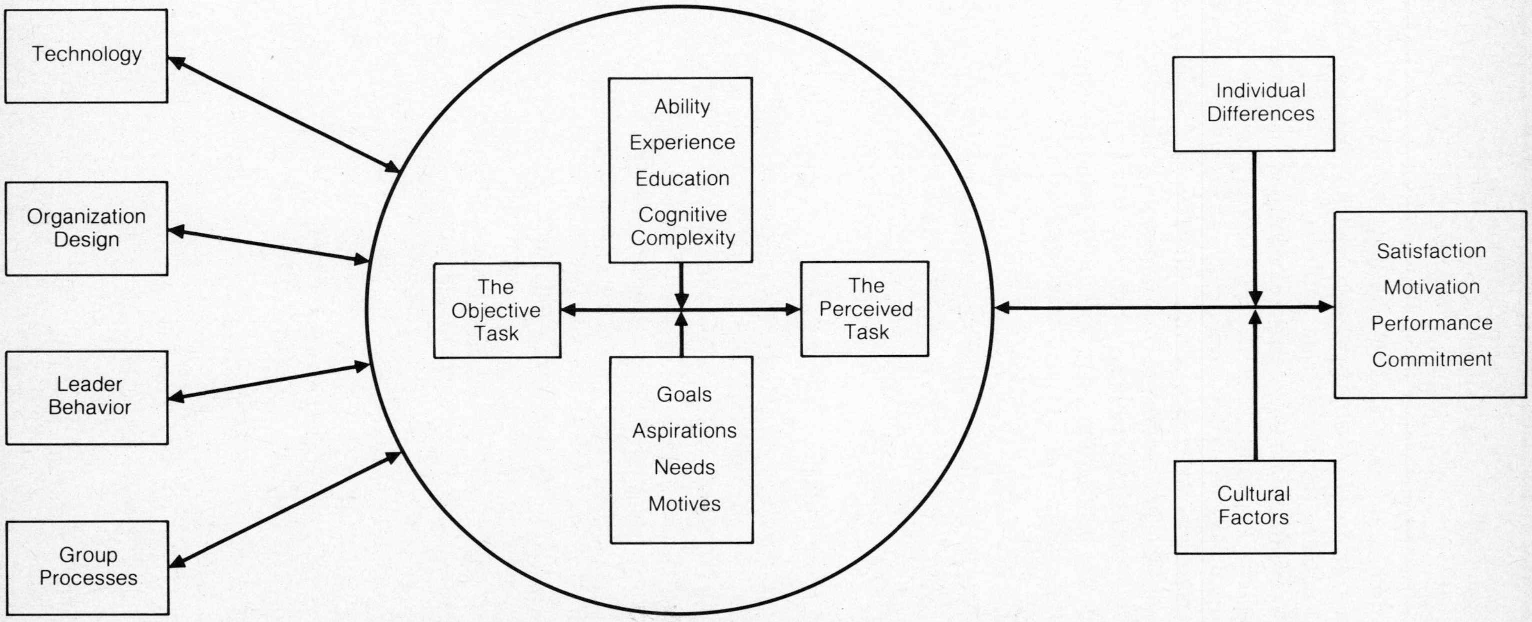

zation design configurations and task design variables are explored. Chapter 8 is concerned with task design and leader behavior. The emphasis is on ways in which task design variables influence leader behavior and, conversely, how various aspects of leader behavior affect task design. Chapter 9 focuses on task design and group processes. Attention is directed at how group and interpersonal processes influence task variables, how social and informational variables affect task design processes, and how jobs can be designed for work groups and teams. Included in each of these chapters is a discussion of future research needs and directions.

Chapter 10 ("Implementing Task Redesign") describes ways in which jobs can be changed to enhance work-related outcome variables such as motivation and satisfaction, with special attention devoted to integrating work changes with other organizational systems.

HISTORICAL FOUNDATIONS 2

The purpose of this chapter is to present an overview of significant historical developments in the field of task design. First, we will briefly discuss the pre-1900 period in order to gain a better understanding of subsequent events. Next, we will describe a revolutionary breakthrough in management theory and practice called scientific management. Finally, we will consider two early task design approaches developed by management, job enlargement and job rotation, aimed at improving employee motivation.

TASK DESIGN: EARLY DEVELOPMENTS

Although not termed such, the interest in task design has existed for more than 2,000 years. For example, jobs were specialized and grouped by function during the construction of the pyramids in Egypt and in the general production sector of ancient Rome (Wren, 1979). Current interest in the topic, however, can be traced most directly to the work of Adam Smith and Charles Babbage.

In his classic book, *An Inquiry Into the Nature and Causes of the Wealth of Nations*, Smith (1776) originated the phrase "division of labor" and described its advantages. His book reports on a group of pin-makers who had specialized their tasks to the point where, working together, they could produce many times more pins than if they had worked individually and simply pooled their output. He theorized that the increase in productivity was attributable to three factors: (1) increased individual dexterity, (2) decreased time spent in changing from one task to another, and (3) the invention of specialized machines and equipment. Smith's ideas **13** and theories were primary factors responsible for the widespread move toward industrialization.

Also of great importance was the work of Charles Babbage (1832). His book, *On the Economy of Machinery and Manufactures*, further delineated the advantages of job specialization and division of labor. Beyond the factors described by Smith (1776), he advocated specialization because of decreased learning time, decreased waste, fewer tool changes, and increased skill due to repetition.

A general framework for describing historical trends in the division of labor and job specialization is presented in Figure 2–1. The remainder of this chapter will focus on the first three phases, while Chapter 3 will discuss the current phase.

The first stage of division of labor and job specialization and standardization was characterized by general craft jobs. In the early stages of societal development, it became apparent to some entrepreneurs that demand existed for products previously made on an individual basis. For example, in the agricultural era, families worked their fields to provide for themselves, and also made their own necessities such as furniture, clothes, and shoes. The original craft workers were those who gave up their farms and produced these necessities on a full-time basis. Their products, in turn, were sold or traded to farmers for food. Hence, some people continued to produce food, while others began to produce other products.

As time passed, specialized craft jobs evolved. The general craft job, such as producing an article of clothing from raw materials, was broken up into a few specialized crafts such as weaving, tailoring, and sewing. Hence, jobs were becoming somewhat more specialized. This level of division of labor and job specialization became quite prevalent and dominated industry until the turn of the century. At that time, a management philosophy termed "scientific management" was developed and popularized by Frederick W. Taylor (1911).

SCIENTIFIC MANAGEMENT

As evidenced by Figure 2–1, scientific management was characterized by a very high degree of job specialization and standardization. Taylor believed that, prior to his innovations, workers had enjoyed too much freedom and flexibility in how they worked. In general, he held a somewhat negative attitude toward people. For example, he suggested that people have a natural instinct to work at a level much below their capabilities. Obviously, such lack of effort would lead to a great deal of inefficiency. Scientific management was offered as a solution to this inefficiency. (It should also be noted that there was some resistance to Taylor's ideas; there were even Congressional hearings about this particular management strategy.)

FIGURE 2-1 Historical Development of Task Design

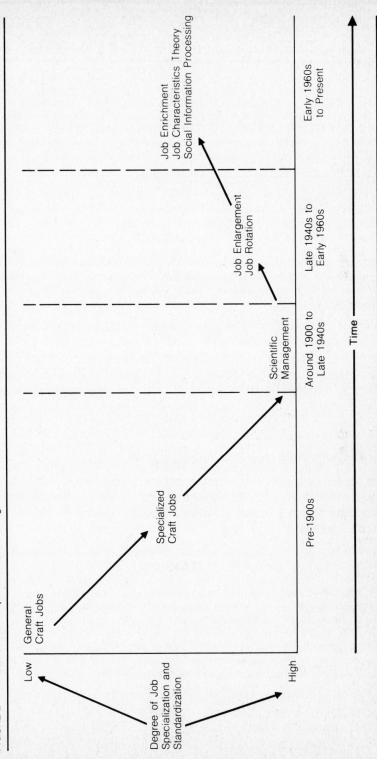

Source: From *Managerial Process and Organizational Behavior*, 2nd ed. by Alan C. Filley, Robert J. House, and Steven Kerr. Copyright © 1976, 1969 by Scott, Foresman and Company. Reprinted by permission.

The design and specification of tasks was a central component in scientific management. As argued by Taylor:

> Perhaps the most prominent single element in modern scientific management is the task idea. The work of every workman is fully planned out by the management at least one day in advance, and each man receives in most cases complete written instructions, describing in detail the task which he is to accomplish, as well as the means to be used in doing the work. And the work planned in advance in this way constitutes a task which is to be solved, as explained above, not by the workman alone, but in almost all cases by the joint effort of the workman and the management. This task specifies not only what is to be done but how it is to be done and the exact time allowed for doing it. And whenever the workman succeeds in doing his task right, and within the time limit specified, he receives an addition of from 30 percent to 100 percent to his ordinary wages. These tasks are carefully planned, so that both good and careful work are called for in their performance, but it should be distinctly understood that in no case is the workman called upon to work at a pace which would be injurious to his health. The task is always so regulated that the man who is well suited to his job will thrive while working at this rate during a long term of years and grow happier and more prosperous, instead of being overworked. Scientific management consists very largely in preparing for and carrying out these tasks (p. 59).

Several characteristics of this quotation are worth additional comment. First, Taylor advocated a clear distinction between management and labor. Second, the task to be performed should be specified precisely both in terms of task requirements and time allotted. Finally, and a very important point for subsequent developments, he felt that a worker exposed to such task specialization would respond favorably over an extended period of time.

Operationalizing Scientific Management

To his credit, Taylor did more than simply espouse a theory and leave it to managers to figure out how to use the concepts. He presented a series of managerially-oriented steps detailing exactly how to implement his concepts and ideas:

1. They develop a science for each element of a man's work, which replaces the old rule-of-thumb method.
2. They scientifically select and then train, teach, and develop the workman, whereas in the past he chose his own work and trained himself as best he could.
3. They heartily cooperate with the men so as to insure all of the work being done in accordance with the principles of the science which has been developed.
4. There is an almost equal division of the work and the responsibility between the management and the workmen. The management takes over all work for which they are better fitted than the workmen, while in the past almost all of the work and the greater part of the responsibility were thrown upon the men (pp. 36–37).

These phases are depicted graphically in Figure 2–2. In the beginning of a work situation, there is a task to be performed, a pool of workers, and a manager. For example, the total task may consist of managing a warehouse. The organization assigns a warehouse manager and five workers to operate the facility.

Phase 2 of the diagram represents management's scientific study, specialization, and standardization of the total task. The warehouse manager may decide that she needs two people to load and unload trucks, two people to transport unpacked merchandise to and from the warehouse bin area, and one person to check and log invoices. Next, she determines exactly how each task is to be performed and the appropriate skill mix necessary to carry out the requirements effectively.

As shown in Phase 3, the manager next matches the required skill mix with the available personnel. For example, she probably selects the two people possessing the greatest physical strength and stamina as truck loaders/unloaders, the two people with the optimal mixture of strength, memory, and attention to detail as transporters, and the person with the highest level of clerical ability, regardless of strength, to handle the invoices. Finally, as represented by Phase 4, the manager cooperates with the workers to insure adherence to standard procedures and maintains the primary role of planner for the group.

Scientific management in general and job specialization in particular have had a profound impact on American society. Through the use of job specialization, manufacturing organizations have come to rely heavily on assembly-line technology. That is, since specialization lends itself especially well to tasks which can be broken down into manageable units, the practice became widespread in mass-production industries. Indeed, one of the United States' most important industries, the automobile industry, still relies very heavily on job specialization. The economies of scale achieved through increased efficiency thus led to large increases in the number of industrial jobs.

For the better part of the first half of this century, little attention was directed at how workers actually felt about specialized tasks. Ignoring the fact that Taylor had warned against hiring over-qualified employees for specialized tasks, managers tended to hire the most qualified people available. The human relations movement (cf., Roethlisberger and Dickson, 1939) had begun to attract considerable attention during this period. However, managers still generally ignored the plight of many talented, motivated employees forced to work at highly specialized, routine tasks. Although some efforts to change this began in the late 1940s (as will be described in another section of this chapter), it wasn't until a classic study was published in 1952 that managers began to realize that job specialization had significant dysfunctional as well as functional consequences.

The Automobile Plant Study

In an attempt to determine how satisfied or dissatisfied workers were with various aspects of their jobs, Walker and Guest (1952) conducted interviews with 180 automobile assembly-line workers. The sample included people who worked on highly specialized and standardized jobs as well as utility workers who performed a variety of different jobs each day. All of the **17**

FIGURE 2–2   Phases of Scientific Management

Phase 1: A Task to be Performed, A Pool of Workers, and Management

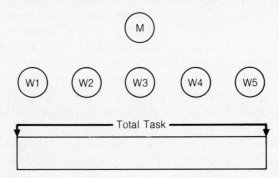

Phase 2: Management Scientifically Studies, Specializes, and Standardizes Tasks

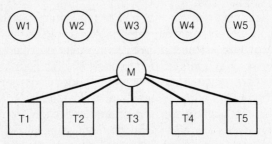

Phase 3: Management Selects, Trains, and Assigns Workers to Tasks

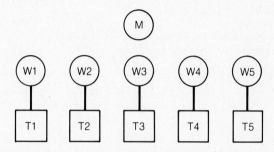

Phase 4: Management Supervises and Maintains Planning Responsibilities

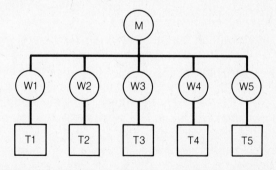

workers were male, and most were relatively young with little work experience. Based on the interviews, the researchers characterized the nature of assembly-line work as follows:

1. *Mechanical pacing.* The speed at which employees work is determined by the speed of the conveyor line rather than by their natural rhythm or inclination.
2. *Repetitiveness.* Individual employees perform the same short-cycle operations over and over again during the work day.
3. *Low skill requirements.* The jobs are designed to be easily learned to minimize training costs and provide maximum flexibility in assigning individuals to positions.
4. *Concentration on only a fraction of the product.* Each job consists of only a few of the hundreds of thousands of operations necessary to complete the product.
5. *Limited social interaction.* The workplace, noise level, and physical separation of workers spaced along a moving line make it difficult for workers to develop meaningful relationships with other employees.
6. *Predetermination of tools and techniques.* The manner in which an employee performs his job is determined by staff specialists. The worker may never influence these individuals (pp. 71–83).

Obviously, each of these characteristics is consistent, either directly or indirectly, with the principles and concepts of scientific management.

However, contrary to Taylor's belief that employees would respond favorably to such work, the automobile workers expressed generally unfavorable reactions. One worker, for example, stated that, "What I can't get used to is the monotony. The job gets sickening, day in, day out, plugging in ignition wires. I get through with one job and have another one staring me in the face" (Guest, 1957, p. 11). Overall, most workers were satisfied with their supervision, job security, and pay. They were generally dissatisfied with their jobs themselves, however.

The specific results of the automobile plant study are summarized in Table 2–1. The "number of operations performed" refers to the number of discrete functions contained within a job. Obviously, the fewer the number of operations in a task, the higher the degree of job specialization and vice versa. The data in Table 2–1 fairly well indicate that the automobile workers preferred a job with more operations over one with fewer operations.

While the automobile plant study served to focus attention on apparent widespread industrial worker dissatisfaction and to launch a variety of managerial efforts to improve conditions, a few managers had recognized

TABLE 2–1 Task Specialization and Employee Interest

NUMBER OF OPERATIONS PERFORMED	NUMBER REPORTING WORK AS VERY OR FAIRLY INTERESTING	NUMBER REPORTING WORK AS NOT VERY OR NOT AT ALL INTERESTING
1	19	38
2–5	28	36
5 or more	41	18

Source: C. R. Walker and R. H. Guest, *The Man on the Assembly Line* (Cambridge: Harvard University Press, 1952), p. 54. Used by permission.

the problem somewhat earlier and had already attempted to reduce dissatisfaction. The strategy which was initially employed has come to be called job enlargement.

JOB ENLARGEMENT

Job enlargement was management's first purposeful attempt to redesign tasks away from the doctrines of specialization and standardization. The technique was first utilized in the late 1940s. Essentially, job enlargement involves horizontal expansion of the task. Recognizing that dissatisfaction in specialized jobs was primarily attributable to the short work-cycle times involved, job enlargement advocates suggested a longer cycle-time brought about by giving the worker more things to do. That is, the worker was given more task variety. In addition, workers were generally given increased responsibility for controlling their own work pace and, occasionally, for inspecting their own work.

Figure 2–3 represents a typical job enlargement change. In a job specialization situation, the total task is broken down initially into components and a worker is assigned to each narrow component. After the job enlargement change, however, each worker has more things to do. For example, after enlargement, Worker 2 performs Task B, as before the change. In addition, however, she or he now also performs parts of Task A and Task C, which were previously the exclusive domain of Worker 1 and Worker 3, respectively.

The Use of Job Enlargement

Apparently, the first systematic use of job enlargement in the United States was at IBM (Walker, 1950). As a result of the job enlargement technique, worker satisfaction improved, production costs decreased, and quality increased. On the negative side, wages were increased and additional inspection equipment was required. Successful job enlargement programs have also been reported at Detroit Edison Company, American Telephone and Telegraph, the Colonial Insurance Company, the Civil Service, the Social Security Administration, and Maytag (Filley, House and Kerr, 1976). Further, the majority of job enlargement efforts probably went unreported in the literature; during the late 1940s and through the 1950s, job enlargement was apparently utilized by a large number of organizations.

Empirical Evidence

A great deal of information about the results of job enlargement is available from a series of studies conducted at Maytag. One study involved the production of washing machine water pumps (Kilbridge, 1960). The enlargement change progressed through three stages:

Stage 1. Six workers assembled the pump as it moved along a conveyor belt. (Note: high   **21**

FIGURE 2–3   Job Enlargement

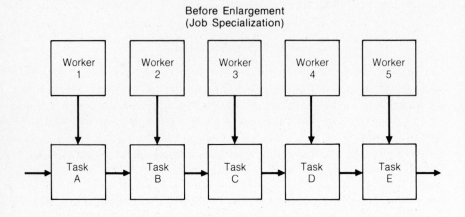

**Before Enlargement
(Job Specialization)**

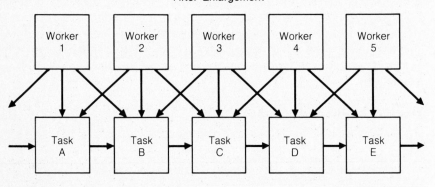

After Enlargement

degree of specialization; no worker control over pace of work or work procedures.)

Stage 2. Four workers assembled the pump as it moved along the conveyor belt. (Note: less specialization; still no worker control over pace of work or work procedures.)

Stage 3. Four workers each assembled entire pump at one-person work bench. (Note: low specialization, increased control over pace of work and work procedures.)

As the work progressed from Stage 1 through Stage 2 to Stage 3, the time required to assemble a pump decreased by approximately 16%.

Another Maytag study involved surveying a number of company employees who had worked on both a specialized conveyor belt job and an enlarged work bench job (Conant and Kilbridge, 1965). Most employees preferred the enlarged job. There were, however, some unexpected findings as well. First, a majority of the workers, while preferring the enlarged job, also had a generally favorable attitude toward the specialized job. Second, slightly more than half of the workers liked, rather than disliked, the job specialization aspect of conveyor belt jobs. The results of this study, while supporting the basic premise of job enlargement, do not necessarily refute the concepts of scientific management.

Unfortunately, other than the Maytag studies, few rigorous, scientific evaluations of job enlargement are available in the literature. Clearly, simply providing workers with additional task elements is not and will never be a cure-all for organizational problems. The specific advantages and disadvantages of job enlargement are summarized in the next section.

Conclusions and Summary

As with most behavioral science management strategies, there are positives and negatives associated with job enlargement. On the plus side, job enlargement can be said to have the following advantages:

1. The limited available evidence seems to support the contention that job enlargement is associated with improved satisfaction and motivation.
2. The quality of production appears to be higher under conditions of job enlargement.

Unfortunately, a large number of negative factors also characterize job enlargement:

1. Training costs increase due to larger jobs.
2. Critics claim that job enlargement is a device to get more output from workers and/or eliminate some members of the work force (recall that in the Maytag study, the total number of workers needed to operate the assembly line decreased from six to four as the program moved from Stage 1 to Stage 2).
3. Job enlargement does not really change the essential nature of many routine jobs (for example, a change from a job involving connecting six wires to a job involving connecting ten wires would probably not be particularly motivating).
4. Hiring qualifications may become more stringent due to increased task complexity.
5. No direct relationship between job enlargement and individual employee productivity has been established.

On balance, it appears that while job enlargement was a promising first step in the right direction, it alone is probably not sufficient to have any significant, long-run effects on worker attitudes and/or behaviors. Managers and researchers apparently recognized this shortcoming and soon turned to other, more comprehensive task change strategies to improve conditions. These strategies are discussed in Chapter 3. First, however, it is useful to discuss another technique adopted by managers at about the same time that job enlargement was being popularized. This technique is called job rotation.

JOB ROTATION

Like job enlargement, job rotation was a preliminary attempt to counter boredom and dissatisfaction caused by high levels of job specialization. Unlike enlargement, however, job rotation focuses on changing task as- **23**

FIGURE 2-4   Job Rotation

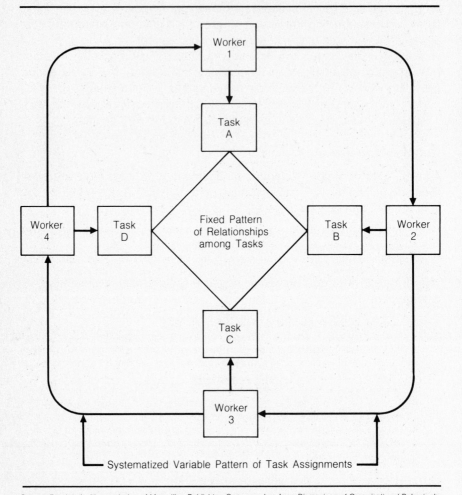

Source: Reprinted with permission of Macmillan Publishing Company, Inc. from *Dimensions of Organizational Behavior* by Theodore T. Herbert. Copyright © 1976, Theodore T. Herbert.

signments as opposed to changing the task itself. The rationale for job rotation appears to have been that if a worker is moved from one task to another, the new task assignment will serve to stimulate renewed interest and motivation on the part of the employee. After a period of time has elapsed, this interest and motivation will subside and workers must be rotated again to renew favorable responses.

A typical approach to job rotation is presented in Figure 2-4. In this situation, we have a group composed of four workers, each with a designated task. On a periodic basis, task assignments are rotated such that, for example, Worker 1 works first on Task A, then rotates through Tasks B, C, and D, and finally rotates back to his or her original task. Then the process is repeated. It is very important to note that the tasks and their interrelationships do not change; we have a fixed pattern of relationships among the tasks and a variable pattern of task assignments.

The Use of Job Rotation

As with job enlargement, many uses of job rotation apparently go unreported in the literature. Companies which have utilized job rotation include American Cyanamid, Baker International, Bethlehem Steel, Ford Motor Company, Prudential Insurance, TRW Systems, and Western Electric. For reasons we will summarize later, few companies use job rotation alone at the present time simply to improve worker motivation and satisfaction. Generally, contemporary managers utilize job rotation in either of two circumstances: (1) job rotation may be a part of a larger task redesign effort based on a more comprehensive approach, or (2) job rotation may be used as a training device to improve worker skills and flexibility.

Empirical Evidence

In one of the few published empirical evaluations of the effectiveness of job rotation, Miller, Dhaliwal, and Magas (1973) present the results of a field experiment. The study was conducted in a plant manufacturing vacuum pumps and utilizing an assembly-line technology. A group of workers was rotated through four different jobs along the line. Results indicated that overall efficiency decreased as a result of the rotation. Other studies of the effects of job rotation on employees have yielded equally disappointing results.

Conclusions and Summary

As indicated earlier, advantages of job rotation include increased worker flexibility. However, other anticipated benefits have generally not materialized. Upon closer scrutiny, the reason for the lack of success of job rotation as a motivational technique becomes apparent: it does nothing to change the nature of specialized jobs.

Recall our rotation example represented in Figure 2–4. Assume that Task A involves plugging a heating element into a toaster and that Task B involves connecting four wires to make the heating element operative. Further assume that the employees are rotated weekly. On Monday morning of Week 2, Worker 1 is rotated and becomes the new wire connector. Certainly, there may be some initial level of interest in the "new" task. However, most people would tend to become proficient at wire-connecting in a very short period of time. Hence, positive benefits may result from the job rotation program for only a few hours each week. Further, if the organization attempted to increase the rotation frequency in order to maintain interest and motivation, the group would probably soon suffer from decreased efficiency due to constant task reassignments. (One interesting **25** point to consider is that extreme, i.e. rapid, job rotation might evolve into job enlargement. For example, consider a worker rotating through a four-task cycle. As the time spent in each task decreases, the worker's perception of his or her job as Task 1, then Task 2, etc. may diminish, and a more macro view of the job actually being the Task 1–4 cycle may develop. The worker may perceive an increase in task variety.)

Overall, then, it appears that job rotation does not really counter the problems associated with job specialization. The nature of the task itself remains unchanged and the dysfunctional consequences of specialization are still present.

SUMMARY

This chapter has traced the historical foundations of task design theory and practice. Scientific management served to focus attention on the task problem and to suggest that organizations could benefit from a more systematic approach to the design of jobs. Although economic benefits did result from job specialization and standardization, managers eventually recognized that narrowly defined tasks had dysfunctional consequences for workers and that alternative approaches to task design were needed to bring about more balance between the goals of the organization and the needs and expectations of its employees.

Two initial strategies that were developed to deal with the problem were job enlargement and job rotation. Neither of these techniques was successful, however, because neither significantly altered the employee's work experience. Hence, boredom, monotony, and dissatisfaction persisted. By the early 1960s and on into the 1970s, other techniques had been developed and implemented by organizations. These strategies and their extensions are still the focus of much task design research and practice and are discussed in Chapter 3.

CONTEMPORARY PERSPECTIVES 3

In Chapter 2, we discussed historical trends in managerial approaches to task design in organizations. The objective of this chapter is to summarize contemporary, state-of-the-art theories and techniques for designing tasks.

First, we will describe one of the behavioral sciences' most widely recognized and discussed managerial techniques, job enrichment. Our coverage will include an analysis of Herzberg's two-factor theory of motivation (Herzberg, Mausner, and Snyderman, 1959), which is the theoretical foundation of job enrichment, as well as a description of the technique itself.

Next, we will summarize a series of empirical and theoretical arguments which suggest that not everyone will respond to the same task in the same fashion. This apparently logical but deceivingly simple supposition has led to the development of the most current theoretical formulation of task design, the job characteristics theory (Hackman and Oldham, 1976). Following a description of this theory, or model, we will critique the "individual difference" position.

Finally, we will briefly summarize a number of other important approaches and considerations relevant to contemporary task design processes in organizations.

THE JOB ENRICHMENT APPROACH

The two-factor theory of motivation (Herzberg, et al., 1959; Herzberg, 1966) and its applied derivative, job enrichment, will be summarized in this section. First, we will describe the theory and relevant evaluative research. Next, job enrichment will be discussed, followed in the same fashion by a **27** summary of the empirical evidence pertaining to the technique's viability as a task design strategy.

The Two-Factor Theory

The two-factor theory was formulated from interview data collected from 200 accountants and engineers working in Pittsburgh (Herzberg, et al., 1959). The objective of the study was to determine what factors caused employees to feel satisfied and/or dissatisfied with their work. Participants were asked, "Can you describe in detail a time when you felt exceptionally good/bad about your job?" Responses as to what caused good or bad feelings were recorded and content analyzed by Herzberg. He concluded that two distinct categories of factors were present in the workplace. The nature of these two sets of factors and their suggested impact on employees are depicted in Figure 3-1.

Specifically, the research findings suggested that there existed one set of factors associated with *job content* which, when present, led to a high level of satisfaction. When these factors were absent, however, the result was not necessarily dissatisfaction. Rather, the employees were simply "not satisfied" with their work. These factors were termed moti-

Figure 3-1 Herzberg's Two-Factor Theory

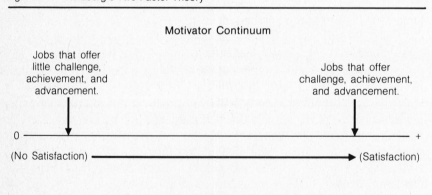

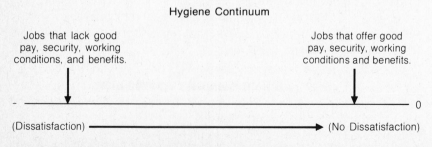

Source: A. D. Szilagyi and M. J. Wallace, *Organizational Behavior and Performance*, 2nd ed. (Santa Monica, California: Goodyear Publishing Co.), p. 111. Used by permission.

vation factors and included the following: 1) achievement, 2) recognition, 3) the work itself, 4) responsibility, 5) advancement, and 6) personal growth and development.

The second set of factors detected in the study was related to the *job context* (i.e., factors tangential to the task itself). When absent (or present at an unacceptable level), these factors led to employees feeling dissatisfied. When these factors were present and acceptable, though, employees were not particularly satisfied; they were simply "not dissatisfied." These factors were called hygiene factors, since they were related to the job context, and included: 1) company policy, 2) quality of supervision, 3) relationship with supervisor, 4) working conditions, 5) salary, 6) relationship with peers, 7) personal life, 8) relationship with subordinates, 9) status, and 10) security.

A summary of how these factors emerged from 12 studies is presented in Figure 3–2. The results generally support the two-factor theory's contention that satisfaction and dissatisfaction are differentially affected by the two sets of factors.

Translating to managerial practice, Herzberg argues that employees cannot be motivated by the hygiene factors themselves. These factors are, however, considered to be of primary importance to employees because of economic and social influences. Hence, managers should first attend to these factors to insure that employees will experience "no dissatisfaction." When a state of "no dissatisfaction" is achieved, though, the theory suggests that further efforts aimed at enhancing the hygiene factors are pointless. Alternatively, the two-factor theory asserts that once a manager has arrived at a level of "no dissatisfaction" among subordinates, he or she should then concentrate on the motivation factors. The result is predicted to be high levels of employee motivation and satisfaction. Operationally, the provision of the motivation factors generally involves enriching tasks along certain lines. Before describing the procedures Herzberg offers for enriching tasks, however, we will summarize the empirical evidence bearing on the validity of the two-factor theory itself.

Relevant Research

The two-factor theory has been the subject of a great deal of empirical research in recent years. As might be expected, some of the results obtained have been supportive, while others have been nonsupportive. Unfortunately, most of the evidence has tended to be negative. A variety of very specific and quite valid criticisms have been directed at the theory.

First, the two-factor theory is concerned with employee *satisfaction*, but makes predictions about employee *motivation*. Yet, the theory does not explain how and why satisfaction and motivation are interrelated. That is, the theory evidently assumes that if employee satisfaction is improved, then increases in motivation to perform will follow. The rationale for this assumption is not clear, and may be a dramatic over-simplification. **29**

FIGURE 3-2 The Role of Motivation and Hygiene Factors

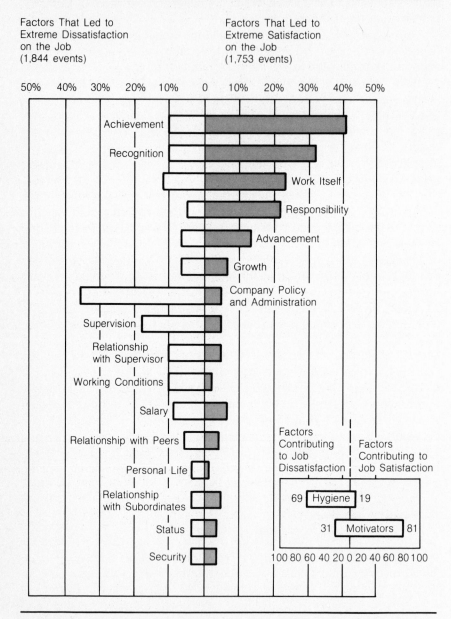

Factors That Led to
Extreme Dissatisfaction
on the Job
(1,844 events)

Factors That Led to
Extreme Satisfaction
on the Job
(1,753 events)

Source: Reprinted by permission of the Harvard Business Review. Exhibit adapted from "One More Time: How Do You Motivate Employees" by Frederick Herzberg (January–February 1968). Copyright © 1968 by the President and Fellows of Harvard College; all rights reserved.

Methodological problems also limit the theory's validity. Recall that Herzberg asked employees to describe factors that caused them to feel particularly good or bad about their work. It has been noted that "people tend to take the credit when things go well, and enhance their own feeling of self-worth, but protect their self-concept when things go poorly by blaming their failure on the environment" (Vroom, 1964, pp. 7–8). Hence, the factors listed by employees might have been, in part, a function of psychological defense mechanisms used to protect self-concepts.

Third, situational characteristics of the original study may preclude generalizing it to other settings. Accountants and engineers tend to take a very professional view of their respective fields and, as a result, may see their jobs in a different light than do many other occupational groups. Further, employees in a heavily industrialized city such as Pittsburgh may see their jobs differently than similar employees in less industrialized cities such as Houston or Miami.

Other criticisms of the two-factor theory include: (1) given factors may cause dissatisfaction for one person and satisfaction for another, (2) whether a given factor serves as a determinant of satisfaction or dissatisfaction is partially a function of occupational level, age, sex, education, culture, and/or status, and (3) intrinsic job factors are probably more important to both dissatisfying and satisfying job events (House and Wigdor, 1967).

The preceding arguments notwithstanding, the fact remains that the two-factor theory has also had some favorable consequences. By describing to managers exactly how they should utilize the theory in organizations, the two-factor theory has focused increased attention on task design issues. Today, the term "job enrichment" is one of the few behavioral science concepts with which the average person on the street has some familiarity.

Job Enrichment

As was described earlier, Herzberg believes that employees can be motivated only by providing them with positive task-related experiences such as achievement, responsibility, advancement, and so forth. In order to accomplish this, he suggests the need to enrich jobs so as to enhance employee satisfaction and motivation.

Specifically, job enrichment involves *vertical job loading*. Rather than simply giving an employee more of the same kinds of tasks to perform (i.e., horizontal job loading or job enlargement), the redesigned task must include factors and components previously held by the employee's supervisor. Job enrichment predicts that meaningful jobs can be characterized by the following six factors:

1. *Accountability*. The worker should be held responsible for his or her performance.
2. *Achievement*. The worker should feel that he or she is accomplishing something worthwhile.

31

3. *Control Over Resources.* If possible, the worker should have control of his or her task.
4. *Feedback.* The worker should receive clear and direct information regarding his or her performance.
5. *Personal Growth and Development.* The worker should have the opportunity to learn new skills.
6. *Work Pace.* Within constraints, the worker should be able to set his or her own work pace (Herzberg, 1974).

The exact manner by which these facets should be operationalized are presented in Figure 3–3. For example, one principle of job enrichment is to give an employee a complete natural unit of work (Principle C). By doing so, the manager is presumably allowing the employee to experience responsibility, achievement, and recognition, all of which are motivational variables according to the two-factor theory.

A number of job enrichment success stories have been presented, most notably from programs at AT&T and Texas Instruments. Ford (1973), for example, describes a variety of experiments at AT&T in which job enrichment was utilized. One change involved a group of eight typists responsible for preparing service orders. Management was faced with problems of high turnover and low output. It was concluded that since the typists worked in relative isolation and since any one of them could be called upon to type an order for any service representative, the typists felt little client responsibility and accountability and received little feedback. The work unit was restructured so as to create a typing team, and specific typists were matched with designated representatives. The task itself was also changed from a series of ten discrete steps to three more complex steps. Finally, job titles were upgraded to reflect increased responsibility

FIGURE 3–3 Operationalizing the Two-Factor Theory

PRINCIPLES OF VERTICAL JOB LOADING

Principle	Motivators Involved
A. Removing some controls while retaining accountability	Responsibility and personal achievement
B. Increasing the accountability of individuals for own work	Responsibility and recognition
C. Giving a person a complete natural unit of work (module, division, area, and so on)	Responsibility, achievement, and recognition
D. Granting additional authority to an employee in his activity; job freedom	Responsibility, achievement, and recognition
E. Making periodic reports directly available to the worker himself rather than to the supervisor	Internal recognition
F. Introducing new and more difficult tasks not previously handled	Growth and learning
G. Assigning individuals specific or specialized tasks, enabling them to become experts	Responsibility, growth and advancement

and status. As a result of these changes, the frequency of on-line orders increased from 27% to 90%, the need for messenger service was eliminated, accuracy improved, and turnover was practically eliminated.

Almost all uses of job enrichment at AT&T have led to improved employee attitudes and, in many cases, better performance (Ford, 1973). One example of the benefits accruing to Texas Instruments was briefly discussed back in Chapter 1. Other organizations which have utilized job enrichment include IBM and General Foods.

Relevant Research

In spite of the successful results summarized above, many criticisms have been directed at job enrichment in the form described by Herzberg. Richard Hackman (1975), for example, has suggested the following problems associated with job enrichment:

1. Reports of job enrichment successes tend to be "evangelical" in nature.
2. The techniques used for evaluation tend to be methodologically poor.
3. Few reports are made of failures, although many likely occur.
4. Situational factors have seldom been assessed.
5. Economic data pertaining to the effectiveness of job enrichment are generally not provided.

Two additional criticisms are that enrichment efforts are generally restricted to a small group of selected employees who are not representative of most other employees, and that all job enrichment efforts have been implemented and controlled by management rather than by workers and/or labor unions (Fein, 1974). Hence, the effectiveness of job enrichment as a task design strategy is questionable on a number of fronts, the most serious being the lack of rigorous, scientific evaluations.

In addition to the weaknesses summarized above, two other problems associated with job enrichment should be noted. First, job enrichment assumes that everyone will respond favorably and in the same fashion to task changes made in accordance with its principles. Certainly, many people will prefer a job with more responsibility, achievement, etc., over one with less. However, it also seems reasonable to argue that some people might respond more favorably than others to job enrichment. Further, a few people might even react negatively to increased responsibility, accountability, and so forth. The job enrichment framework does not take into account differences among individuals in their preferences for and reactions to job enrichment. (By the same token, differences among jobs and organizations are also generally ignored. For example, Herzberg does not specifically acknowledge that some jobs may not be "enrichable," that some jobs may already be too enriched, and/or that what works in one organization may not work in another, for myriad reasons.)

A second problem to be noted about job enrichment is one of theoretical explication. Herzberg tells us that if, for example, we give an em- **33** ployee job freedom, the employee will experience increased responsibility, achievement, and recognition. These factors, in turn, are said to lead to improved motivation and satisfaction, yet we are never told exactly *how* or *why* these processes occur. Such an explanation is clearly needed if true insights into the individual-task interface are to be gained. Hence, the job enrichment framework suffers from problems of *universality* and *precision*.

At about the same time that job enrichment was gaining widespread attention, a stream of research was being initiated that has led to a more refined task design formulation. More specifically, this body of research has not been subject to the universality and precision weaknesses ascribed to job enrichment. While certainly not being above criticism, this formulation has been more widely accepted from a scientific viewpoint and has pointed out new and challenging avenues of research and practice. Before addressing this model, though, we will summarize the research that led to its development.

THE ROLE OF INDIVIDUAL DIFFERENCES

Requisite Task Attributes

In 1965, Turner and Lawrence reported the results of a large-scale task design study. The researchers were originally interested in determining how differences in tasks affected employees. They predicted that a positive relationship would exist between task complexity and employee satisfaction and attendance.

This particular study made two primary contributions to contemporary task design theory. The first contribution was a multi-faceted approach to the description and measurement of tasks as a method for differentiating one job from another. Based on a review of the literature and an a priori conceptual framework, Turner and Lawrence identified six requisite task attributes, which they called (1) variety, (2) autonomy, (3) required social interaction, (4) opportunities for social interaction, (5) knowledge and skill required, and (6) responsibility.

The six attributes were measured by field observations and interviews with 470 employees working in 47 different jobs. The measures of the six attributes were then combined into a summary measure of complexity called the Requisite Task Attribute Index (RTA Index). Analysis of the data confirmed the predicted relationship between complexity and attendance, but *not* between complexity and satisfaction. Because of these unexpected findings, the research team subjected their data to further scrutiny.

These analyses led to the second primary contribution of the study: it was found that for some workers the predicted relationship held, but for others it did not. More specifically, it was found that the predicted relationship between RTA Index and satisfaction did exist, but only for workers from factories located in small towns. For employees working in urban settings, satisfaction was generally unrelated, and in some cases negatively related, to the RTA Index. As an explanation for these findings, Turner and Lawrence suggested that working in an urban setting, characterized by diverse cultures, high mobility, and a general lack of community identification, may lead to a feeling of anomie, or a lack of norms. Hence, urban workers would be expected not to react favorably to complex jobs because of a lack of norms conducive to such a favorable reaction. Alternatively, rural workers, because of lower mobility and stronger community identification, would have the opportunity to develop and react to norms consistent with a more favorable response to complex work.

Worker Alienation

The supposition that individual differences may intervene between task variables and employee reactions prompted considerable interest. An early refinement and extension of this argument was made by Hulin and Blood (Blood and Hulin, 1967; Hulin and Blood, 1968; Hulin, 1971). These researchers suggested that the rural/urban differences were actually caused by adherence to or alienation from the middle-class work norm. This norm was defined as "a positive affect for occupational achievement, a belief in the intrinsic value of hard work, a striving for the attainment of responsible positions, and a belief in the work-related aspects of Calvinism and the Protestant ethic" (Hulin and Blood, 1968, p. 48). It was predicted that workers who adhered to this norm would respond favorably to a complex task, whereas workers who were alienated from the norm would respond less favorably.

Initially, communities were classified in order of expected alienation (expected alienation was seen as a function of standard of living, the existence of slums, population density, and similar indices). Data from approximately 1,300 blue-collar workers in these communities were collected and analyzed in terms of job level and satisfaction. It was found that in the most highly alienated community, higher level jobs were associated with low satisfaction. Conversely, employees in higher level jobs in the least alienated community indicated higher levels of satisfaction (Blood and Hulin, 1967).

The alienation hypothesis was more clearly elaborated in Hulin and Blood (1968). It was argued here that urban workers do not necessarily exhibit a total absence of work norms. Rather, the urban worker may be a member of a subculture sufficiently diverse to develop its own norms. Specifically, it was noted that:

> Blue-collar workers living in small towns or rural areas would not be members of a work group large enough to develop and sustain its own work norms and values and would be more likely to be in closer contact with the dominant middle class. On the other hand, blue-collar workers living and working in large metropolitan areas would likely be members of a working-class population large enough to develop a set of norms particular **35**

FIGURE 3–4   The Universal and Individual Difference Models

THE UNIVERSAL MODEL

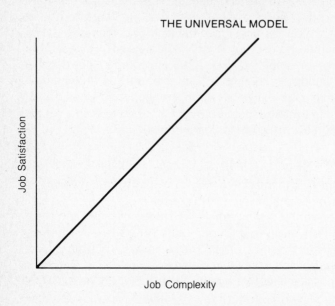

Job Satisfaction

Job Complexity

THE INDIVIDUAL DIFFERENCE MODEL

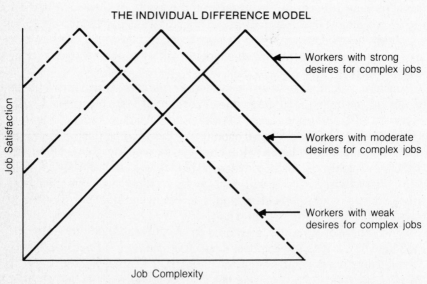

Job Satisfaction

← Workers with strong desires for complex jobs

← Workers with moderate desires for complex jobs

← Workers with weak desires for complex jobs

Job Complexity

Source: From *New Perspectives in Job Enrichment*. edited by John R. Maher © 1971 by Van Nostrand Reinhold Company. Reprinted by permission of the publisher.

to that culture. There is no compelling reason to believe that the norms developed by an urban working-class subculture would be the same or similar to those of the middle class (p.52).

Finally, the alienation hypothesis is further developed by Hulin (1971). He summarizes the basic difference between the universal job enrichment model and the individual difference perspective graphically, as shown in Figure 3–4. Whereas job enrichment assumes a universally linear relationship between increasing task complexity and employee satisfaction, the alternative formulation suggests a nonlinear, nonuniform relationship. In his summary comments, it is noted that, "A more reasonable conclusion would be that either positive or negative results might be expected from a program of job enrichment and the type of result depends to a great extent on the motivations of the work force involved (among other things)" (p. 182).

Higher-Order Needs

The next major breakthrough in research on individual differences and task design was reported by Hackman and Lawler (1971). These researchers suggested that, rather than looking at cultural and/or sociological factors, a more reasonable argument would be that psychological variables are the most logical differentiating factor among individuals. Using an expectancy theory framework, they suggested that some individuals can be characterized by a strong desire for higher-order (i.e., personal growth, feelings of worthwhile accomplishment, etc.) need satisfaction, while others have a weaker desire for this need satisfaction. The former worker is expected to respond favorably to a complex task, while the latter is expected to respond less favorably.

These researchers modified the RTA framework by conceptualizing four "core" job characteristics: (1) variety, (2) autonomy, (3) feedback, and (4) task identity. The predictions were tested on a sample of 208 employees working at 13 different jobs in a telephone company. The job characteristics were rated by the researchers, company managers, and the employees themselves. Measures of higher-order need strength, satisfaction, motivation, absenteeism, and performance were taken from questionnaires, company records, and supervisory evaluations.

Analysis of the data indicated generally positive relationships between each of the four job characteristics and the outcome variables, although the relationships involving performance were less consistent and of lower magnitude. The moderating effects of higher-order need strength were then examined by looking at employees in the top and bottom one-third of the distribution of need strength scores. Results indicated that relationships between variety, autonomy, and feedback and the four dependent variables were generally stronger for those employees with high scores on the need strength measure and were generally weaker for those employees with the low scores. It was concluded that, "The results of this study **37** suggest that there are important interdependencies among the character-istics of individuals and the characteristics of jobs which must be taken account of in the development of any full understanding of the impact of various kinds of job design" (Hackman and Lawler, 1971, p. 280).

The role of individual differences in task design, then, appears to be quite important. While there is still considerable controversy over the true nature of these differences, as will be discussed later in this chapter, the major contemporary perspective on task design builds primarily upon this study and the higher-order need strength variable. This model will be summarized in the next section. The discussion will be followed by an analysis of the "individual difference" concept and its utility in task design research and practice.

THE JOB CHARACTERISTICS THEORY

Based upon the pioneering research described in the previous section, Hackman and Oldham (1976, 1980) present a comprehensive framework of task design processes. This framework, called the job characteristics theory, is presented in Figure 3–5. At the core of the job characteris-tics theory are what are called "critical psychological states." These psych-ological states are seen as primary determinants of employee motivation and satisfaction, as defined below:

1. *Experienced meaningfulness of the work.* The degree to which the individual expe-riences the job as one which is generally meaningful, valuable, and worthwhile.
2. *Experienced responsibility for work outcomes.* The degree to which the individual feels personally accountable and responsible for results of the work he or she does.
3. *Knowledge of results.* The degree to which the individual knows and understands, on a continuous basis, how effectively he or she is performing the job (Hackman and Oldham, 1976, pp. 256–257).

To the extent that these conditions are present, employees should expe-rience favorable feelings about themselves when they perform well.

The emergence of these psychological states is described as being a function of the presence of five core task dimensions. These dimensions are the four characteristics suggested by Hackman and Lawler (1971), plus one additional characteristic:

1. *Skill variety.* The degree to which a job requires a variety of different activities in carrying out the work, involving the use of a number of different skills and talents of the person.
2. *Task identity.* The degree to which the job requires completion of a "whole" and identifiable piece of work; that is, doing a job from beginning to end with a visible outcome.
3. *Task significance.* The degree to which the job has a substantial impact on the lives or work of other people, whether in the immediate organization or in the external environment.
4. *Autonomy.* The degree to which the job provides substantial freedom, independence, and discretion to the individual in scheduling the work and in determining the proce-dures to be used in carrying it out.

FIGURE 3–5   The Job Characteristics Theory

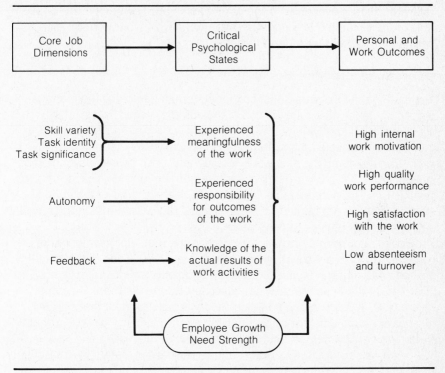

Source: J. R. Hackman and G. R. Oldham, "Motivation Through the Design of Work: Test of a Theory," *Organizational Behavior and Human Performance* (Vol. 16, 1976), pp. 250–279. Used by permission.

5. *Feedback*. The degree to which carrying out the work activities required by the job results in the individual obtaining direct and clear information about the effectiveness of his performance (Hackman and Oldham, 1976, pp. 257–258).

As noted in Figure 3–5, specific characteristics are seen as influencing specific psychological states. Jobs which can be characterized as having relatively high degrees of these dimensions are seen as being more motivating and satisfying and are termed high scope tasks. Conversely, low scope tasks are those characterized by lower levels of each dimension and are seen as less motivating and satisfying.

The job characteristics theory further suggests an important role for the moderating variable, individual growth need strength. Need strength is seen as intervening between the job dimensions and the psychological states and between the psychological states and the outcome variables. Specifically, the theory asserts that people with high growth needs are more likely to experience the psychological states when their jobs are relatively high in scope than are people with less strong growth needs. Further, high growth need strength people are more likely to react favorably to the psychological states.

39

Finally, the model makes predictions regarding five organizationally relevant outcome variables. High scope tasks are seen as having a favorable impact on internal work motivation, quality of work performance, job satisfaction, absenteeism, and turnover.

Operationalizing the Model

Translating the job characteristics model from the abstract into managerial practice generally involves the use of the Job Diagnostic Survey (JDS). The JDS (Hackman and Oldham, 1975), more fully discussed in Chapter 5, is a measure of perceived task variables. Specifically, the instrument provides indices of each of the five core task-dimensions, critical psychological states, individual growth need strength, internal work motivation, and job satisfaction. The primary purposes of the JDS are to provide a diagnosis of existing jobs before beginning planned task redesign efforts and to evaluate the effects of such task redesign efforts.

Scores obtained from the JDS on the five core task dimensions are combined to yield a motivating potential score (MPS). Jobs with a low MPS are seen as likely candidates for task redesign efforts. For example, profiles of a high and low scope task, as assessed by the JDS, are presented in Figure 3–6. The job characteristics theory would suggest that Job B is a reasonable candidate for task redesign efforts, while Job A is probably already at its maximum level of enhancement for motivating employees.

Once target jobs for redesign efforts have been determined by their MPS, the next step in operationalizing the job characteristics theory is to redesign the tasks according to five action principles (Hackman, Oldham, Janson, and Purdy, 1975). These principles are: (1) form natural work units, (2) combine tasks, (3) establish client relationships, (4) vertical loading, and (5) opening feedback channels. Figure 3–7 represents how each of these principles is seen as influencing or improving each of the five core task characteristics.

Validity of the Model

It has been noted that, "The job characteristic model has rapidly become the dominant paradigm in organizational psychology's search for the alchemist's stone . . ." (Evans, Kiggundu, and House, 1979, p. 354). That is, the model has been the subject of a substantial amount of attention in recent years, both in terms of verbal discussion and scientific analysis. It is with the latter area that we are primarily concerned.

While there is an abundance of studies available dealing with individual differences and task design, few assessments of the complete job characteristics theory have been presented. In their initial presentation of the theory, Hackman and Oldham (1976) present evidence generally supportive of the theory's propositions. They tested the model on a heterogeneous **40** sample of 658 employees working on 62 different jobs in seven organiza-

FIGURE 3–6   JDS Profile of a "Good" and a "Bad" Job

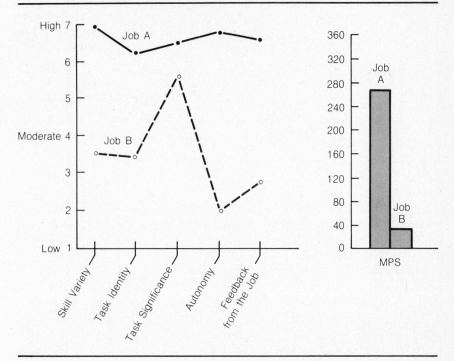

Source: J. R. Hackman, "Work Design," in J. R. Hackman and J. L. Suttle (eds.), *Improving Life At Work: Behavioral Science Approaches to Organizational Change* (Santa Monica, California: Goodyear Publishing Co., 1977), p. 135. Used by permission.

tions. Predictions involving performance and absenteeism were not as strongly supported as were other predictions of the theory. Overall, the moderating effects of growth need strength and the role of the psychological states were also supported.

The job characteristics model has also been tested in an industrial setting, with results suggesting generally weak but statistically significant relationships among variables (Evans, et al., 1979). Perhaps the most rigorous test of the theory to date, however, has been the field experiment conducted by Orpen (1979). He randomly assigned clerical employees to one of two groups. One group had their jobs redesigned in accordance with the job characteristics theory, while the other group experienced no task changes. After six months, it was found that: (1) employees in the redesigned condition perceived their jobs as having higher scope, (2) these perceptions caused increased employee satisfaction, (3) these perceptions caused decreased absenteeism and turnover, but (4) these perceptions had no impact on rated or actual employee performance. Other evidence of an inferential nature provides some additional support for the job **41**

FIGURE 3–7 Operationalizing the Job Characteristics Theory

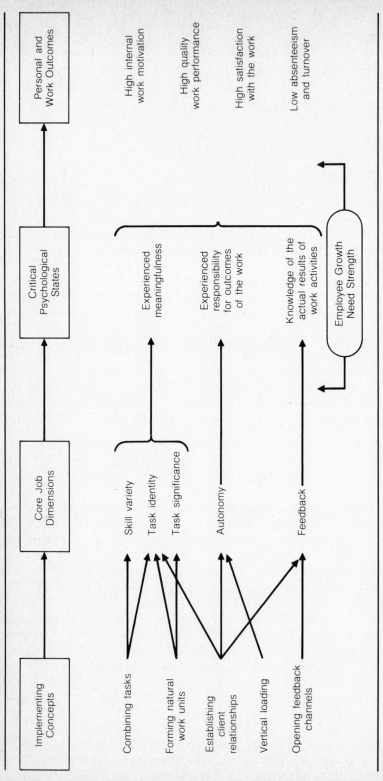

Source © 1975 by the Regents of the University of California. Reprinted from *California Management Review*, volume xvii, no. 4, p. 62 by permission of the Regents.

characteristics theory, although nonsupportive evidence is also available, especially in terms of individual differences (cf., Stone, 1975, 1976).

Recently, Hackman and Oldham (1980, p. 97) have noted that, "While there is support in the research literature for the basic job characteristics model, it would be inappropriate to conclude that the model provides a correct and complete picture of the motivational effects of job characteristics." The author believes that this is a generally accurate observation. The job characteristics theory has made a very significant contribution to the task design literature. While not the alchemist's stone alluded to by Evans, et al. (1979), the theory has succeeded in synthesizing previous research, focusing increased attention on the task design issue, and pointing out future research needs and directions. Further, the theory has not fallen victim to the problems of universality and precision characteristic of the job enrichment framework. Indeed, a primary proposition of the theory is that task design relationships are not universal and that situational and individual variables must be considered. Further, interrelationships among variables have been more completely explicated in terms of both how and why they might exist.

Hackman and Oldham have not attempted to over-sell their model, nor have they ignored or attempted to hide its deficiencies and shortcomings. These weaknesses, however, are all too real. Researchers and managers must take care to not stop searching for better, more complete, and more accurate formulations for task design and to continually evaluate current formulations, such as the job characteristics theory.

A common folk saying heard quite frequently is that you must learn to walk before you can run. Scientific management was our first attempt at crawling. During the job rotation and job enlargement era, we tried to struggle to our feet. Job enrichment found us standing on our feet and moving forward, although we frequently stumbled and fell. Finally, we learned to walk confidently and steadily with the job characteristics theory. Now, we must learn to run.

INDIVIDUAL DIFFERENCES: A CRITIQUE

The role of individual differences and task design processes is perhaps best illustrated as in Figure 3–8. The first category of moderating variables will be dealt with in Chapters 5 through 9. Category 2 is our primary concern at this point. At the time Figure 3–8 was first developed, Schwab and Cummings (1976, p. 32) noted that, "Research is just beginning on the second linkage and its moderators, but is nonexistent on the first." As if in response to this observation, a large number of studies have recently appeared addressing these issues. Over the past few years, in addition to the individual differences summarized earlier, the following variables have been investigated as potential task design moderating variables:

FIGURE 3–8   Individual Differences and Task Design

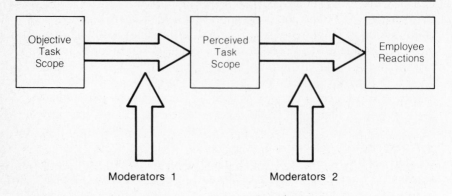

Source: Adapted from D. P. Schwab and L. L. Cummings, "A Theoretical Analysis of the Impact of Task Scope on Employee Performance," *Academy of Management Review* (Vol. 1, No. 2, 1976), p. 32. Used by permission.

1. Knowledge and skill (Hackman and Oldham, 1980)
2. Context satisfactions (Hackman and Oldham, 1980)
3. Demographic variables (Aldag and Brief, 1975a)
4. Socialization congruence (Aldag and Brief, 1975a)
5. Authoritarianism (Aldag and Brief, 1975a)
6. Need for autonomy (Stone, Mowday, and Porter, 1977)
7. Work-related values (Stone, 1976)
8. Locus of control (Sims and Szilagyi, 1976)
9. Occupational level (Sims and Szilagyi, 1976)
10. Need for achievement (Steers and Spencer, 1977)
11. Age (Aldag and Brief, 1975b)
12. Tenure (Lawler, Hackman, and Kaufman, 1973)

As might be expected, some of these studies found support for the individual difference point of view, while others did not. Inconsistencies abound among published empirical investigations. It is interesting to note that even when researchers attempt to review, synthesize, and integrate the available body of literature with respect to the individual difference argument, contradictions still arise. For example, one recent review concluded that, "Individual differences are likely to influence both the way the employee perceives characteristics of a job and the way he or she responds to those perceptions" (Aldag and Brief, 1979, p. 100). On the other hand, another review has noted, "Nineteen years of theory building and empirical research have not provided much hope in finding generalizable individual difference moderators of the relationship between job quality and worker responses. Why continue?" (White, 1978, p. 278).

An additional complication arises when we consider the argument that the moderating effects of individual differences may be present, but may change, either predictably or unpredictably, over time. On the "predictable" side, it has been suggested that one key variable to consider may be knowledge and skill (Hackman and Oldham, 1980). Hence, we might "predict" that as a worker acquires knowledge about a task and improves his or her skills with respect to that task, his or her perception that the task is complex (i.e., high in scope) should diminish. However, even this argument doesn't consider differences in learning abilities, transfer effects, and so forth. A "predictable" pattern, then, actually becomes quite "unpredictable," dependent upon a network of still other individual differences.

Another variation on the stability of individual difference effects has been demonstrated in a manufacturing setting (Griffin, 1981c). This study looked at the moderating effects of growth need strength over time. At the first time point, growth need strength moderated the relationships between job satisfaction and identity and autonomy but not variety and feedback. However, three months later, moderating effects were found between job satisfaction and variety but not autonomy, feedback, or identity.

Perhaps part of the difficulty arises from the conceptualization of the need strength variable itself. It was originally developed from a motivational framework. Implicit in its development was the assumption that need satisfaction would somehow affect other aspects of employee satisfaction. At the same time, however, the task design framework suggests interactive effects between task characteristics and need strength as a determinant of satisfaction. Hence, there is some theoretical confusion as to exactly how and why the need strength variable is expected to operate within the task design perspective. These issues will be further explored and developed in a later section of this chapter and also in Chapter 9.

Overall, it seems that one positive and five negative comments can be made with respect to the individual difference position. On the plus side, intuitive logic and some scientific evidence would indicate that individual differences are an important consideration in task design; that is, some people prefer a high scope task to a low scope task; some people are indifferent with respect to high versus low scope tasks; and a very few people prefer a low scope task to a high scope task. On the other hand, research has *not* identified what the key individual difference variables are, how they operate, why they operate, or how they track over time. Finally, the research has not been successfully translated into managerial practice by identifying for managers how individual differences should be accounted for in task redesign programs. Certainly, much remains to be done.

OTHER CONTEMPORARY PERSPECTIVES ON TASK DESIGN

This section will briefly summarize other contemporary approaches, developments, and breakthroughs in the task design area. Two of these areas will be explored at greater depth in later chapters, while the others are beyond the scope of this book. The topics in the latter group are simply included to provide the reader with a more complete framework for understanding the task design area.

Task Design in Other Countries

At the same time that American companies have been experimenting with alternative forms of task design, organizations in other countries have also explored ways in which jobs can be made more meaningful, motivating, and satisfying to employees.

The best-known and most widely discussed task design techniques adopted in other countries are the Swedish experiments. In response to high levels of turnover and absenteeism in Sweden in the late 1960s and early 1970s, both Saab and Volvo turned to task design as a potential solution. Saab, for example, installed changes in an engine factory leading to more emphasis on work teams. Under the new system, workers decided which members would perform which tasks, the pace of work, and the rest break schedule (Dowling, 1973). While results of this program were mixed, Saab has continued to experiment with task design strategies in other plants.

Volvo's approach to task design has also been well documented (Gyllenhammar, 1977; Foy and Gadon, 1976). In response to the problems referenced above, Volvo management, led by Pehr Gyllenhammar, designed its new Kalmar plant in a manner conducive to maximizing employee potential. Employees at Kalmar, opened in 1974, are grouped into teams of 15 to 25 each. The teams are responsible for a large variety of tasks, with a total cycle time of slightly less than 30 minutes per team. As at Saab, each team has considerable latitude over job assignments, etc.

In addition, the traditional automobile assembly line has been replaced by movable platforms for each auto. The platform moves along a computerized track. The speed of each platform can be varied by the team, it can be moved aside, and it can also tilt the auto to facilitate assembly underneath. In terms of effectiveness, turnover and absenteeism both decreased markedly, and production quality improved. On the negative side, the facility costs several million dollars more than a conventional plant, and output capacity is also considerably lower than a U.S. plant (more information about the Volvo experience is found in Chapter 9).

Other countries have also developed innovative task design approaches. In Norway, experiments have taken place in the paper industry and also in shipping (Thorsrud, 1977). Breakthrough strategies of work participation have been reported from Israel (Kanovsky, 1965). Worker-managed companies have been somewhat successful in Denmark (Moller, 1977). Clearly, then, the interest in task design is not confined to the United States. Around the world, governments, organizations, and people are constantly working toward improving the employee's work experience.

The preceding illustrations are offered simply to provide the reader with some of the flavor of the foreign studies. One specific aspect of task design findings in other countries that deserves special note, however, is the socio-technical systems concept. This viewpoint will be briefly introduced here; a more complete treatment is found in Chapters 6 and 9.

The Socio-Technical Systems Approach

The socio-technical systems approach to organizing work was first advanced by the Tavistock Institute of Human Relations in London. The term "socio-technical" indicates, quite correctly, that the concept is a synthesis of the social (i.e., human) and technical (i.e., mechanical) systems within organizations. On the one hand, a basic concern of management must be the efficient conversion of inputs into outputs. The technical aspects of the organization are crucial; at the same time, however, management must not neglect the human side of the organization—individual and group needs and motives are also very important.

Operationally, the utilization of the socio-technical systems approach in organizations has often been through the use of autonomous work groups or teams. Many organizational tasks lend themselves more effectively to a group or team approach than to an individual approach to task accomplishment. Under such an arrangement, work groups are generally given considerable autonomy in planning what is to be done and allocating work among group members, and compensation is often based on group performance rather than individual performance.

While developed abroad, the socio-technical systems approach in general, and the autonomous work group arrangement in particular, have also been utilized in the United States. The most notable use of these concepts in this country has been at the General Foods pet food plant in Topeka, Kansas. As indicated earlier, a more thorough discussion of socio-technical systems theory is found in Chapter 6; Chapter 9 includes an in-depth description of the use of autonomous work groups and teams, as well as more information on the General Foods experience.

The Social Information Processing View

Another recent approach to the study and description of task design processes has been termed the social information processing approach (Salancik and Pfeffer, 1977, 1978). This view takes exception to the basic task design framework represented by the job characteristics theory (Hackman and Oldham, 1976, 1980). Specifically, this theory and similar formulations assume that objective task properties exist, that employees perceive these properties, and that employees then respond to their perceptions in predictable ways. In effect, then, the framework is derived from need-satisfaction models of job attitudes. This derivation would suggest that individuals have stable and identifiable attributes, including needs, and that jobs also have stable and identifiable characteristics relevant to those needs (Salancik and Pfeffer, 1977).

In their initial critique of need-satisfaction models, Salancik and Pfeffer (1977) call into question the theoretical underpinnings of this view. They note, for example, that many such models are formulated in such a way as to be almost impossible to refute. Further, it is argued that studies investi- **47** gating such models have been characterized by methodological problems. At the core of their criticism, however, is the assumption of rational choice and perception inherent in need-satisfaction models. They argue that the models fail to consider the idea that people may be able to provide their own satisfactions by cognitively reconstructing relevant situations.

As an alternative view, Salancik and Pfeffer (1978) offer a social information processing approach to job attitudes and task design. This perspective argues that employee task perceptions are actually socially constructed; employees are assumed to receive informational cues about their jobs from others in their social network (i.e., co-workers, supervisors, etc.) and to react as much or more to these informational cues as to objective task properties. This process is reflected, to a certain extent, in the Category 1 moderating variables in Figure 3–8. This view of task design is currently the focus of a substantial amount of empirical research and will be discussed in more detail in Chapter 9.

Peripheral Task Design Strategies

This final section will examine a number of peripheral or secondary task design strategies currently utilized in organizations. Actually, the task design label is somewhat of a misnomer for several of these strategies, because they don't really focus on the task itself. They are, however, concerned with the individual-organization interface and, therefore, should at least be summarized in a discussion of contemporary task design approaches.

Modified workweek. The modified workweek is a term applied to restructuring work schedules away from the traditional eight-hours-per-day, five-days-per-week arrangement. More specifically, the modified workweek allows employees to work a full 40 hours in less than five days. Generally, this is accomplished by having employees work four ten-hour days per week. Some organizations have all employees on the same four-day schedule and simply don't do business on the other three days. More common, however, are organizations that stagger work schedules such that employees work a four-day week, but the organization remains in operation other days as well (Cohen and Gadon, 1978).

The rationale for using a modified workweek is generally couched in terms of advantages for both the individual and the organization. Advocates suggest that organizations can save money due to fewer weekly start-ups and lower absenteeism and tardiness. Individual employees are also expected to experience more satisfaction, have more leisure time, and spend less time commuting. On the negative side, employees generally experience more fatigue due to longer working days and often complain that longer work days cut into evening activities. Organizations also encounter scheduling difficulties when interacting with firms on traditional work schedules.

In the early 1970s, many firms adopted the modified workweek. Since the mid-1970s, however, the number of organizations adopting the system has leveled off. Current estimates are that approximately 750,000 American workers are on some form of modified work schedule.

Some empirical evidence exists as to the effectiveness of the modified workweek. In a field experiment, it was found that employee satisfaction and performance initially increased after a firm adopted a four-day, 40-hour workweek. However, after slightly more than two years, satisfaction and performance had declined back to their original levels (Ivancevich and Lyon, 1977). Cohen and Gadon (1978) also describe how companies are discontinuing programs at a rate of approximately 4 to 5%, leaving the future outlook uncertain. In summary, then, it appears that the benefits of a modified workweek may not be as great as originally hoped, but many employees will continue to operate under the system.

Flexible working hours. The modified workweek does not give the employee any more control over when he or she works; the organizations simply rearrange the required times of attendance. Under a flexible working hours, or flexi-time, arrangement, however, the employee has considerable latitude over working hours. Typically, organizations utilizing flexi-time divide the workday into two components: core time, when everyone must be present, and flexible time, when employees choose their hours.

An example of a flexi-time program might be characterized by the firm having flexible time from 6:00 a.m. to 9:00 a.m., 11:00 a.m. to 1:00 p.m., and 3:00 p.m. to 6:00 p.m. Core time, therefore, would be 9:00 a.m. to 11:00 a.m. and 1:00 p.m. to 3:00 p.m. The individual employee can come to work any time between 6:00 a.m. and 9:00 a.m. After eight hours of work, which must include the four core hours, the employee's work day is complete.

The anticipated benefits of flexi-time are obvious. The employee is given considerable latitude in choosing working hours and can schedule his or her work day in a manner most convenient for his or her particular situation. Depending on the individual's preferences, the employee can come to work early in the morning and leave at midday, or else come in at midmorning and leave later in the afternoon. The individual can also take as long as two hours at lunch.

A flexi-time arrangement is a very real attempt to allow employees the opportunity to balance their work life and their personal life. From the organization's viewpoint, numerous examples have been documented whereby flexi-time resulted in lower absenteeism and turnover and improved performance (Cohen and Gadon, 1978). On the negative side, flexi-time may necessitate more controls to insure that employees are putting in the required number of hours per week. Also, since the firm is open a longer number of hours per day, utility expenses may increase. Finally, some constraints are placed on flexi-time efforts by government regulations.

49

In contrast to the modified workweek trend, the number of organizations utilizing flexi-time appears to be increasing at a fairly constant rate. Organizations adopting flexi-time include the United States government, Metropolitan Life, and Control Data Corporation. It is estimated that in the United States, there are more than 400,000 people on some type of flexible work schedule (Cohen and Gadon, 1978).

As was stated above, many organizations have reported favorable results from the adoption of flexi-time. A recent scientific assessment of the effects of flexi-time on productivity provides additional information. Schein, Maurer and Novak (1977) describe the use of flexi-time in five different units of a large financial institution. After four months, two groups had experienced significant productivity gains, although other factors could have led to the gains in one group. The fact that productivity did not decline in any of the groups led Schein, et al. (1977, p. 465), to conclude that, "At a minimum then, flexible working hours appear to have no adverse impact on productivity and may be an employee benefit that can be introduced at little cost to the organization."

Job sharing.   A relatively new approach to work is the concept of job sharing. Just as the name implies, job sharing involves having two or more people share one job. The people sharing the job may be husband and wife, friends, or total strangers. A typical example of job sharing might find one person coming into the office or plant at 8:00 a.m. and working until 12:30 p.m. The other person comes in at 12:30 p.m. and works until 5:00 p.m. If the job is complex, of course, the two employees may need to spend some time communicating with one another and coordinating their activities.

Employees might opt for job sharing for a variety of reasons, including a desire for more leisure time, more time for family, and the opportunity for both husband and wife to pursue careers in tight job markets. From the organization's viewpoint, job sharing may allow the utilization of a broader spectrum of talent and increased flexibility with respect to scheduling and staffing.

Since job sharing is a relatively new technique, there are no accurate estimates as to the number of people operating under the system. However, as more and more women enter the workplace and, concomitantly, more and more men find it appealing and/or necessary to work fewer hours (i.e., to share household duties), job sharing seems likely to become more common in organizations. It would appear that the technique may be one situation for allowing employees to have more control over their work experiences.

SUMMARY

This chapter has presented a variety of contemporary task design strategies and considerations. First, Herzberg's two-factor theory and job enrichment were discussed. Next, we described Hackman and Oldham's job characteristics theory. In the final section, we briefly summarized four other contemporary topics pertaining to task design: task design in other countries, socio-technical systems theory, the social information processing approach, and peripheral task design strategies.

In summary, then, it appears that what Frederick Taylor started in 1911 as a narrowly defined topic of managerial concern and interest has mushroomed into a diverse area of study and practice. This area of study is characterized by a multiplicity of theoretical viewpoints, managerial approaches, and research perspectives. In all likelihood, this trend will continue as organizations identify and implement other methods of task design with the potential for enhancing the employee quality of working life and improving organizational productivity and effectiveness.

In Chapter 4, we will turn our attention back toward a topic briefly introduced in Chapter 1. Specifically, we will discuss the outcomes of appropriate and inappropriate task design configurations from the point of view of both the individual and the organization.

4 WORK-RELATED OUTCOMES

The objective of this chapter is to discuss more fully and expand some ideas introduced in Chapter 1. Earlier, we justified an in-depth treatment of task design because of its potential for enhancing both individually- and organizationally-relevant outcomes. The primary outcome variables which have been related to task design variables, either descriptively and/or empirically, include satisfaction, motivation, and performance (Hackman, 1977; Hackman and Oldham, 1980). It has been further suggested that task design may also be related to other outcome variables such as commitment, stress, and attendance. In this chapter, we will examine each of these potential outcome variables in detail.

First, we will present the rationale for expecting to find a relationship between task characteristics and the outcome variable under discussion. Next, we will summarize the relevant research evidence pertaining to the variable. We will then present our conclusions with respect to the appropriateness of the outcome variable as a viable consideration for future task design research and practice. In the final section of the chapter, we will present an integrative framework of all expected relationships among task characteristics and the outcome variables.

Before proceeding, however, two additional points of clarification may be needed. Our emphasis is on task design and work-related outcomes. It should be clearly understood, however, that all of these work-related outcomes are a function of a large number of factors, of which task design is only one. Hence, changes in task design alone are not likely to dramatically influence any outcome variable. Any such effects are likely to be constrained and bounded by the other variables. Second, we will generally imply, for the sake of parsimony, that task design variables have a causal impact on work-related outcomes. At specific points, however, and in later chapters, it will become apparent to the reader that many of the work-related outcome variables also influence task design variables and processes. For example, highly satisfied employees may perceive their task differently than highly dissatisfied employees. The rationale for our approach is that we are describing the potential benefits that might accrue to organizations and their employees when they adopt contemporary task design strategies.

TASK DESIGN AND MOTIVATION

One primary outcome variable included in most contemporary task design formulations is employee motivation. At this point, the term motivation will be taken as a general construct subsuming more specific motivational components such as internal work motivation. We will define motivation to include those factors and processes which initiate, channel, and sustain individual behavior. Within the organizational setting, then, we are essentially concerned with two behaviors. First, we are interested in what motivates a person to select and maintain one type of job over another. For example, why do some people accept and keep jobs on an assembly line when other people refuse to do that type of work? Second, we are concerned with those factors that cause one person to exert effort on a particular job in order to exceed expected performance levels, as opposed to the individual who chooses to do just enough to get by.

Rationale

Since the groundbreaking study by Hackman and Lawler (1971), task design research has explicitly or implicitly been conducted within an expectancy theory framework. Expectancy theory (Vroom, 1964) is a model of individual choice behavior. In its present form, expectancy theory includes a number of important variables. These variables are summarized below:

1. *Expectancy*. The individual's perception regarding the likelihood that a particular act (i.e., behavior) will be followed by a particular outcome; hence, expectancy is a subjective probability estimate.
2. *Valence*. The strength of the individual's preference for a particular outcome; valence may be positive for desired outcomes and/or negative for undesired outcomes.
3. *Outcomes*. The results of the individual's behavioral choice; first-level outcomes can generally be described as organizationally-relevant factors such as pay, performance, etc.; second-level outcomes include individually-relevant factors such as need satisfaction.
4. *Instrumentality*. The individual's perception of the causal linkages between first- and second-level outcomes; hence, instrumentality is viewed as being correlational in nature.
5. *Motivation*. The force on a person to behave in certain ways as a function of interactions among expectancies, valences, instrumentalities, and first- and second-level outcomes.

53

Specific relationships among the variables of expectancy theory are presented in Figure 4–1.

Expectancy theory has progressed through a number of modifications and refinements since its initial development (cf., Vroom, 1964; Graen, 1969; Porter and Lawler, 1968). The current formulation (Campbell and Pritchard, 1976) is an integrated model building on the previous viewpoints. The primary dependent (i.e., outcome) variables of the theory are behavioral choices, goal-directed efforts, and the change in either choice or effort resulting from experience. Behavioral choice and effort are seen as being directed at alternative tasks and at performance levels within tasks respectively. Specific performance levels for specific tasks are referred to as task goals. Note from Figure 4–1 that a task goal has an accompanying valence and that the linkage between effort and the task goal is characterized as an expectancy.

The model then specifies the consequences of reaching (or not reaching) the task goal. More precisely, a number of other outcomes may

FIGURE 4–1   The Expectancy Model of Motivation

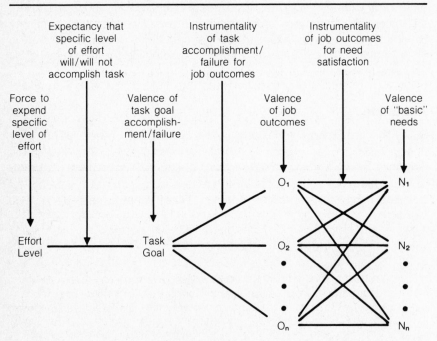

For purposes of simplicity this schematic portrays only one level of effort and one level of success on one task goal. A similar set of relationships exists for alternative levels of effort and alternative tasks or alternative levels of success.

Source: J. P. Campbell and R. D. Pritchard, "Motivation Theory in Industrial and Organizational Psychology," in M. D. Dunnette (ed.), *Handbook of Industrial and Organizational Psychology*, Boston, Houghton-Mifflin, 1976, p. 80.

be contingent upon achieving the desired task goal (i.e., a certain level of performance). External outcomes are those established by the organization (i.e., pay) or other people (i.e., recognition), while internal outcomes are those defined by the individual (i.e., self-esteem). These outcomes also have valences, and the linkages between task goal accomplishment and job outcomes are described in terms of instrumentalities.

Finally, the model suggests a second level of outcomes which are dependent upon first-level job outcomes. The example used by Campbell and Pritchard to illustrate this point is pay as a first-level outcome potentially resulting from task goal accomplishment, and the ability to purchase a new home as a second-level outcome potentially resulting from the first-level outcome. First- and second-level outcomes are linked by instrumentalities.

At a general level, then, the process may be illustrated by tracing through various behavioral decisions made by a person. Further, the process may actually be more understandable by looking at the various steps in reverse order. Assume that an individual employee strongly desires to buy a new sportscar (positive valence for a second-level outcome). In order to have the money for the car, the employee needs to get a pay raise. Further, he has determined that he *must* get the raise in order to buy the car and that if he gets the raise, he *can* definitely afford to make the purchase. Hence, the first-level outcome (the pay raise) also has a positive valence, and since the attainment of the first-level outcome will lead directly to the second-level outcome, the relationship between the two has a positive instrumentality (i.e., the pay raise leads directly to the ability to purchase the car).

The employee then assesses strategies for getting the desired pay increase. Fortunately, his organization has a well-designed and equitable reward system. Specifically, he knows that rewards follow performance. Therefore, the accomplishment of task goals also takes on a positive valence, since there is a positive instrumentality between the attainment of the task goals (performance) and the desired first-level outcome (pay).

Finally, the employee determines how best to reach relevant task goals. If the task has been properly designed, and if our hypothetical employee has been properly selected and trained by our personnel system, then the appropriate level of effort should lead to task goal attainment. If the employee perceives this to be the case, then a positive expectancy will exist between effort and performance. Hence, our employee will be motivated to exert effort because he realizes that: (1) his effort will lead to successful performance, (2) successful performance will result in a pay increase, and (3) the pay increase will enable him to buy the sportscar.

Of course, the overall process is much more complex (and probably less rational) than this, because of the existence of a myriad of first- and second-level outcomes, many of them mutually exclusive (i.e., a student who must choose among going to summer school, taking a full-time job for the summer in another city, or having a European vacation). Further, **55** each outcome probably has a different valence, and the associated expectancies and instrumentalities will be less clear-cut than in our simple example.

Early task design theorists offered five propositions developed from expectancy theory that explain, in a general sense, how task variables may influence motivation. These propositions are:

1. To the extent that an individual believes that he or she can obtain an outcome he or she values by engaging in some particular behavior or class of behaviors, the likelihood that he or she will actually engage in that behavior is enhanced.
2. Outcomes are valued by individuals to the extent that they satisfy the physiological and psychological needs of the individual, or to the extent that they lead to other outcomes which satisfy such needs or are expected by the individual to do so.
3. Thus, to the extent that conditions at work can be arranged so that employees can satisfy their own needs best by working effectively toward organizational goals, employees will in fact tend to work hard toward the achievement of these goals (McGregor, 1960).
4. Most lower level needs (e.g., physical well-being, security) can be and often are reasonably well satisfied for individuals in contemporary society on a continuing basis and, therefore, will not serve as motivational incentives except under unusual circumstances.
5. Individuals who are capable of higher order need satisfaction will in fact experience such satisfaction when they learn that they have, as a result of their own efforts, accomplished something that they personally believe is worthwhile or meaningful (Hackman and Lawler, 1971, p. 262).

The job characteristics theory (Hackman and Oldham, 1976) implicitly retains this expectancy framework, although variable interrelationships are not specifically identified.

Unfortunately, most empirical studies of task design have not operationalized the expectancy theory variables. Perhaps one reason for this shortcoming has been the lack of an a priori framework predicting how the variables may influence one another. One framework that does specify some variable interrelationships, however, has recently been developed (Aldag and Brief, 1979). This viewpoint is presented in Figure 4–2.

The Aldag and Brief framework suggests that task attributes (i.e., task characteristics) will have a positive impact on employee motivation if, in fact, the employee perceives the task attributes to have a positive valence. They also note that the valence of each task attribute will be weighted by the perceived likelihood (i.e., instrumentality) that performance will lead to experiencing the attribute. Hence, Aldag and Brief view the valence and instrumentality of task attributes as crucial intervening variables between the employee's perceptions of the task attributes and the employee's self-perception of job behavior caused by the task attributes. Overall, however, while this framework does explicitly attempt to relate task design and expectancy theory variables, some predicted relationships are ambiguous and the rationale for others is not fully developed.

56

FIGURE 4–2 The Aldag and Brief Model of Task Design and Motivation

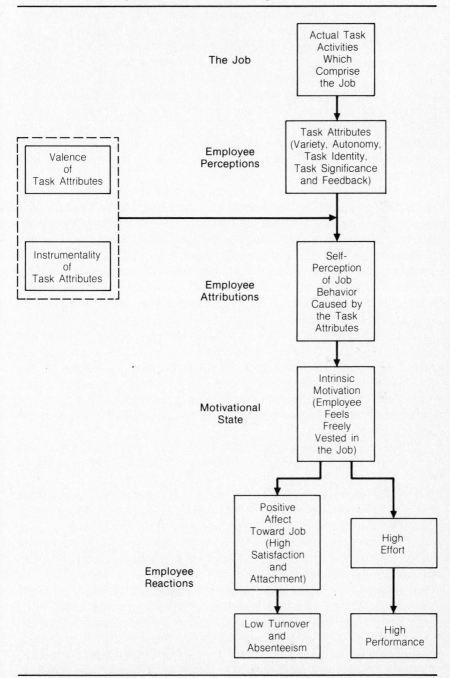

Research Evidence and Conclusions

This section will summarize the research evidence and draw appropriate conclusions pertaining to the task design—motivation relationship. While generally not operationalizing expectancy theory concepts, a large number of studies have tested a direct task design—motivation linkage. Overall, most of these studies have tended to support such a linkage. For example, positive relationships have been found in a number of field surveys (i.e., Hackman and Oldham, 1976). Studies that have attempted to include explicitly some expectancy theory concepts (i.e., Evans, Kiggundu, and House, 1979) have also yielded encouraging results. A positive relationship between task variables and motivation has also been found in a well-designed field experiment (Orpen, 1979).

The Orpen study, in particular, provides considerable insight into the role of task design in the motivational process. Using the job characteristic theory as a framework, he introduced task changes in an experimental group of 36 clerical employees. The tasks of 36 employees in a control group were unchanged. Worker assignments to groups were on a random basis, an unusual characteristic of organizational field research. After a six-month period, it was found that "employees in altered jobs were more involved in their work and more highly motivated to perform well than those in unaltered jobs" (p.204).

Empirical findings, then, are generally consistent with the assertion that task attributes are positively associated with employee motivation. Of course, when dealing with complex human attitudes and behaviors, any conclusions are somewhat speculative. Nevertheless, the evidence supporting such a relationship is quite convincing and leads us to suggest that increases in task scope will usually be accompanied by increases in employee motivation.

It would also be useful at this point to attempt a more precise statement of task characteristics and motivation relationships from an expectancy theory perspective. By integrating the basic expectancy model (Figure 4–1) and the Aldag and Brief refinement (Figure 4–2) with the job characteristics theory (Hackman and Oldham, 1976), Figure 4–3 emerges. As indicated, the framework suggests that employees may exert effort aimed at task performance if such performance has a positive expectancy for experiencing relevant task attributes such as variety, autonomy, feedback, identity, and/or significance.

These task attributes, in turn, may be expected to result in certain first-level outcomes such as perceived significance of the task, perceived accountability for task performance, and knowledge of results pertaining to task performance. (It should be noted that these outcomes are similar to the critical psychological states in the job characteristics theory.) The experienced task attributes and first-level outcomes are linked by

instrumentalities.

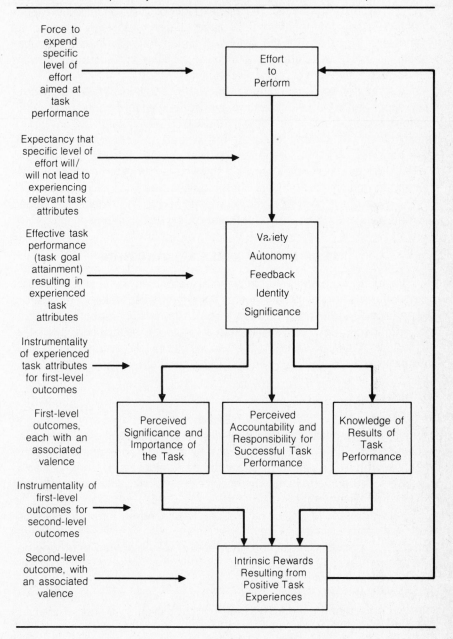

Next, the attainment of the first-level outcomes is expected to result in intrinsic rewards from positive task experiences. Again, instrumentality intervenes between the first- and second-level outcomes. Finally, the framework suggests that the extent to which intrinsic rewards actually result will influence future efforts to perform. That is, the intrinsic reward serves as positive reinforcement for motivated effort.

In summary, then, in addition to our earlier conclusion that increases in task scope will enhance motivation, two somewhat more specific generalizations can be drawn. First, employees will be motivated to exert effort on the job to the extent that: (1) this effort is seen as leading to experienced task attributes, (2) the experienced task attributes are seen as leading to valued first-level outcomes, and (3) the first-level outcomes are seen as leading to valued second-level outcomes such as intrinsic rewards. Second, this level of motivation will be maintained to the extent that valued second-level outcomes are, in fact, realized by the employee.

TASK DESIGN AND SATISFACTION

A second outcome variable generally included in most task design formulations is employee satisfaction. As with the discussion of motivation, we will initially refer to satisfaction from a general perspective, encompassing specific facets of satisfaction such as job satisfaction, pay satisfaction, etc. Later, however, it will be necessary to take a more precise view of satisfaction.

Rationale

In contrast to the motivation variable, there does not exist any one clearly delineated theoretical framework relating task design and employee satisfaction. Rather, the variables are generally related from a position of common sense and/or intuition. The automobile plant study summarized in Chapter 2 is a prime reason why researchers typically link task design and satisfaction. Recall that Walker and Guest (1952) found workers to be generally satisfied with their pay, supervision, and so forth, but dissatisfied with the real nature of their jobs. Hence, managers began to search for cures for this dissatisfaction; task design was assumed to be one potential cure.

While a well-developed framework for analysis is not available, the logic behind an anticipated task design and satisfaction relationship is fairly simple and straightforward. This logic might be organized and summarized as follows:

1. When tasks are highly specialized (i.e., low variety, autonomy, feedback, identity, and significance), the typical employee will master task-related procedures in a short period of time.
2. For most people, mastery over a simple and routine task will generally result in feelings of monotony and boredom.

3. A feeling of boredom and a lack of task-relevant challenge will generally cause a person to express feelings of dissatisfaction and unhappiness about his or her job.
4. In contrast, when tasks are more complex and challenging, employees will find task mastery a more difficult endeavor; in fact, nuances of many high scope tasks may effectively constrain complete task mastery.
5. When the employee is spending longer periods of time in learning a task, the task appears to be much less boring and routine.
6. Hence, the employee performing a complex task has less reason to express feelings of dissatisfaction about the task.

Of course, the preceding arguments assume that people generally prefer to not be bored; rather, the logic would argue that most people prefer to be challenged at work and to have the opportunity to learn new skills. These assumptions, while open to argument, appear to be generally reasonable.

Hackman and Oldham (1980) make a final important point in regard to employee satisfaction. As was noted in the introduction of this section, it is eventually necessary to consider different facets of satisfaction and their role in task design. In their job characteristics theory, they specify that *growth satisfaction* and *general satisfaction* are appropriate outcome variables to consider. They go on to point out that other facets of satisfaction, such as satisfaction with pay, supervision, etc., may either be unaffected or negatively affected by task design variables. Whether or not these elements of satisfaction are really unrelated to task design, however, is still an open question. In some settings, for example, task-related satisfactions may overlap and/or be related to other facets such as satisfaction with supervision (see Chapter 8) and satisfaction with co-workers (see Chapter 9). Clearly, however, the assertion that both the magnitude and the direction of influence between task variables and satisfaction will vary across facets of satisfaction seems reasonable and justified.

Research Evidence and Conclusions

As with motivation, there exists a fairly large body of research relating task characteristics and satisfaction. Positive relationships between these variables have been found in a large number of studies, although a few non-supportive studies also exist. Based on a review of the literature through 1976, Pierce and Dunham (1976, p. 87) conclude that "satisfaction with work is more strongly related to task design than are other affective, behavioral or motivational variables." The literature since that time also seems to support this conclusion.

Particularly compelling, again, is the Orpen (1979) study. Just as in the case of employee motivation, he found significant improvements in employee satisfaction over a six-month period in an experimental group whose jobs were redesigned. Finally, Griffin (1981c) also provides support for the task design–satisfaction relationship in one of the few longitudinal field studies available. He found a positive relationship between task characteristics and job satisfaction in the same industrial sample at two **61** different points in time three months apart. This finding suggests that the predicted relationship is essentially stable over time.

Overall, therefore, the available evidence supports the argument that employee satisfaction is related to task variables. The suggested relationship seems logical and reasonable and has been almost universally supported by researchers. A few questions, however, remain to be answered.

First, it has been argued that, in fact, individual satisfaction differences may cause employees to describe their jobs in different ways (O'Reilly, Parlette, and Bloom, 1980). While most other studies generally support the assumed direction of causality, this alternative view deserves more consideration. Second, the role of other facets of satisfaction in task design research and practice is still uncertain for two reasons: (1) as mentioned earlier, recent task design formulations include important nontask variables such as the social setting and leader behavior, and (2) relationships among facets of satisfaction themselves may confound predicted relationships. For example, it seems reasonable to suggest that satisfaction with pay will generally be unrelated to task characteristics. However, a particular worker may be so dissatisfied with his or her pay so as to cause the worker to not fully perceive, appreciate, and respond to a well-designed task.

In summary, however, these two problems do not seem to be of sufficient concern or importance to detract significantly from the strong research support suggesting a task design–satisfaction relationship. Rather, they just point to comparatively small areas in need of further refinement.

TASK DESIGN AND PERFORMANCE

The final primary outcome variable generally considered by task design theorists is performance. Our discussion of this variable will be in somewhat more depth and will also take a more critical stance for the following reasons: (1) performance is a variable which is often linked theoretically with organizational variables such as leader behavior, motivation, and so forth, but which is seldom supported empirically, and (2) performance determinants are of tremendous practical importance to managers. Hence, the suggestion that a task design–performance relationship exists warrants careful analysis.

Rationale

The rationale for predicting such a relationship can be approached from two different perspectives. More specifically, it can be argued that task design variables influence employee performance directly or indirectly. The research of Richard Hackman provides justification for expecting to find a direct task design–performance relationship.

As summarized earlier in this chapter, expectancy theory was used as a basis for the job characteristics theory. The initial framework (Hackman and Lawler, 1971) suggested that to the extent that organizational goals and individual needs are congruent, employees will work hard to achieve such goals. Since expanded task scope was seen as a vehicle for obtaining individual and organization congruence, Hackman and Lawler predicted a task scope–employee performance relationship.

This initial viewpoint was more clearly explicated by Hackman and Oldham (1976). In their job characteristics theory, they state that all outcome variables, including quality of work performance, "are expected to be more positive for jobs with high motivating potential . . ." (p. 259), i.e., jobs with high scope.

Finally, the most current available presentation of the job characteristics model (Hackman and Oldham, 1980) also includes performance as a specific outcome variable. The term used to represent performance is work effectiveness. Work effectiveness, in turn, consists of both quality and quantity of output. The rationale for assuming a *quality* relationship is: "When a job is high in motivating potential, people who work on that job tend to experience positive affect when they perform *well*. And performing well, for most people, means producing high-quality work of which one can be proud" (p. 91). The *quantity* prediction is based on three factors: (1) high scope tasks are generally not characterized as routine and boring; hence, employees aren't as likely to search for ways of avoiding work, (2) as a result of task changes aimed at increasing scope, hidden inefficiencies in the work system may be corrected, and (3) such change efforts may simplify and refine the total work system. Hence, the rationale for expecting a direct task design–performance linkage has been logically developed from a theoretical point of view.

An alternative formulation, offered by Schwab and Cummings (1976), suggests an indirect relationship between the variables. As shown in Figure 4–4, this particular approach is also based on expectancy theory. Expectancy theory postulates that employee performance is directly attributable to individual motivation and ability (Vroom, 1964). Schwab and Cummings, in turn, suggest that task scope influences performance indirectly by operating through motivation and/or ability. Specifically, they predict that task scope will influence performance in conjunction with ability, and will also operate as an independent variable in influencing motivational factors such as expectancies, instrumentalities, and valences. Note that these latter predictions are generally consistent with Figures 4–2 and 4–3.

The prediction of an interactive relationship between task scope and ability is based on the theory of work adjustment (Dawis, England, and Lofquist, 1968). Schwab and Cummings note that the work adjustment theory focuses on the optimal balance of individual abilities and task demands (i.e., task scope). Hence, if task scope is too high or too low with respect to the employee's ability, performance will suffer. In contrast, per- **63**

FIGURE 4–4 The Schwab and Cummings Model of Task Scope and Employee Performance

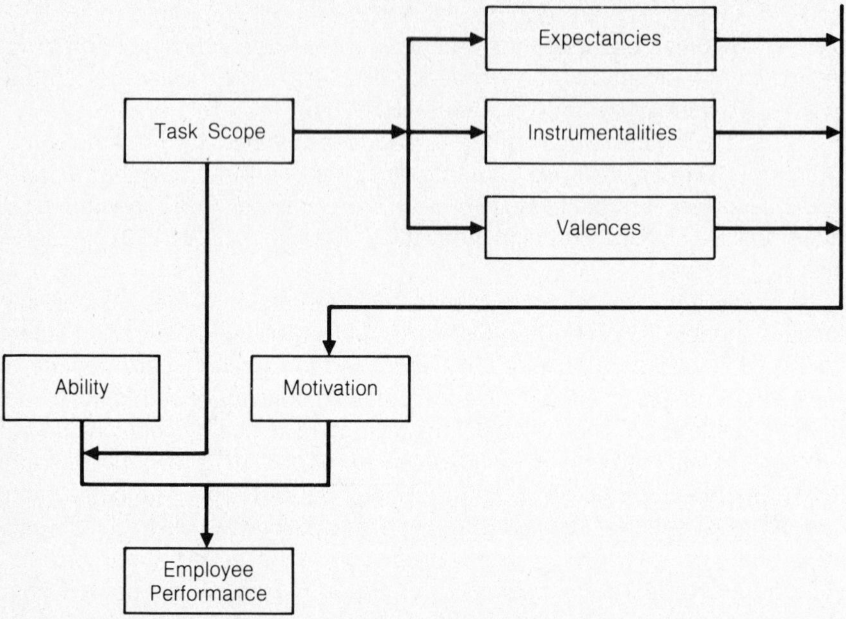

Source: D. P. Schwab and L. L. Cummings, "A Theoretical Analysis of the Impact of Task Scope on Employee Performance," *The Academy of Management Review* (Vol. 1, 1976), pp. 23–35. Used by permission.

formance will be enhanced to the extent that task scope and relative ability are congruent.

This framework also suggests that task scope will serve as an independent variable influencing motivation factors. While a number of predictions are made in the Schwab and Cummings article, the key hypotheses are summarized below:

1. Increases in task scope beyond the individual's current task level will cause a reduction in expectancy perceptions.
2. Increases in task scope will cause an increase in instrumentality perceptions pertaining to task-administered outcomes (i.e., the interaction between the individual and accomplishment).
3. Increases in task scope will cause an increase in the valence of performance.

Hence, these predictions serve to indicate more precisely expected relationships among task design and performance within an expectancy theory framework.

Research Evidence and Conclusions

The research evidence pertaining to the task design–performance linkage will be reviewed in two parts. First, we will examine studies based on a job enlargement/enrichment framework. Next, we will summarize research focusing on the perceived task characteristics–performance linkage.

Job enlargement/enrichment. A number of researchers have assessed the impact of job enlargement and/or enrichment on employee performance. In one of the first longitudinal studies, it was found that three organizational factors similar in concept to task dimensions were associated with employee performance over a two and one-half year period (Farris, 1969). Paul, Robertson and Herzberg (1969) summarize five job enrichment programs conducted in British firms. In all five studies, job enrichment led to an increase in employee performance levels. The American Telephone and Telegraph studies (Ford, 1973) found positive increases in employee productivity as a result of 19 job enlargement programs. Positive relationships between job enrichment/enlargement efforts and performance have also been reported by Maher (1971) and Merrens and Garrett (1975). On the negative side, nonsupporting evidence has been obtained from a laboratory experiment (Robey, 1974) and a field experiment (Bishop and Hill, 1971).

At face value, then, the evidence would appear to support a predicted relationship between task design and performance from a job enrichment/enlargement perspective. A closer examination of these studies, however, raises a number of questions. Two critical flaws characterize most of these studies. First, many of the studies were one-shot investigations. Second, and even more of a problem, most studies did not measure any aspects of the focal jobs themselves. By failing to assess the nature of jobs before and after a presumed job change, for example, researchers leave open to question the following points: (1) did employees actually recognize that a job change had taken place, and (2) couldn't behavioral changes have been caused by other, uncontrolled factors? Hence, the research findings pertaining to job enrichment/enlargement and performance are generally supportive, but are open to alternative explanations.

Perceived task characteristics. As summarized in Chapter 3, a major research thrust in recent years has focused on employee perceptions of their jobs. Griffin, Welsh and Moorhead (1981) have reviewed studies focusing on task characteristics perceptions and performance, and this section is condensed from that review. The criteria for inclusion in the Griffin, et al. (1981) review were: (1) the study must include measures of employee perceptions of tasks, and (2) the degree of association between these task perceptions and some primary facet of employee performance must have been empirically tested.

A total of 13 studies were located which met these criteria. These studies are summarized in Table 4–1. Column 2 refers to the research instrument used to measure task perceptions. These instruments are described in Chapter 5. Column 3 summarizes the measure of performance utilized in the study. The next column indicates the inclusion of any po- **65**

TABLE 4–1   Summary of Task Characteristics—Performance Studies

STUDY	MEASURE OF TASK CHARACTERISTICS[a]	MEASURE OF PERFORMANCE[c]	MODERATOR(S) TESTED[d]
1. Hackman and Lawler (1971)	YJI	SE	GNS
2. Wanous (1974)	YJI	SE	GNS PWE RU
3. Hackman and Oldham (1976)	JDS	SE	GNS
4. Oldham, Hackman, and Pearce (1976)	JDS	SE	GNS
			CS
			GNS × CS
5. Sims and Szilagyi (1976)	JCI	SE	GNS
			LC

TABLE 4–1 Summary of Task Characteristics—Performance Studies (*continued*)

TYPE OF STUDY[e]	SAMPLE SIZE	NATURE OF SAMPLE[f]	MAIN EFFECTS[g]	INTERACTIVE EFFECTS[h]
FS	208	HE	6 of 12 correlations between task characteristics and performance positive and significant	No support for total sample; modest support only for high scope tasks
FS	80	HO	Main effects not reported	No support for any moderating variable; most correlations non-significant[i]
FS	658	HE	4 of 5 task characteristics and MPS scores significantly correlated with performance	Correlations for high and low GNS groups different in predicted direction but differences not significant
FS	201	HO	MPS and performance significantly correlated	Correlations for high and low GNS groups different in predicted direction but differences not significant
				Correlations for high and low CS groups different in predicted direction; 1 of 5 pairs significantly different
				Correlations for high GNS/high CS and low GNS/low CS groups all significantly different and in predicted direction
FS	766	HE	6 of 6 correlations between task characteristics and performance positive and significant	3 of 6 pairs of correlations for high and low GNS groups different in predicted direction (1 pair significantly different); remaining 3 pairs of correlations significantly different in opposite direction
				No moderating effects detected

(*continued*)

TABLE 4–1   Summary of Task Characteristics—Performance Studies (continued)

STUDY	MEASURE OF TASK CHARACTERISTICS[a]	MEASURE OF PERFORMANCE[c]	MODERATOR(S) TESTED[d]
6. Umstot, Bell, and Mitchell (1976)	JDS[b]	DI	GNS
7. Steers and Spencer (1977)	YJI	SE	NA
8. Evans, Kiggundu, and House (1979)	JDS	SR	GNS NA
9. Orpen (1979)	JDS[b]	SE DI	GNS CS
10. White and Mitchell (1979)	JDS[b]	DI	None
11. Griffin (1981c)	JCI	DI	GNS
12. Griffin (1981d)	JCI	DI	GNS
13. Pierce (1979)	JDS	SE	None

[a] JCI = .Job Characteristic Inventory, JDS = Job Diagnostic Survey, YJI = Yale Job Inventory
[b] Used as a manipulation check
[c] SE = Supervisory evaluation, SR = Self-rated, DI = Direct measure of quantity and/or quality
[d] GNS = Growth need strength, CS = Contextual satisfaction, NA = Need for achievement, PWE = Protestant work ethic, RU = Rural/urban background, LC = Locus of control
[e] FS = Field survey, FE = Field experiment, LE = Lab experiment, LFS = Longitudinal field survey

TABLE 4–1 Summary of Task Characteristics—Performance Studies (continued)

TYPE OF STUDY[e]	SAMPLE SIZE	NATURE OF SAMPLE[f]	MAIN EFFECTS[g]	INTERACTIVE EFFECTS[h]
LE	42	HO	No main effects between task charteristics/MPS and performance detected	4 of 6 pairs of correlations for high and low GNS groups different in predicted direction but differences not significant; autonomy significantly correlated with performance for high GNS group
FS	115	HO	No significant correlations between task characteristics and performance	5 of 6 pairs of correlations for high and low Nach groups significantly different in predicted direction
FS	343	HO	5 of 7 correlations between task characteristics/MPS and performance positive and significant	No moderating effects detected
FE	72	HO	No significant correlations between task characteristics and performance	No moderating effects detected
LE	41	HO	No significant relationships found	Not applicable
LFS	109 160	HO HO	No significant correlations between task characteristics and performance	No moderating effects detected
FS	80	HO	3 of 4 task characteristics significantly correlated with performance	No moderating effects detected
FS	397	HO	Significant R obtained with 3 task characteristics regressed on performance	Not applicable

[f] HE = Heterogeneous, HO = Homogeneous
[g] Extent to which statistical relationships were found between task characteristics and performance
[h] Extent to which predicted moderator effects were found
[i] Specific results not presented in article: interpretation is based on author's discussion of results

Source: R. W. Griffin, A. Welsh, and G. Moorhead, "Perceived Task Characteristics and Employee Performance: A Literature Review," *The Academy of Management Review* (Vol. 6, 1981). Used by permission.

tential individual difference variable in the study (see Chapter 3 for a review of the individual difference literature). Column 5 indicates the type of study, while sample sizes and sample homogeneity are summarized in Columns 6 and 7 respectively. The column labeled "Main Effects" summarizes the extent to which direct relationships were found between task perceptions and performance. The last column summarizes the extent to which any predicted moderating effects were found.

In general, Studies 3, 4, 5, and 12 provide strong support for main effects predictions. Studies 1, 8, and 13 provide mixed support. Studies 6, 7, 9, 10, and 11 provide no support whatsoever for main effects. Individual difference predictions were supported less frequently, with mixed support provided in Studies 4 and 7, weak support provided in Studies 1, 3, 5, and 6, and no support provided in Studies 2, 8, 9, 11, 12, and 13. Once again, the evidence is inconclusive.

One important point raised by the review pertains to the manner in which performance was operationalized in these studies. Specifically, performance has been defined and measured in several different ways. Hence, generalizations about task design and performance from Table 4–1 are tenuous due to significantly different operationalizations of the performance variable.

In contrast to the task design–motivation and task design–satisfaction linkages reviewed earlier, the evidence pertaining to task design and performance is much more difficult to interpret. About the only "conclusion" that is appropriate is that research findings are inconclusive. On the one hand, enough support has been found to be encouraging and to warrant additional attention. On the other hand, many studies have yielded no support at all for a task design–performance relationship.

It is possible, however, to draw some tentative generalizations about the effects of task variables on performance. First, improvements in task design may result in moderate performance improvements in some cases. This improvement, however, is likely to result most specifically from increased motivation. That is, task improvements may have a direct and positive impact on motivation, which in turn may result in performance improvements.

Second, it is unrealistic to expect task design improvements always to increase performance. For example, in many cases (e.g., on an assembly line), the quantity of output is not directly a function of employee effort. That is, the production process may dictate output.

Third, improved performance may occur at the aggregate level (i.e., group or organization) as opposed to the individual level. This might occur, for example, because task changes may result in a more efficient production system. Finally, even if identifiable performance increases do not follow task design changes, the organization may still realize direct-cost savings due to lower turnover and absenteeism resulting from improved levels of satisfaction and motivation.

TASK DESIGN AND OTHER VARIABLES

Motivation, satisfaction, and performance are considered to be primary potential outcome variables by most task design researchers. This section will summarize three secondary variables which may also be influenced by task design. These variables are considered to be secondary not because of a lack of importance or relevance, but because they are seldom included in task design research. However, they have been linked to task variables by some researchers, and for this reason they will be summarized here.

Task Design and Attendance

Rationale. The rationale for originally predicting a task design–attendance relationship is somewhat ambiguous. The Turner and Lawrence study (1965) found a positive relationship between task complexity and attendance, and many subsequent investigations have assumed that such a relationship might exist. A logical argument, however, might be that the effects of task design on employee attendance would tend to be indirect. Specifically, as has already been summarized, task scope tends to be related to employee satisfaction and motivation. Satisfaction and motivation, in turn, might logically be expected to lead to improved employee attendance. That is, employees who are satisfied with their work and who are motivated by their jobs might be expected to make fewer excuses to avoid working.

Research evidence and conclusions. As mentioned earlier, employee attendance was positively related to task scope in the Turner and Lawrence study (1965). Since that time, however, no consistent pattern of findings has emerged. In fact, one study (Hackman, Pearce, and Wolfe, 1978) found increased absenteeism following a task redesign program. The probable reason for such disappointing results would be the point raised earlier: attendance is more a function of satisfaction and motivation than of task design.

The obvious conclusion to be reached is that there is little theoretical or empirical support for a direct task design–attendance relationship. Rather, the effects of task design on employee attendance are probably indirect and operate through the affective variables satisfaction and, perhaps, motivation. Further, due to this indirect relationship, if improved attendance does result from changes in task design, such changes will presumably take an extended period of time to manifest themselves.

Task Design and Commitment

Rationale. Another variable that has recently been linked to task design is organizational commitment. Commitment has been defined as "the relative strength of an individual's identification with and involvement **71**

in his or her employing organization'' (Porter, Steers, Mowday, and Boulian, 1974). The rationale for predicting a task design–commitment relationship is that commitment has been shown to be interrelated with a variety of personal, motivational, behavioral, and organizational variables. Since task design has been related to many of these same variables, the expectation is that task design and organizational commitment may be related to one another.

Research evidence and conclusions. To date, one study has empirically tested the prediction that task scope will be associated with organizational commitment. Both variables were measured in a sample of 115 managers in a manufacturing firm (Steers and Spencer, 1977). It was found that four of six perceived task characteristics were positively correlated with commitment.

Since only one study has tested the relationship in question, any conclusions must, by definition, be drawn with considerable caution. We will tentatively state that increases in task scope will potentially result in increased organizational commitment on the part of employees. However, much additional research is needed to have any reasonable degree of confidence in this conclusion. Because of the nature of the commitment variable, this research is certainly justified.

Task Design and Experienced Stress

Rationale. A final outcome variable which may conceivably be related to task design is experienced stress on the part of subordinates. The task design–stress connection can be described from an activation theory framework (Scott, 1966). Activation theory refers to the degree of physical and/or psychological activation or stimulation acting on a person. Hence, it seems plausible to suggest that a low scope task will result in low levels of activation, while a high scope task will cause higher levels of activation. Unfortunately, a method for operationalizing activation theory is unavailable.

Two specific questions of interest arise from this approach, however, which have implications for task design. First, it seems plausible that in some cases, activation from task attributes may be too high. That is, an employee may, for example, experience so much variety, autonomy, feedback, and significance from a task as to be over-stimulated. A logical result of such over-stimulation might be experienced stress by the employee. A second issue, really a corollary of the first, pertains to task changes. Even if a redesigned task is properly structured, until the employee becomes familiar with the new task demands, he or she may also experience stress through over-activation and role-overload (cf., Kahn, Wolfe, Quinn, Snoek, and Rosenthal, 1964).

One approach has been developed that is both tentative and speculative, but it does describe potential interrelationships among task scope,

72

FIGURE 4–5   Task Scope, Activation, Experienced Stress, and Job Satisfaction

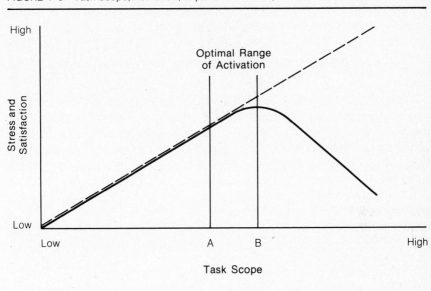

experienced stress, activation levels, and employee satisfaction (Quick and Griffin, 1980). The predicted pattern of interrelationships is presented in Figure 4–5. As task scope is increased, employee satisfaction and experienced stress also increase. Initially, this increase in stress is seen as desirable. At some point A, however, satisfaction increases come at a decreasing rate, while experienced stress continues to steadily increase. At some point B, employee satisfaction begins to decrease due to over-activation; however, experienced stress maintains an increasing trend. The range in task scope between points A and B is seen as causing the optimal level of activation. Task scope below point A produces under-activation and levels of satisfaction below optimum. Alternatively, task scope higher than point B leads to over-activation, a great deal of experienced stress, and, consequently, decreases in employee satisfaction.

Two additional points should also be made at this time. First, this framework is assumed to be individual-specific. The optimal level of activation varies considerably from one person to another (Scott, 1966); further, the A–B range also varies considerably between people. Second, the framework is also time-specific. The optimal level of activation varies for any one individual according to experience, fatigue, motivation, etc.

Research evidence and conclusion.   As indicated earlier, this framework is both tentative and speculative. No empirical evidence exists in regard to the relationships summarized in Figure 4–5; hence, no conclu-   **73**

sions are warranted. Due to the significance of the stress variable (cf., Ivancevich and Matteson, 1980), however, research is clearly needed to explore formulations such as the one summarized here.

TASK DESIGN AND OUTCOMES: AN INTEGRATION

This chapter has explored the effects of task design on work-related outcome variables. At this point, we will present an integrative framework that will tie things together somewhat and provide additional insight into the effects of task design on outcome variables. The framework is presented in Figure 4–6. (Note that the stress variable is not included due to its speculative nature and lack of empirical study.)

At a general level, the framework assumes that task design variables and processes tend to influence the relevant outcome variables in either a direct or indirect fashion. The strongest relationships are predicted to be between task design and employee satisfaction and motivation. Task de-

FIGURE 4–6   An Integrative Model of Task Design and Work-Related Outcome Variables

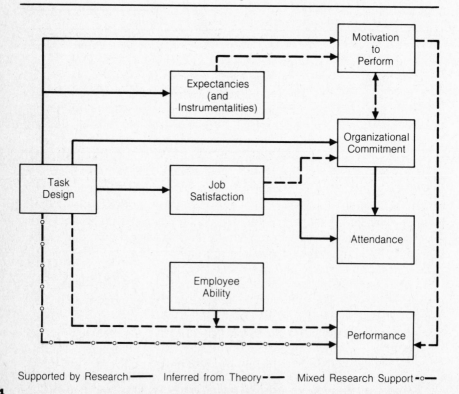

Supported by Research —— Inferred from Theory ‑‑ Mixed Research Support ‑o‑

sign is also predicted to have a direct impact on commitment and performance. Finally, task design is predicted to have four interactive relationships: (1) with expectancies and instrumentalities on motivation, (2) with satisfaction on commitment, (3) with satisfaction on attendance, and (4) with ability on performance.

The basis for each predicted relationship will be briefly summarized below (in each case, the assumed antecedent variable is listed first):

1. *Task Design and Motivation*: strong empirical support summarized earlier in this chapter.
2. *Task Design and Expectancy*: empirical support found in Sims and Szilagyi (1976) and Evans, et al. (1979), as summarized earlier.
3. *Expectancy and Motivation*: assumed from expectancy theory (Vroom, 1964; Schwab and Cummings, 1976), as summarized earlier.
4. *Task Design and Satisfaction:* strong empirical support as summarized earlier.
5. *Task Design and Performance*: mixed empirical findings as summarized earlier.
6. *Ability and Performance*: assumed from expectancy theory.
7. *Task Design / Ability and Performance*: assumed from expectancy theory.
8. *Motivation and Performance*: assumed from expectancy theory.
9. *Task Design and Commitment*: empirical support found in Steers and Spencer (1977), as summarized earlier.
10. *Satisfaction and Commitment*: assumed from discussion of commitment found in Steers (1977a, p. 121); commitment is seen as resulting from, among other things, positive past experiences in the organization.
11a. *Motivation and Commitment*: assumed from Steers (1977a, p. 121); commitment is seen as resulting from, among other things, variations in need strengths.
11b. *Commitment and Motivation*: assumed from Steers (1977a, p. 123); commitment is seen as a cause of willingness to expend effort on behalf of the organization.
12. *Satisfaction and Attendance*: assumed from discussion of satisfaction found in Hamner and Organ (1978, p. 229).
13. *Commitment and Attendance*: empirical support found in Porter, et al. (1974), and Steers (1977a).

It should also be noted that this framework is somewhat incomplete. Specific elements that are missing include: (1) the determinants and/or causes of task design, (2) possible reverse causality among variables such as the impact of satisfaction on employee task perceptions, and (3) other potential outcome variables. As indicated earlier in this chapter, task design will not be the only determinant of any of these variables. Rather, each will be influenced by a variety of individual and organizational factors.

However, the framework is not really intended to completely describe the individual's work environment. It is simply offered as a summary device for understanding the existing evidence regarding task design and key outcome variables. As additional insights are gained, by both managerial practice and empirical research, further refinements may be needed. At the present time, though, the framework may serve as a useful device for better understanding the role of task design in influencing employee reactions to work, and it justifies further attempts at improving the employee's work experience.

5 THE MEASUREMENT OF TASKS

Task measurement is a fairly widespread practice in many organizations. However, specific aspects and characteristics of tasks may be measured by a variety of techniques and for a number of different reasons. The following scenarios should serve to highlight these differences.

Bill Saunders is the president of a medium-sized manufacturing company in the Southwest. His company, Atlas Incorporated, has recently been plagued with a decline in the quality of their finished goods and an overall problem of poor employee morale. Mr. Saunders has contracted with Dr. Helen Winthrop, a management consultant, to help alleviate these problems. After a three-month assessment, Dr. Winthrop has recommended a task redesign program. She has concluded that two factors have contributed to a mismatch between jobs and employees in the company. First, during a sustained period of rapid growth, Atlas had inadvertently created many highly specialized jobs to facilitate efficiency. At the same time, the personnel manager had raised hiring standards in order to get "a better quality work force." What Atlas actually did, then, was to develop an intelligent, highly motivated group of employees and then assign them to simple, highly-specialized tasks.

After reading Dr. Winthrop's analysis and recommendations, Mr. Saunders was in general agreement with the need for task redesign. He recalled reading about something called job enrichment when he was in college, and this seems like just what Atlas needs to turn things around. One thing is puzzling Mr. Saunders, however: the recommendations suggest having employees fill out some kind of questionnaire before their jobs are redesigned, and then again about six months later. As far as he's concerned, this is not really necessary. He is ready to "get the show on the road" and doesn't want to worry about questionnaires. Mr. Saunders has just called Dr. Winthrop and asked her to explain why this questionnaire is needed.

Dr. Winthrop replies: "The questionnaire is going to provide us with a great deal of relevant information. Obviously, we can use it to find out if morale, or satisfaction, actually increases after the jobs are changed. After all, improving satisfaction is a major reason for the whole program, and if we don't measure satisfaction, we won't really know if we've solved the problem or not. It will also give us important information about the task changes themselves.

"The questionnaire I've recommended measures employee perceptions of the amount of variety, autonomy, feedback, identity, and significance in the present jobs. Scores we get on these characteristics will help us in two ways. First, by comparing different jobs within the company to national norms that are available, we can identify the jobs most deficient in motivational properties. That is, we can get a feel for which jobs to start on, which ones can wait a while, and so forth. Second, some people have found that even when they thought they had changed a group of jobs, the employees themselves did not perceive any changes. By measuring perceptions before the change, and then again afterward, we'll know if we really accomplished our objectives. Yes, measuring employee perceptions of their jobs is really important if task redesign is to be successful."

One of Atlas' primary customers, King Wholesalers, is also experiencing human resource problems. Over the last two years, turnover has increased from around 10% per year to over 30%. The personnel manager, Tom Campbell, is concerned about this dramatic increase and has set about investigating the problem. Over the last few months, he has conducted in-depth exit interviews with every employee resigning from the firm. In almost every case, the employee cited pay as the primary factor behind the departure from King. There are a number of other wholesalers in the area, and the employees all said they could make more money by changing jobs.

After doing more research, Tom schedules an appointment with the company president, Albert King. During the meeting, Tom outlines the situation and recommends a job evaluation study with the intent of changing the firm's salary structure. Mr. King asks Tom to clarify what he means by a job evaluation study.

"A job evaluation study," Tom states, "is a process by which we can determine the worth or value of different jobs in the company. You see, over the past few years, a great deal of inequality has crept into our system. Until recently, all of our jobs were essentially manual in nature, and any one person could pretty well learn to do any of the jobs in the warehouse. Now, though, many of the jobs have been integrated with our computer system. For some people, these new jobs involve entering data directly into the computer and then interpreting printouts. Some people even have to know some basic computer programming. Yet we're still paying everyone about **77** the same wage. Clearly, some of our jobs now require more expertise than others, and if we want to attract and keep good people for those jobs, we're going to have to pay them a fair salary. The job evaluation study, then, is going to tell us which jobs are the most significant in terms of our overall operation. Then we'll be able to compete with these other companies for the talent we need, because we'll know how much to pay people for different jobs.

"Over the long run, we're also going to have to think about a job analysis study. Job evaluation focuses on determining how much to pay a person to do a job; job analysis, on the other hand, is concerned with determining exactly what the job duties in a particular situation consist of. This will help us better match jobs and people. We'll know what skills to look for in a job applicant, and we'll also lower the risk of discrimination charges."

Another local manufacturer, Moorhead Metals, is also initiating a study of jobs, but for still a different reason. Moorhead Metals is a machine shop that fabricates metal parts to customer specifications. Because of a healthy local business climate, Moorhead has grown steadily over the years. The company has recently purchased ten new sophisticated fabricating machines in order to better meet customer demand. The company's industrial engineer, Paul Hamm, must now develop a set of production specifications for the machines. A recent visitor to the shop asked Paul what is involved in developing these specifications.

Paul says, "Well, we actually do two things. First, we study the job itself to determine the most efficient way of doing things. We try to minimize unnecessary movements by the employee and develop the best techniques for doing the jobs that need to be done. The second thing our study does is to determine the production quota for the machine. Our employees are paid on a production-bonus system. They receive a base rate for turning out a certain number of units per hour. They also get a bonus for each unit above that number that they can produce. So, setting that production quota is extremely important. On the one hand, the quota has to be low enough to give the machinist something to shoot for. If it's too high, the machinist will know it can't be reached and won't even try. On the other hand, if the quota is too low, the employees will break it so often and by such a large margin that the company will end up losing money.

"To make the job even tougher, you almost have to get it right the first time. If you set the quota too low, and then try to raise it, the employees accuse you of trying to squeeze more work out of them. If you set it too high to start with, that's not quite so bad, but the employees still get discouraged because they can't meet the quota. I've even known some employees who would purposely fall below a new quota just so you'd lower it and make their jobs easier."

Each of the companies discussed in the preceding paragraphs is engaged in an activity requiring task measurement. However, each firm is measuring tasks for different reasons and through different methods. Atlas is measuring employee *perceptions* of task *characteristics* in order to enhance *outcome variables* such as *satisfaction*. King is concerned with *task content* in order to adjust salary schedules and selection criteria to reflect the *value* and *requirements* of the job to the firm. Moorhead is measuring *operational properties* of tasks in order to train employees in *efficiency* and to set anticipated levels of *output*.

The following sections of this chapter will discuss these different approaches to task measurement. Much of our discussion will center on the measurement of task perceptions, since this topic is most relevant to task design as we have defined it. Following these discussions, a final section will describe how the techniques might be used in conjunction with one another to facilitate task redesign programs.

THE MEASUREMENT OF TASK PERCEPTIONS

As evidenced by the literature summarized in Chapters 3 and 4, most task design research over the last several years has focused on employee perceptions of certain task characteristics. This research was stimulated by the Turner and Lawrence (1965) study. At the present time, most task design investigations employ one of two instruments created to assess task perceptions. One instrument is referred to as the Job Diagnostic Survey, or JDS (Hackman and Oldham, 1975). This measure represents a revision and refinement of an earlier instrument called the Yale Job Inventory (Hackman and Lawler, 1971). This latter instrument will not be described here since the JDS is viewed as its successor. The second instrument to be discussed in this section is the Job Characteristic Inventory or JCI (Sims, Szilagyi, and Keller, 1976). The JCI is used less frequently than the JDS, but is viewed by many as an acceptable alternative.

The Job Diagnostic Survey

The Job Diagnostic Survey was first described by Hackman and Oldham (1975). The instrument was designed to measure relevant variables in the job characteristics theory (as summarized in Chapter 3). Specifically, the JDS was intended "to be of use both in the *diagnosis* of jobs prior to their redesign, and in *research and evaluation* activities aimed at assessing the effects of redesigned jobs on the people who do them" (Hackman and Oldham, 1975, p. 159).

The researchers spent approximately two years developing the JDS. During the developmental stages, over 1,500 employees from 15 different organizations responded to the instrument. Modifications were made by adding, deleting, and/or changing items. The following section will describe the JDS itself in more detail.

Description.   The total JDS includes 83 items. Besides the task   **79**

TABLE 5-1 The Job Diagnostic Survey

SECTION ONE

This part of the questionnaire asks you to describe your job, as *objectively* as you can.

Please do *not* use this part of the questionnaire to show how much you like or dislike your job. Questions about that will come later. Instead, try to make your descriptions as accurate and as objective as you possibly can.

A sample question is given below.

A. To what extent does your job require you to work with mechanical equipment?

$$1 - - - - - - - 2 - - - - - - - 3 - - - - - 4 - - - - - - - 5 - - - - - - - \textcircled{6} - - - - - 7$$

| Very little; the job requires almost no contact with mechanical equipment of any kind. | Moderately | Very much; the job requires almost constant work with mechanical equipment. |

You are to *circle* the number which is the most accurate description of your job.

If, for example, your job requires you to work with mechanical equipment a good deal of the time—but also requires some paperwork—you might circle the number six, as was done in the example above.

If you do not understand these instructions, please ask for assistance. If you do understand them, turn the page and begin.

1. To what extent does your job require you to *work closely with other people* (either "clients," or people in related jobs in your own organization)?

$$1 - - - - - - - 2 - - - - - - - 3 - - - - - - - 4 - - - - - - - 5 - - - - - - - - 6 - - - - - - - 7$$

| Very little; dealing with other people is not at all necessary in doing the job. | Moderately; some dealing with others is necessary. | Very much; dealing with other people is an absolutely essential and crucial part of doing the job. |

2. How much *autonomy* is there in your job? That is, to what extent does your job permit you to decide *on your own* how to go about doing the work?

$$1 - - - - - - - 2 - - - - - - - 3 - - - - - - - 4 - - - - - - - 5 - - - - - - - - 6 - - - - - - - 7$$

| Very little; the job gives me almost no personal "say" about how and when the work is done. | Moderate autonomy; many things are standardized and not under my control, but I can make some decisions about the work. | Very much; the job gives me almost complete responsibility for deciding how and when the work is done. |

3. To what extent does your job involve doing a *"whole" and identifiable piece of work*? That is, is the job a complete piece of work that has an obvious beginning and end? Or is it only a small *part* of the overall piece of work, which is finished by other people or by automatic machines?

$$1 - - - - - - - 2 - - - - - - - 3 - - - - - - - 4 - - - - - - - 5 - - - - - - - - 6 - - - - - - - 7$$

| My job is only a tiny part of the overall piece of work; the results of my activities cannot be seen in the final product or service. | My job is a moderate-sized "chunk" of the overall piece of work; my own contribution can be seen in the final outcome. | My job involves doing the whole piece of work, from start to finish; the results of my activities are easily seen in the final product or service. |

(Continued)

4. How much *variety* is there in your job? That is, to what extent does the job require you to do many different things at work, using a variety of your skills and talents?

1 - - - - - - - 2 - - - - - - - 3 - - - - - - - 4 - - - - - - - 5 - - - - - - - 6 - - - - - - - 7

Very little; the job requires me to do the same routine things over and over again.	Moderate variety.	Very much; the job requires me to do many different things, using a number of different skills and talents.

5. In general, how *significant or important* is your job? That is, are the results of your work likely to significantly affect the lives or well-being of other people?

1 - - - - - - - 2 - - - - - - - 3 - - - - - - - 4 - - - - - - - 5 - - - - - - - 6 - - - - - - - 7

Not very significant; the outcomes of my work are *not* likely to have important. effects on other people.	Moderately significant.	Highly significant; the outcomes of my work can affect other people in very important ways.

6. To what extent do *managers or co-workers* let you know how well you are doing on your job?

1 - - - - - - - 2 - - - - - - - 3 - - - - - - - 4 - - - - - - - 5 - - - - - - - 6 - - - - - - - 7

Very little; people almost never let me know how well I am doing.	Moderately; sometimes people may give me "feed-back"; other times they may not.	Very much; managers or co-workers provide me with almost constant "feedback" about how well I am doing.

7. To what extent does *doing the job itself* provide you with information about your work performance? That is, does the actual *work itself* provide clues about how well you are doing—aside from any "feedback" co-workers or supervisors may provide?

1 - - - - - - - 2 - - - - - - - 3 - - - - - - - 4 - - - - - - - 5 - - - - - - - 6 - - - - - - - 7

Very little; the job itself is set up so I could work for-ever without finding out how well I am doing.	Moderately; sometimes doing the job provides "feedback" to me; some-times it does not.	Very much; the job is set up so that I get almost constant "feedback" as I work about how well I am doing.

(Continued)

TABLE 5–1   (Continued)

Listed below are a number of statements which could be used to describe a job.

You are to indicate whether each statement is an *accurate* or an *inaccurate* description of *your* job.

Once again, please try to be as objective as you can in deciding how accurately each statement describes your job—regardless of whether you like or dislike your job.

Write a number in the blank beside each statement, based on the following scale:

How accurate is the statement in describing your job?

1	2	3	4	5	6	7
Very Inaccurate	Mostly Inaccurate	Slightly Inaccurate	Uncertain	Slightly Accurate	Mostly Accurate	Very Accurate

_____ 1. The job requires me to use a number of complex or high-level skills.

_____ 2. The job requires a lot of cooperative work with other people.

_____ 3. The job is arranged so that I do *not* have the chance to do an entire piece of work from beginning to end.

_____ 4. Just doing the work required by the job provides many chances for me to figure out how well I am doing.

_____ 5. The job is quite simple and repetitive.

_____ 6. The job can be done adequately by a person working alone—without talking or checking with other people.

_____ 7. The supervisors and co-workers on this job almost *never* give me any feedback about how well I am doing in my work.

_____ 8. This job is one where a lot of other people can be affected by how well the work gets done.

_____ 9. The job denies me any chance to use my personal initiative or judgment in carrying out the work.

_____ 10. Supervisors often let me know how well they think I am performing the job.

_____ 11. The job provides me the chance to completely finish the pieces of work I begin.

_____ 12. The job itself provides very few clues about whether or not I am performing well.

_____ 13. The job gives me considerable opportunity for independence and freedom in how I do the work.

_____ 14. The job itself is *not* very significant or important in the broader scheme of things.

characteristics, the JDS also measures experienced psychological states, affective outcomes (general satisfaction, growth satisfaction, and internal work motivation), context satisfactions, and individual growth need strength (these variables were discussed in Chapters 3 and/or 4). The task characteristics questions of the JDS are presented in Table 5–1. The scoring key for the task characteristics themselves is summarized below:

1. Variety: Item 4 (Section 1); Items 1 and 5 (Section 2)
2. Identity: Item 3 (Section 1); Items 3 and 11 (Section 2)
3. Significance: Item 5 (Section 1); Items 8 and 14 (Section 2)
4. Autonomy: Item 2 (Section 1); Items 9 and 13 (Section 2)
5. Feedback (from job): Item 7 (Section 1); Items 4 and 12 (Section 2)
6. Feedback (from agents): Item 6 (Section 1); Items 7 and 10 (Section 2)
7. Dealing with others: Item 1 (Section 1); Items 2 and 6 (Section 2)

Characteristics 6 and 7 are not actually a part of the job characteristics theory, but are included in the JDS for informational purposes. The other five dimensions are scored by averaging the three items specified above (note also that some items are "reverse scored," i.e., worded in such a way so that high scores reflect a low level of that particular dimension; these item values are subtracted from 8 before scoring). The five scores, in turn, are combined in the following fashion to yield a Motivating Potential Score:

$$\left\{\begin{array}{l}\text{Motivating} \\ \text{Potential} \\ \text{Score (MPS)}\end{array}\right. = \left[\dfrac{\text{Skill Variety} + \text{Task Identity} + \text{Task Significance}}{3}\right] \times \text{Autonomy} \times \text{Job Feedback}$$

The lower the resultant MPS the more potential there is for redesigning the job (see Chapter 3 for additional information regarding the JDS).

In our first hypothetical scenario presented at the beginning of this chapter, Dr. Helen Winthrop probably was recommending the use of the JDS to Bill Saunders at Atlas, Inc. For reasons that will become apparent through our discussion, the JDS is used in more organizations than are alternative measures.

Empirical assessment. As noted above, the JDS has been the most widely used questionnaire in task design research. Accordingly, there exists a fairly large body of information regarding the instrument's reliability and validity. A recent review of several studies concludes that the instrument can be characterized by acceptable levels of reliability, questionable convergent validity, and uncertain substantive validity (Aldag, Barr, and Brief, 1978).

One particular shortcoming of the JDS, also noted by Aldag, et al. (1978), pertains to the instrument's dimensionality. The JDS is assumed to measure five distinct constructs, i.e., task dimensions. Yet numerous studies (cf., Dunham, 1976; Dunham, Aldag, and Brief, 1977) have found that factor analytic procedures often yield solutions involving fewer than or more than five factors. Hence, the extent to which the instrument is actually measuring variety, autonomy, feedback, identity, and significance is not known. **83**

Advantages of the JDS.   There are two distinct advantages to organizations using the Job Diagnostic Survey. First, the JDS offers organizations a package of scales measuring most, if not all, relevant task design variables. Hence, a manager who administers the JDS for task design or redesign purposes doesn't necessarily have to be concerned with locating other scales to measure satisfaction, motivation, etc. (As we will see in the next section, there are also disadvantages associated with this method.)

A second significant advantage of the JDS is the existence of a pool of normative data. Hackman and Oldham (1980) present average data obtained from the JDS for nine different job families. A manager utilizing the JDS for jobs included in one of these families will have a basis for comparison in making task design decisions.

Disadvantages of the JDS.   The JDS also has some disadvantages and weaknesses. First, there is a problem of common-method variance. When employees complete the entire instrument, data analysis will typically involve correlating task characteristics scores with other scores such as satisfaction. However, since both sets of data are based on individual perceptions and are obtained at the same time by the same method, there is a very real danger that statistical relationships may be artifically inflated.

A second shortcoming of the JDS is its dimensional instability. That is, the extent to which the instrument actually is measuring specific characteristics seems to vary across settings. It has even been suggested that the instrument's dimensionality should be assessed for each setting where it is used (Dunham, 1976), yet many managers may lack the time and/or computational facilities for such analysis. Other relatively minor drawbacks to the JDS include: (1) it is not appropriate for people with an eighth-grade education or less, and (2) it is designed to be administered anonymously; hence, performance relationships would be difficult to assess, and (3) the instrument is easily faked.

The Job Characteristic Inventory

The Job Characteristic Inventory (JCI) was originally presented by Sims, Szilagyi and Keller (1976). The instrument was first administered to a sample of 1,161 paramedical and support personnel at a major medical center. A slightly revised version was next administered to 192 manufacturing managers. Results of this study provide the basis for the instrument. Hence, the development of the JCI was less systematic and intensive than was the development of the JDS.

Description.   The JCI consists of 30 items. Employees respond to the questions on 5-point Likert-type scales. The instrument is presented in Table 5–2. The task characteristics themselves are scored as follows:

1. Variety: Items 1, 7, 12, 17, 22
2. Autonomy: Items 2, 8, 13, 18, 23, 28
3. Feedback: Items 4, 9, 14, 20, 25, 30
4. Identity: Items 3, 19, 24, 29
5. Dealing with others: Items 6, 11, 16, 27
6. Friendship opportunities: Items 5, 10, 15, 21, 26

In contrast to the JDS, the JCI is not a self-contained assessment package. The only variables tapped by the instrument are the six task characteristics themselves.

Empirical assessment. The JCI has been used less frequently than the JDS in task design research, so there is less empirical evidence available for assessing the instrument's psychometric properties. The evidence that does exist, however, indicates that the JCI has acceptable reliability, reasonable convergent validity, and unknown substantive validity (Aldag, et al., 1978).

Further, the dimensionality of the JCI has generally been more consistent than that of the JDS. Specifically, it has been shown that the dimensionality of the JCI generally is stable over time (Griffin, 1981c) and also across diverse samples (Griffin, Moorhead, Johnson, and Chonko, 1980).

Advantages of the JCI. The primary advantage of the JCI is that it appears to be more stable than the JDS. The instrument is also somewhat simpler, both in format and content. Hence, the JCI may be more appropriate for a more diverse group of employees.

Disadvantages of the JCI. Unfortunately, the JCI is also characterized by several deficiencies. First, the instrument and its use are not guided by any well-developed theoretical framework. Second, managers are not given any indication as to other supporting instruments that may be needed, such as measures of satisfaction, etc. Finally, there is no systematically developed pool of normative data for comparative purposes.

Summary

In the only published direct comparison of the JCI and the JDS, Pierce and Dunham (1978a) found that the JCI had better reliability and more stable dimensionality than the JDS. They conclude that, "Perhaps the optimal approach for job design researchers focusing on perceived job characteristics would be the use of multiple methods" (p. 128). This appears to be a reasonable and justifiable conclusion. When conditions preclude the administration of multiple questionnaires, however, the JDS would appear to be the most logical choice, simply because more is known about its psychometric properties.

This is not to imply, of course, that either the JDS or the JCI is a truly ideal instrument. The previous discussion highlights many of the short- **85**

TABLE 5–2   The Job Characteristic Inventory

The following questions concern certain aspects of your job. Please *circle* the number to the right of each question which indicates how you feel about that question.

	VERY LITTLE	LITTLE	A MODERATE AMOUNT	MUCH	VERY MUCH
1. How much variety is there in your job?	1	2	3	4	5
2. How much are you left on your own to do your own work?	1	2	3	4	5
3. How often do you see projects or jobs through to completion?	1	2	3	4	5
4. To what extent do you find out how well you are doing on the job as you are working?	1	2	3	4	5
5. How much opportunity is there to meet individuals whom you would like to develop friendships with?	1	2	3	4	5
6. How much of your job depends upon your ability to work with others?	1	2	3	4	5
7. How repetitious is your job?	1	2	3	4	5
8. To what extent are you able to act independently of your supervisor in performing your job function?	1	2	3	4	5
9. To what extent do you receive information from your superior on your job performance?	1	2	3	4	5
10. To what extent do you have the opportunity to talk informally with other employees while at work?	1	2	3	4	5
11. To what extent is dealing with other people a part of your job?	1	2	3	4	5
12. How similar are the tasks you perform in a typical work day?	1	2	3	4	5
13. To what extent are you able to do your job independently of others?	1	2	3	4	5

TABLE 5-2 (continued)   Job Characteristic Inventory

Below are a number of statements describing job characteristics. Indicate HOW MUCH THE CHARAC-
TERISTIC IS PRESENT in your job by circling the number to the right of each statement.

	VERY LITTLE	LITTLE	A MODERATE AMOUNT	MUCH	VERY MUCH
14. The feedback from my supervisor on how well I'm doing.	1	2	3	4	5
15. Friendship from my co-workers.	1	2	3	4	5
16. The opportunity to talk to others on my job.	1	2	3	4	5
17. The opportunity to do a number of different things.	1	2	3	4	5
18. The freedom to do pretty much what I want on my job.	1	2	3	4	5
19. The degree to which the work I'm involved with is handled from beginning to end by myself.	1	2	3	4	5
20. The opportunity to find out how well I am doing in my job.	1	2	3	4	5
21. The opportunity in my job to get to know other people.	1	2	3	4	5
22. The amount of variety in my job.	1	2	3	4	5
23. The opportunity for independent thought and action.	1	2	3	4	5
24. The opportunity to complete work I start.	1	2	3	4	5
25. The feeling that I know whether I am performing my job well or poorly.	1	2	3	4	5
26. The opportunity to develop close friendships in my job.	1	2	3	4	5
27. Meeting with others in my work.	1	2	3	4	5
28. The control I have over the pace of my work.	1	2	3	4	5
29. The opportunity to do a job from beginning to end (i.e., the chance to do a whole job).	1	2	3	4	5
30. The feedback about my performance that I receive from people other than my supervisor.	1	2	3	4	5

comings and deficiencies of each questionnaire. It is also possible that other task dimensions (for example, difficulty and predictability) exist, but are not measured by either the JCI or JDS. Finally, since these instruments are based on employee *perceptions* of their jobs, little *objective* information about jobs is obtained.

Objective measurements of tasks are important, however, for a number of reasons. First and foremost, even though an employee reacts (in terms of behaviors and attitudes) to his or her own perceptions of the task, a manager must contend with objective qualities when designing and redesigning tasks. Hence, the manager will likely want and need as much objective data as possible when dealing with task design issues.

A second reason for describing objective task measures in this discussion is their potential importance following a task change. Labor leaders, for example, have argued that if a task redesign effort increases job duties, then additional compensation may be warranted. Whether this is correct or not, however, can only be determined by analyzing objective task properties. Similarly, the manager may wish to ascertain the extent to which the task change may have had an impact on performance. The nature of the change, though, may have altered the appropriate level or base of output; therefore, it may be necessary to study and redefine expected output levels for redesigned tasks.

A final reason for describing objective task measures is somewhat more theoretical in nature. As described in Chapter 3, an important issue to be resolved is the nature of the linkage or interface between the objective task and the perceived task. Most task design research to date, however, has focused only on perceived task properties. Attention should be drawn to objective measurement techniques that may be useful for further understanding of task design properties. As we shall see, some researchers have already begun to address these issues on an exploratory basis.

In the following sections we will describe two broadly defined objective task measurement perspectives. First, we will consider techniques focusing on job value such as job evaluation and analysis. Next, we will discuss techniques dealing more directly with operational task properties.

JOB EVALUATION AND ANALYSIS

Atlas, Inc. was interested in measuring employee task perceptions so that jobs could be redesigned to be more motivating and satisfying. King Wholesalers, on the other hand, was more interested in assessing objective task content so that appropriate levels of compensation could be developed and relevant selection criteria could be adopted. We will first summarize four basic job evaluation techniques and then direct our attention to job analysis procedures. Finally, we will relate the measures of job content to employee task-characteristics perceptions.

Job Evaluation

Job evaluation, as indicated above, is concerned with the value of the job to the organization. Each of the four techniques to be described are generally utilized by the personnel manager and/or a job evaluation specialist.

The point system. The point system, developed in the 1920s, is probably the most widely used of all job evaluation techniques. The point system focuses on specific job factors or components. The first step in utilizing this system is to identify key factors that will be used as a basis for comparison. Commonly used factors include responsibility, effort, skill, and working conditions. For managerial employees, factors might include responsibility, decision-making requirements, and knowledge.

After key factors have been defined, a range of potential points is established for each factor for each job. For example, a managerial job might be allocated a range of 150–500 points for responsibility, 100–400 for effort, and so forth. Next, each factor is broken down by degrees on which jobs can be compared. A managerial job with a great deal of responsibility might be assigned 500 points, a similar job with slightly less responsibility 400 points, etc. Qualitative decisions regarding points for degrees of significance are sometimes difficult to make. Discrete or quantitative degrees, such as level of education, are somewhat easier to establish.

Point values for each degree of each factor are next combined into an overall assessment index for purposes of the actual evaluation. Finally, each job is compared against each factor by degree, resulting in the determination of a total number of points for that particular job. The relative worth or value of the job is reflected in its point total; the more points a particular job has, the more compensation should be attached to that particular job.

Factor comparison method. The factor comparison method of job evaluation also involves breaking the total job down into factors or components. Rather than developing a scale for comparison purposes, however, jobs are compared directly to one another. The first step in the procedure is to identify a set of key jobs for evaluation. This selection process is very important, because the results of this evaluation will serve as the basis for subsequent evaluations. One important aspect of the selection process is that the evaluators be completely satisfied with the appropriateness of the current relative pay levels for the key jobs.

As with the point system, primary factors of each job are identified. However, unlike the point system, degrees are not taken into account. Each of these factors is then ranked according to its importance in each of the focal jobs. This is accomplished by determining a rank for every job, one factor at a time. That is, rather than ranking one job at a time across all factors, rankings are done on a factor-by-factor basis.

89

After this ranking has been completed, salary dollars are assigned to each job according to its ranking by factors. Since an initial criterion in job selection was agreement on current salary levels, it is important that the assignment of dollars by ranking be consistent with current salaries.

Finally, a salary scale is developed for each factor. The scales establish the relative differences in pay for the jobs. Other jobs in the organization are then evaluated according to current job descriptions and specifications and plotted on the salary scale for each factor. The total value for a particular job is then established by adding the amounts associated with each factor.

Job ranking method. Whereas the point system is the most widely used method of job evaluation, the job ranking method is the oldest system. It is also comparatively simple and straightforward. Rather than break jobs down into factors, or components, the job ranking method focuses on the total job.

Essentially, the job evaluator ranks all jobs in the organization in order of importance. Obviously, in a large organization with many different jobs, this would be a difficult procedure. After the ranking has been completed, salary levels are specified for each job by rank. This process is also somewhat difficult, because the job ranking method does not take into account relative differences between rankings. For example, jobs ranked 1 and 2 might actually be very similar to one another, whereas jobs 2 and 3 might be substantially different. Yet, the ranking method does not specifically address this issue.

Job grading method. The final technique for job evaluation to be summarized is the job grading method. This technique is perhaps best known because of its use by the Federal Civil Service System. As with the ranking method, job grading focuses on the total job rather than on job factors. However, rather than comparing jobs against one another, they are compared against a scale composed of grades.

The job evaluator first defines a series of grades or job classifications. Next, jobs in the organization are assigned to particular grades. The basis for this assignment is typically job descriptions and/or specifications. Salary ranges are developed for each grade, and jobs within those grades paid accordingly.

These four methods of job evaluations are summarized in Table 5–3. For more information on any or all of these procedures, the interested reader should consult Dunn and Rachel (1971), Famularo (1972), and/or Nash and Carroll (1975). We now direct our attention at the other personnel-based approach to task measurement, job analysis.

Job Analysis

Job analysis focuses on task-relevant requirements. A variety of techniques is currently available for job analysis; we will describe this method of task

TABLE 5–3 Summary of Job Evaluation Techniques

BASIS FOR COMPARISON	SCOPE OF COMPARISON	
	Job as a Whole	Job Factors
Job versus Job	Job Ranking Method	Factor Comparison Method
Job versus Scale	Job Grading Method	The Point System

Source: H. J. Chruden and A. W. Sherman, Jr., *Personnel Management*, 5th edition (Cincinnati, Ohio: South-Western Publishing Co., 1976), p. 445. Used by permission.

measurement at a general level and then discuss one specific technique in more detail.

The two essential components in job analysis are: (1) to specify the job-related behaviors and tasks needed to produce an output or service, and (2) to determine the skills, ability, and knowledge necessary to carry out the behaviors and tasks. One common approach to job analysis incorporating both of these elements is the development of *job descriptions and/or specifications*. Such descriptions specify what the job entails and imply what skill requirements are necessary for successful task accomplishment. The job analysis in general and the job description in particular are generally developed by trained job analysts and/or personnel specialists. Data to be used are obtained from observation, interviews, supervisory conferences, critical incidents, work sampling, and/or questionnaires (Heneman, Schwab, Fossum, and Dyer, 1980).

91

Since the questionnaire technique is closest in nature to the general area of task design, we will focus more attention on one particular instrument that has been widely used. This instrument, called the Position Analysis Questionnaire, or PAQ, was developed and presented by Ernest McCormick (McCormick, Jeanneret, and Mecham, 1972; McCormick, 1976). MCormick suggests that all jobs can be characterized by an underlying structure of components or dimensions; that is, jobs have a basic commonality of attributes or dimensions. However, jobs can be differentiated by their varying degrees of each of these attributes. This concept, then, is similar to the basic perceived task design framework. The dimensions, however, are assumed to be objective.

The PAQ identifies 194 job attributes that are described as worker-oriented. That is, they evolve from the various individual behaviors associated with task performance. The various categories of behaviors are summarized in Table 5–4. As indicated, worker-oriented task attributes include information input, mediation processes, work output, and other behavioral aspects of the work environment. The PAQ has been generally accorded favorable evaluations by empirical research. Specifically, the instrument has been used for job evaluation purposes and for establishing aptitude requirements for various types of jobs (Aldag and Brief, 1979).

Job evaluation and analysis procedures in general and the PAQ in particular may also have considerable utility for increasing our understanding of the task design process. For example, the JDS, the JCI, the point system, the factor comparison method, and the PAQ all focus on dimensions, attributes, and characteristics of tasks. It seems reasonable to suggest that considerable overlap may exist among some of these dimensions, at least at a conceptual level.

A few available research studies support this contention. One early study found positive relationships between job difficulty, measured by the point system, and employee satisfaction (Svetlik, Prien, and Barrett, 1964). Since a high scope task may well be more difficult than a lower scope task, job difficulty as assessed by job evaluation techniques may be an important element to consider in task design research and practice.

Randall Dunham (Dunham, 1977a; Dunham, Pierce, and Kolenko, 1979) has also provided some interesting insights into relationships between perceived task characteristics (as assessed by the JDS) and objective job analysis indices (as assessed by the PAQ). Data from a sample of 256 employees at a pharmaceutical plant indicated that job ability requirements and compensation values varied systematically with perceived task characteristics. Specifically, jobs with low perceived task attributes (i.e., low scope perceptions) were also viewed as having lower ability requirements and also lower compensation values. Alternatively, higher scope tasks had correspondingly higher ability requirements and compensation values (Dunham, 1977a).

92 Another study (Dunham, Pierce, and Kolenko, 1979) also found that while some overlap exists, perceptual and objective measures were tapping

TABLE 5–4   The Position Analysis Questionnaire
(Numbers of Items are in Parentheses)

INFORMATION INPUT (35)

Sources of job information (20): Use of written materials
Discrimination and perceptual activities (15): Estimating speed of moving objects

---

MEDIATION PROCESSES (14)

Decision making and reasoning (2): Reasoning in problem solving
Information processing (6): Encoding, decoding
Use of stored information (6): Using mathematics

WORK OUTPUT (50)

Use of physical devices (29): Use of keyboard devices
Integrative manual activities (8):Handling objects, materials
General body activities (7): Climbing
Manipulation, coordination activities (6): Hand-arm manipulation

---

INTERPERSONAL ACTIVITIES (36)

Communications (10): Instructing
Interpersonal relationships (3): Serving / catering
Personal contact (15): Personal contact with customers
Supervision and coordination (8): Level of supervision received

---

WORK SITUATION AND JOB CONTEXT (18)

Physical working conditions (12): Low temperature
Psychological and sociological aspects (6): Civic obligations

---

MISCELLANEOUS ASPECTS (36)

Work schedule, method of pay, and apparel (21): Irregular hours
Job demands (12): Specified (controlled) work pace
Responsibility (3): Responsibility for safety of others

---

unique constructs and that both approaches to task measurement hold considerable utility for task design considerations. This notion will be addressed more specifically in a later section of this chapter. We now turn our attention to the third form of task measurement, referred to as work measurement.

WORK MEASUREMENT

Whereas job evaluation and analysis focus on job value and are generally associated with the personnel function in organizations, work measurement is concerned with operational properties of tasks and is usually the responsibility of industrial engineers and other efficiency specialists. The objective of work measurement is to determine the most time- and cost-efficient method for performing a task and to establish quotas or other productivity standards. This is the approach to work measurement being considered by Moorhead Metals, as summarized at the beginning of this chapter. This section will briefly summarize a number of major work measurement techniques that might be used by Moorhead Metals and other firms.

Time Study

Time study involves the direct observation of jobs in order to determine how much time a worker should be allotted to complete a specified task. An initial step in a time study is to determine the scope of the analysis. Care must be taken so that the time frame studied is representative of normal conditions. Further, it is important to select an employee for observation who has about average or normal levels of ability and output. After these activities have been completed, the observer determines elements of the total task. That is, rather than simply determining the total time needed for a task, it is generally more useful to determine appropriate times for each meaningful, discrete step in the total task.

During the actual time study, the observer records such things as job conditions and, of course, the time spent on each task activity. The observer also determines the performance rating for the task; that is, he or she establishes the number of units that an average employee should generate over any specific time period. This expectation may then play a role in the performance evaluation process, the distribution of rewards in the organization, and so forth.

Work Sampling

Work sampling, as the name suggests, involves sampling job activities with the objective of estimating the proportion of time associated with each element of the task. First, the observer identifies activity elements of the job. For example, activities for a secretary would typically include typing, filing, greeting visitors, and so forth. These activities should be easily observable, reasonable in number, mutually exclusive, and collectively exhaustive (Smith, 1978).

After determining the scope of the work sampling assessment, the observer makes randomly scheduled observation tours. During these tours, he or she records which task activities the employee was engaged in. Assuming a reasonable number of such tours, the observer should eventually be able to specify the proportion of time associated with each key activity.

Hence, work sampling takes a more holistic view of the job than does the time-study approach. In particular, its flexibility makes it especially appropriate for reasonably complex jobs. It should also be noted that rather than attempting to establish specific production quotas, work sampling is more descriptive in nature.

Standard Data

Standard data techniques focus on normal or expected time values for different task activities. In many ways, standard data techniques are like time studies. However, rather than focusing on productivity quotas for existing tasks, the objective of a standard data study is to provide expected productivity levels for a proposed method and/or a new task.

The starting point in a standard data analysis is to gather existing time-study data for the focal task. This focal task must be similar to the proposed task in terms of normal work pace, essential activities, and so forth.

The focal task is usually broken down into four elements: (1) fixed set-up time, (2) variable set-up time, (3) fixed operating time, and (4) variable operating time. These various components are then extrapolated onto the proposed task, with appropriate adjustments made. These estimates, in turn, provide the observer with the necessary information for estimating productivity levels for the proposed task. Decisions can then be made regarding whether or not to adopt the new method. A primary benefit of the standard data approach is that a representative focal task that is well understood can be used to establish estimates for a variety of proposed tasks. Also, the new task can be implemented with estimated productivity quotas already known.

Flow Charts

Flow charts involve specifying the role of each task in the total work system. In many ways similar to a PERT diagram, a flow chart (also referred to as an operation process chart, man-machine process chart, etc.) is, therefore, a higher level of analysis than the previously discussed measurement techniques; the focus is on the total work system rather than specific jobs.

First, the total work-system plan is established. This plan specifies total **95** work time, movement time between operations, interface time, and so forth. Next, the specifications for each task are developed. While other techniques may be used for this purpose, individual task specification is generally not that precise or detailed. The resultant chart can then be used to focus on and/or eliminate bottlenecks, hidden inefficiencies, and so forth.

Summary

This section has summarized four major work measurement approaches. Organizations have generally utilized these approaches for one or more of the following purposes: (1) methods improvement, (2) cost reduction programs, (3) employee training, (4) workplace layout, (5) assembly-line balancing, (6) indirect evaluation, (7) equipment and/or tool selection and (8) human factors design (Karger and Bayha, 1977). As with our discussion of job evaluation and analysis approaches, each technique was summarized in a very cursory manner. For additional information regarding work measurement, the reader should consult Karger and Bayha (1977) or Smith (1978).

The next section will describe how the various approaches to the measurement of tasks could be used to complement one another.

AN INTEGRATIVE SYSTEM OF TASK MEASUREMENT

For the most part, the three forms of task measurement described in this chapter (task perceptions measures, job analysis and evaluation, and work measurement) are used independently of one another. Yet, logic would indicate that, in many instances, the three approaches should be used in concert. Some examples should illustrate this point.

First, as indicated earlier, one of the primary arguments that some unions use against job enrichment is that workers will be doing more complex and demanding tasks for the same compensation. And, in some cases, this is indeed the case. Hence, job evaluations may be needed to determine appropriate compensation adjustments for task redesign. Job analysis may also be needed to ascertain the extent to which selection criteria must be modified in view of a more complex task following work redesign. Further, task redesign may also alter acceptable levels of performance. After a redesign including a big increase in task variety, fewer units of output may be a logical expectation. Therefore, work measurement may be needed to determine new quotas and so forth for the redesigned task.

A potential framework for integrating task measurement approaches is presented in Figure 5–1. It should be noted that this system will not always be appropriate, either in content or sequence. Rather, this system represents a logical flow when task design as defined in this book is the focus. Given other situations, a different framework may be called for.

FIGURE 5-1   An Integrative System of Task Measurement

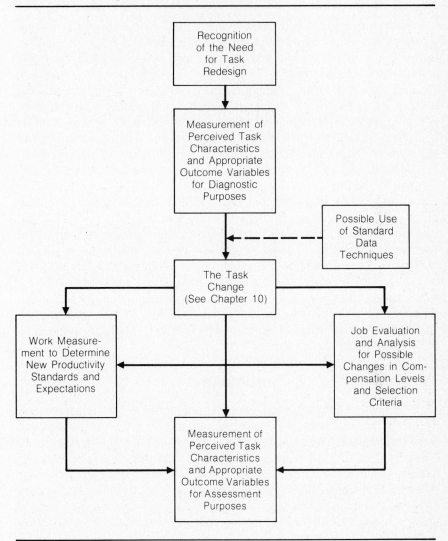

The catalyst for the system is the recognition of a need for task redesign. This recognition may take the form of declines in employee morale, a desire to improve quality of work life, or similar circumstances. An instrument designed to measure perceived task characteristics, such as the JDS and/or JCI, is administered to determine employee perceptions of their current tasks. These data are gathered for diagnostic purposes. At the same time, base-line data are gathered to assess employee satisfaction, motivation, and/or performance. In some cases, standard data techniques **97**

may also be useful to extrapolate expected performance levels after the change.

Next comes the actual task change itself. Since an entire chapter (Chapter 10) will be devoted to task change implementation, no further discussion is necessary at this point. Following implementation, however, at least three issues remain.

First, job evaluation techniques may be utilized to determine new compensation levels. As indicated earlier, some people feel that "en-riched" jobs deserve higher levels of compensation. Of course, the organization should have anticipated this adjustment in advance and factored in potentially higher labor costs in its cost/benefit analysis of the project. Job analysis may also be necessary to determine new selection criteria to be used by the firm.

At about the same time that job evaluation and analysis are taking place, work measurement approaches may also be useful in establishing new productivity quotas. Even if standard data techniques were used earlier to estimate new levels of output, these estimates may need to be fine-tuned by use of another technique. Finally, the perceived task characteristics and outcome variables should be measured again. These measures will be for evaluation purposes. In some cases, task changes have not really been perceived as such by employees. Further, it is important to ascertain the extent to which anticipated gains in affective and behavioral outcomes actually are realized.

SUMMARY

This chapter has discussed different approaches to task measurement. First, methods for assessing employee perceptions of task characteristics were summarized. Next, we looked at job evaluation and analysis proce-dures for determining the value of jobs to an organization and appropriate selection criteria to be used in filling them. We then described work mea-surement techniques that are useful for investigating operational properties of tasks, including anticipated levels of output. Finally, we discussed a system through which the techniques could be used together to enhance work-system effectiveness.

As indicated at various spots in this chapter, clear and logical linkages between perceived and objective task properties do not always exist. In many cases, comparing a perceived and an objective task component may be somewhat akin to forcing the proverbial round peg into a square hole. Yet, logic would indicate the importance of not emphasizing either the perceptual or the objective task to the exclusion of the other. The objective task is of concern to the manager because it must be the basis for em-ployee selection criteria, compensation, and productivity measurement, as well as being a framework for redesign efforts. The employee, on the other hand, primarily reacts to her or his own perceptions of the task. Future attention to task design issues, then, needs to include efforts to better integrate both objective and perceived task perspectives.

The preceding points also lead to an additional concern of considerable importance. The research summarized to this point in the book has generally focused on the interface between the employee and the task. While this is undoubtedly a critical concern, it should also be recognized that this interface does not exist in a vacuum—it is not the only point to be considered. More precisely, the individual employee and his or her task co-exist in a complex organizational milieu consisting of a variety of other jobs, employees, groups of jobs, and groups of employees, as well as supervisors, subordinates, formal systems like the pay and promotion system, and informal systems like the status system.

Hence, it is important at this point to broaden our orientation. We must begin to describe and attempt to understand the role of task design in its broader context. Specifically, we need to investigate interrelationships among task design processes and other important organizational factors. Beginning in the next chapter, we will discuss potential relationships among task design and four other categories of organizational variables: technology, organization structure, leader behavior, and group and interpersonal processes.

TASK DESIGN
6 AND
TECHNOLOGY

As indicated at the end of Chapter 5, we are now ready to expand our discussion of task design to include other important organizational factors.

The task performed by the employee influences and is influenced by the surrounding work environment; yet, little is known about the nature of these relationships. The integrative framework presented in Chapter 1 suggested primary interrelationships among task design elements and technology, organization design, leader behavior, and group processes. This chapter will relate task design and technology; subsequent chapters will deal with the other factors.

Potential relationships among task design and technology are relatively obvious. For example, as Timex begins to produce more quartz and digital watches relative to conventional timepieces, new machines and work procedures are needed. Each change is likely to be accompanied by a change in relevant tasks. That is, the operation of a new machine will probably require a redesigned task for the employee. Similarly, a task change may influence the overall work-flow in the organization, thereby influencing or altering technology.

Some of the material presented in this chapter will be well grounded in theory and research, while in other areas we will, of necessity, be more conjectural. First, we will describe the nature of organizational technology and its role in modern organization and management theory. Next, attention will be focused on how technological variables act to constrain and/or facilitate the task design process. The discussion will then become somewhat theoretical as various typologies of technology are summarized. These various categories will be related specifically to task design variables to the extent possible. The socio-technical systems approach to task design will then be presented. Having outlined and summarized a number of task design and technology perspectives, an integrative view of how the variables interact will be described. Finally, we will offer some speculative comments about future technologies.

THE NATURE OF TECHNOLOGY

The nature of an organization's technology is perhaps best understood when viewed from a systems theory perspective. Systems theory is concerned with interdependent objects (i.e., physical components, theoretical concepts, etc.) that interact with one another and with a broader environment. Systems theory was originally developed in the physical and biological sciences (cf. Bertalanffy, Hempel, Bass, and Jonas, 1951), but has recently been applied to social systems such as organizations (cf., Johnson, Kast, and Rosenzweig, 1973).

As presented in Figure 6–1, the systems model is composed of four basic elements: (1) inputs from the environment, (2) one or more transformation processes, (3) outputs into the environment, and (4) feedback from the environment into the system. Inputs to the organizational system include material resources (raw materials, physical facilities, etc.), human resources (operating employees, managerial talent, etc.), financial resources (stockholder investments, product sales, etc.), and information resources (market forecasts, economic indices, etc.). Outputs include the products and/or services of the organization (an automobile, a haircut, an educated student, etc.), profits and/or losses of the organization (improved standards of living for a community, increased taxes resulting from a university's financial overruns, etc.), and employee behaviors (feelings of accomplishment translating into positive societal contributions, a manager's heart problems resulting from job-related stress, etc.).

FIGURE 6–1   A Systems Model of Organizations

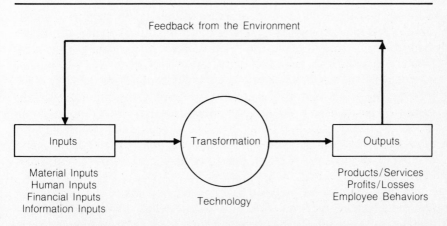

101

The intervening process between inputs and outputs of the system represents the organization's technology. Hence, technology can be defined as the conversion processes utilized by an organization in the transformation of inputs into outputs.

It is useful to note that different kinds of organizations emphasize different categories of inputs in their transformation processes. Most people think of material resources when describing technology. An automobile plant, for example, is dominated by the assembly line, where thousands of component parts are systematically integrated to eventually yield a finished product. Many service organizations, however, emphasize human inputs. A barber shop, for example, involves one person cutting another person's hair. The tools and techniques may vary, but the barber and the customer are essentially a given.

Financial institutions would seem to emphasize monetary or financial resources. A bank focuses primarily on attracting funds in the form of customer demand deposits and savings and on managing these funds through wise investments in various financial markets. Other firms emphasize information inputs. A marketing research firm, for example, relies heavily on economic indicators, consumer surveys, etc., and may offer no tangible output other than recommendations about the feasibility of various products and services.

It is useful to note that, in some instances, the conversion process may be simply the movement of various resources from one place to another. A wholesale firm, for example, typically does not make any changes in products. Rather, the firm buys the output of a manufacturer in bulk and sells the product in smaller quantities to retailers. Hence, the technology of the wholesale firm is to provide *place utility* by facilitating exchanges between producers and retailers.

The preceding examples allow us to generalize a number of different perspectives on organizational technologies. First, organizational technologies vary in terms of the *focus of the conversion*. Any combination of material, human, financial, and/or informational inputs might be emphasized in the conversion process. Second, technologies vary in terms of the *magnitude of the conversion*. The transformation of raw materials into steel beams is a substantial alteration of the inputs into an entirely new output. Alternatively, the earlier wholesaler example described a technology characterized by no actual materials conversion. Third, many organizations can be said to have *multiple technologies*. Sears, for example, produces some of its own merchandise and operates a consumer credit department, an insurance division, and a property development unit. Hence, the *focus* and *magnitude* of the conversion process may vary both *between* and *within* organizations.

A final point to be made in this section pertains to the problem of assumed technological differences and similarities. Many people might assume, for example, that because two firms produce competing products of a similar nature, the firms would use similar technologies. Skinner (1979)

TABLE 6–1   Contrasting Production Systems for Manufacturing Metal versus Plastic Flashlight Casings

	METAL DRAWING	PLASTIC MOLDING
Equipment	Punch press	Injection molding machine
Raw materials	Metal sheets	Plastic resin pellets
Tools	Die set—male or female	Split halves of a mold
Building	Heavy foundations to handle weight and impact	Ordinary floor
Manufacturing engineering	Mechanical, metal expertise	Plastics, hydraulics expertise
Maintenance	Mechanical, hydraulic	Mechanical, hydraulic
Operator	Heavier work, higher skill	Lighter work, lower skill
Supervisory skills	Managing male work force, scheduling	Mixed work force, machine troubleshooting, quality checking
Inventory	Sheet metal and work-in-process	Plastic powder and finished goods
Operations	May require several plus finishing	One
Scheduling	Potentially complex	Simple
Safety	Dangerous	Safer
Quality/precision	Depends on die and machine setup	Depends on molds, timing set into machine
Costs	Depends especially on die conditions and setup	Depends especially on short cycle and change-overs
Flexibility-product change	Die change necessary	Mold change necessary
Volume change	Add dies, machines, shifts or move to higher speed equipment	Add dies, machines, shifts; cycle limited
Potential for automation	Combine operations with transfer dies, install part location sensors, etc.; can be largely automatic	Largely automatic

Source: from *Work in America: The Decade Ahead*, Edited by Clark Kerr and Jerome M. Rosow © 1979 by Litton Educational Publishing, Inc. Reprinted by permission of Van Nostrand Reinhold Company.

provides a useful example to illustrate the fallacy of this assumption. The two firms in question may be producing battery-powered flashlights. One firm, however, may make the flashlight case out of plastic, while the other might use a metal case. The plastic case would be created by injection molding of plastic resin, whereas the metal case would involve drawing the metal out in a press with a die. Basic differences in the two processes are summarized in Table 6–1. As noted by Skinner, the production of the metal case involves much more complicated scheduling and inventory control systems, more operations, and probably takes place in a less appealing work environment.

Thus, it is important to remember that technologies vary significantly between firms, even in the same industry. The next section will relate how technological factors, such as the focus and magnitude of the conversion process, act to constrain and/or facilitate the task design process.

TECHNOLOGY AS A CONSTRAINING AND A FACILITATING VARIABLE

When managers attempt to redesign tasks within the organization, technology is a major variable that must be considered. Depending upon the circumstances, an organization's technology may substantially constrain or facilitate the extent to which meaningful task changes can be introduced.

Technology as a Constraining Variable

Oldham and Hackman (1980, p. 251) note that, "The technology of an organization can constrain the feasibility of work redesign by limiting the number of ways that jobs within the technology can be designed." Clearly, in many instances technology will limit potential task changes that may be available to the manager. This would appear to be most likely when equipment and machinery investments are substantial. By their very nature, most pieces of industrial machinery define the jobs that their operators perform. A company such as an automobile manufacturer actually defines most of the jobs in its plants by the kind of equipment that is purchased and installed.

To consider task redesign, then, is to consider huge capital outlays for new machines. Further, since most machines would be interrelated, the entire technological process would probably require redesign. A good example of how this process might work is the Volvo plant described in Chapter 3. That plant cost approximately 10% more than a conventional automobile plant and has a much lower capacity. Before managers would consider such an option, they must believe that substantial benefits will result.

Technology as a Facilitating Variable

In other industries, technology may act as a facilitating variable in redesigning tasks. The processing of insurance claims, for example, is a job typically not amenable to automation. In the claims division of a large insurance company, a task redesign effort was recently implemented with little difficulty. This ease of implementation was primarily a function of the organization's technology. Prior to the change, claims were sequentially passed from one clerk to another, with each clerk doing one small part of the total task. After the change, each clerk processed one complete claim from first step to last.

Since the initial task arrangement was not defined by expensive equipment and machinery, the only costs incurred in the change were for minimal down-time during transition and some on-the-job training. Further, the latter cost was particularly low, because the company had already been practicing job rotation and thus most clerks were already proficient at most

FIGURE 6–2   Technology as a Constraining and Facilitating Variable in Task Design

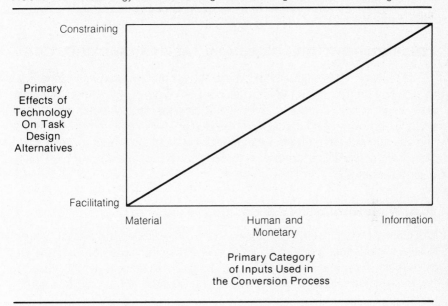

of the tasks. The organization's technology, then, facilitated management's attempts at redesigning tasks.

Summary

In general, it appears that, in some cases, technological factors constrain task design processes while in other cases technology facilitates task design. One way of conceptualizing these relationships is presented in Figure 6–2. Figure 6–2 suggests that when the primary inputs used in the conversion process are material, technology will predominantly serve as a constraint to task design alternatives. The rationale for this is that materials conversions will typically require a great deal of equipment and machinery. The auto assembly line is a good example.

At the other extreme, technology will generally facilitate task design processes when information inputs are dominant. In this case, work would usually be performed by people and/or information-processing units such as high-speed computers. Due to the relative ease in changing work-flow processes between people (i.e., the insurance example) and/or reprogramming a computer, task design alternatives would probably be more diverse.

At the mid-range are human and financial input-based organizations. Such organizations would usually have some investment in equipment that would moderately constrain task design alternatives. However, this investment would generally not be overwhelming, relative to the overall worth of **105** the organization. Therefore, technology might both constrain and facilitate task design processes in these types of organizations.

TECHNOLOGY TYPOLOGIES AND TASK CHARACTERISTICS

At this point, it is useful to take a more theoretical stance with respect to technology. In the preceding discussion, both technology and task design were dealt with at a general level. We will now begin to focus more specifically on how technological and task design variables interact. This section will summarize a number of technology typologies and suggest possible interrelationships among technological types and appropriate task design variables.

Joan Woodward and Task Design

Woodward (1958, 1965) developed one of the earliest and most widely used technological typologies. Initially, her research was concerned with the effects of organizational size on organizational structure. After finding few meaningful relationships, however, she directed her attention towards technological differences among various organizations. Woodward found that when organizations were placed into one of three categories of technology, interpretable patterns of structural variation emerged. These three categories were termed small batch (or unit) production, mass production, and continuous process production, and are defined as follows:

1. *Small batch or unit production.* The product is made to customer specifications. Production runs are typically short, and the operations performed on each unit are generally nonrepetitive. Examples include airplane manufacturers, print shops, and many machine and metal fabricating shops.
2. *Mass production.* The product is manufactured with an assembly-line arrangement. Products are typically made for inventory rather than for specific customers. Operations are generally repetitious, predictable, and routine. Examples include automobile plants.
3. *Continuous process production.* The product moves through a sequence of machine (process) transformations as it is changed from raw material to a finished good. Examples include petroleum refineries and chemical plants.

Two additional characteristics of the typology are relevant at this point. First, the classification scheme is intended only for industrial firms using a traditional production process. Second, the categories are listed in order of assumed technical complexity. That is, Woodward felt that a mass production technology is more complex than a small batch technology, but less complex than a continuous process technology. In many cases, though, obvious exceptions to this assumption can be found. A manufacturer of large commercial aircraft, such as Boeing, would fall into Woodward's small batch category. Yet, constructing a 747 would probably involve as much technological complexity as most other manufacturing processes.

Perhaps a more realistic view, and the one adopted here, is that the categories fall along a production "smoothness" continuum (Starbuck, 1965). Specifically, a small batch organization would tend to be characterized by production irregularity. Mass production, in turn, would have a much more regular (or smooth) production flow. Finally, the continuous process organization would have still more regularity. The following paragraphs will relate each category of production smoothness to task design considerations.

Small batch organizations are typically characterized by nonstandard, or ad hoc, output. Therefore, the various tasks within that form of work system would also tend to be nonstandard. More specifically, jobs in a small batch firm are likely to be structured as a function of worker skills. Hence, any particular set of jobs is likely to be nonstandard, nonroutine, nonspecialized, and nonformalized. Translating to task design terms, the jobs are likely to have relatively high degrees of variety, autonomy, feedback, identity, and significance.

The mass production organization, on the other hand, produces much more of a standard output on a more routine basis. The tasks within the firm are likely to be structured as a function of the work system. Since a mass production work system is typically designed to maximize efficiency, it follows that jobs within the firm will generally be highly standard, routine, specialized, and formalized: they will have little variety, autonomy, feedback, identity, and significance.

Continuous process organizations are essentially automated systems of conversion. Relatively few employees would be needed to operate the continuous process plant, and their jobs would essentially be to serve as observers. A scenario for a sample job might involve a skilled technician seated before an instrument panel. Most of the time, the technician simply monitors the various dials and indicators. Occasionally, however, she may adjust a control knob or lever when some gauge moves beyond allowable limits. In terms of task characteristics, the job may have little variety and identity, since the same functions are performed repeatedly. However, the job may also have substantial autonomy (due to the technician's expertise), significance (due to the importance of proper control), and feedback (from the instrument panel itself).

James Thompson and Task Design

Thompson (1967) proposed a somewhat more general typology applicable to a wider range of organizations. The basis for his typology is the manner in which individuals or work groups are arranged. The three categories in this typology are:

1. *Long-linked technology.* Characterized by serial interdependence of a number of different operations. Similar to Woodward's (1958) mass production technology.
2. *Mediating technology.* Characterized by processes that link or join together relatively

FIGURE 6–3   Thompson's Technological Typology

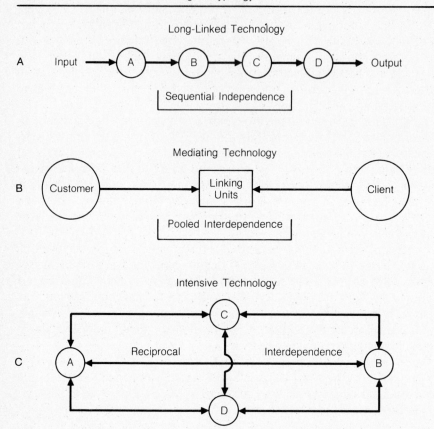

independent elements of a system. The various units are integrated (i.e., mediated) by standard policies and procedures. Examples include a bank where different categories of borrowers (i.e., consumer, commercial, and agricultural) are separated and then handled by standard procedures.

3. *Intensive technology.* Characterized by a variety of techniques that the organization may employ to solve problems. The choice of techniques and their sequence are varied as a function of the project itself. For example, both a construction company and a general hospital would be illustrative of intensive technology.

These categories are depicted in Figure 6–3. As noted above, and illustrated by the examples following each definition, Thompson's categories of technology are more general than Woodward's and can be used to classify a diverse group of organizations. While the Woodward groupings are essentially limited to manufacturing firms, Thompson's framework can also be used to categorize service organizations, hospitals, and so forth.

Also in contrast to Woodward's typology, some limited evidence exists that provides insights into Thompson's (1967) technologies and task design. Before discussing this evidence, however, we will first look at potential relationships that appear to be conceptually and intuitively apparent. This discussion is based substantially on the logic of Miles (1980).

One category of technology offered by Thompson was mediating technology. Since such a technology would seem to make relatively few demands on decision-making and communications processes (due to the nature of such *pooled* interdependence), the appropriate structure for the firm would probably be a bureaucratic organization characterized by a high degree of standardization. Tasks within the firm would probably be comparatively low in scope.

Long-linked technologies, on the other hand, would seem to place greater demands on decision-making and communications processes due to the increased complexities of a *sequential* form of interdependence. However, these complexities would probably also be dealt with by standardization and formalization of procedures. Again, task scope would tend to be fairly low.

Finally, intensive technologies, due to *reciprocal* interdependence, would probably be extremely complex in terms of decision-making and communications processes. Further, mutual adjustment processes characteristic of reciprocal interdependencies would tend to preclude the use of standardization and formalization as a management strategy in such organizations. A less formal, more organic style of functioning would tend to evolve, thereby bringing about tasks generally of higher scope and complexity. In summary, then, it seems that task scope would be fairly low in both mediating and long-linked systems and fairly high in intensive systems.

The exact nature of these relationships has been empirically tested by Rousseau (1977). A measure of perceived task scope did in fact reflect low task scope scores for ten long-linked technology systems and high task scope scores for six intensive technology systems. However, high scope tasks were also found in three mediating technology organizations. Of course, one study doesn't really provide any definitive answers. Rousseau's findings, however, do offer an empirical base for arguing that tasks vary across different technologies.

The Aston Group and Task Design

Whereas the typologies offered by Woodward (1965) and Thompson (1967) represent mutually exclusive categories, the Aston Group framework consists of three technological elements that can be used to characterize organizations. The Aston Group framework, so-named because it was developed by a group of researchers (e.g., Hickson, Pugh and Pheysey, 1969) at the University of Aston, is based on work-flow integration and includes:

109

1. *Operations technology.* Refers to the equipping and sequencing of work-flow activities.
2. *Materials technology.* Refers to materials used in the work flow.
3. *Knowledge technology.* Refers to the quality, quantity, level of sophistication, and dispersion of information and knowledge used in the work flow.

An example of how these elements might be used to describe an organization can be developed from the chemical industry. Fairly simple chemicals obtained from suppliers, mines, and so forth (materials technology) are managed by a skilled work force of chemists and engineers (knowledge technology) and transformed into soft drink containers, fertilizers, etc. (operations technology). Since the framework does not provide a basis for differentiating organizations, we cannot differentiate potential task design configurations in terms of the framework. We can, however, draw some generalizations about task design variables and the Aston dimensions from a different perspective.

It would seem that task design variables would be most strongly related to operations technology, moderately related to knowledge technology, and essentially unrelated to materials technology. Since operations technology focuses on specific work techniques and procedures, it follows that a task change would probably change the operations technology of the system, and, conversely, an operations technology change would probably change the nature of tasks within the work system.

Second, it seems reasonable to assume that a task change might lead to moderate changes in the amount, quality, and level of sophistication of the information needed for successful task accomplishment. Similarly, a change in knowledge technology (i.e., the addition of a new computer system) might also cause changes in some of the tasks themselves. A task change in and of itself, however, would not likely affect the system's materials technology, since material inputs are likely to remain unchanged. Of course, it should also be noted that a materials technology change would probably necessitate a new operations technology that could, in turn, affect certain task variables.

Charles Perrow and Task Design

Perrow (1967) has presented still another conceptualization of technology that has task design implications. Perrow's conceptualization includes two critical dimensions of technology: (1) the number of exceptional cases that are encountered in the work system and (2) the nature of the search process undertaken when such exceptions are encountered.

The number of exceptional cases is generally a function of the material inputs (i.e., raw materials, etc.) being converted by the organization. In the automobile assembly-line situation, the raw materials are essentially uniform. Therefore, few exceptional cases arise. Alternatively, in a research and development laboratory, exceptional cases would tend to be the rule. Regardless of the number of exceptional cases encountered in the

FIGURE 6–4   Perrow's Model of Technology

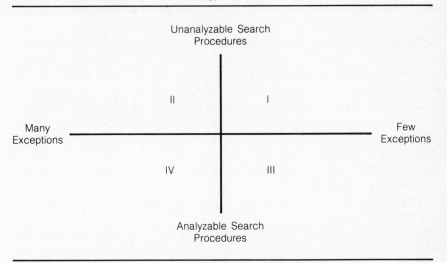

Source: Adapted from C. Perrow, "A Framework for the Comparative Analysis of Organizations," *American Sociological Review* (Vol. 32, 1967), pp. 194–208.

work system, the nature of the search process may range from a clear and analyzable pattern to one of ambiguity and uncertainty. For example, when a problem (i.e., exceptional case) arises in the automobile plant, plant managers and engineers generally have a logical and systematic procedure established to deal with the situation. At the other extreme, a leak in a nuclear power plant may not have an obvious solution. To the contrary, even equally well-trained experts may disagree as to how to deal with the crisis.

These two dimensions may be combined to form four quadrants of routineness, as presented in Figure 6–4. Quadrant 1 represents the *few exceptions—unanalyzable search* situation (example: craft work). Quadrant 2 is the extreme nonroutine situation characterized by *many exceptions—unanalyzable search* processes (example: research and development laboratories). The other extreme of routineness, *few exceptions–analyzable search* procedures, falls in Quadrant 3 (example: manufacturing). Finally, Quadrant 4 represents the *many exceptions–analyzable search* situations (example: engineering production).

In contrast to the Aston framework, Perrow's (1967) typology can be related to task design variables in a fairly straightforward manner. Recall that Perrow's framework is based on the two dimensions labeled *number of exceptional cases* and *nature of the search process*. These two dimensions, in turn, define four situations based on extremes of each dimension.

The *many exceptions–unanalyzable search* situation (Quadrant 2 of Figure 6–4) would more than likely have the highest level of task uncertainty, complexity, and scope. A research and development scientist, for **111** example, would probably be involved in several projects at once, would have considerable control over those projects, and would receive feedback from the projects themselves (i.e., successful breakthroughs), complete entire projects himself, and feel that the projects were important. This task, obviously, would be characterized by relatively high degrees of variety, autonomy, feedback, identity, and significance.

Quadrant 3 of Perrow's model (*few exceptions–analyzable search procedures*) would represent the opposite extreme. A task in this situation (the automobile assembly job is an example) would probably be highly standardized and structured and, therefore, low in scope. This is further reinforced by the Rousseau (1977) study.

Perrow's "mixed" categories (Quadrants 1 and 4) would tend to have intermediate levels of task scope. In the *few exceptions–unanalyzable search* situation, some task dimensions (i.e., variety) may be deficient, while others (i.e., feedback) may be comparatively high. Similarly, the *many exceptions–analyzable search* situation might be characterized by high variety and little feedback.

Slocum and Sims and Task Design

The final technological typology to be discussed is also the most recent in origin. Slocum and Sims (1980) suggest that technology can be described along three dimensions: work-flow uncertainty, task uncertainty, and task interdependence. These dimensions are defined as follows:

1. *Work-flow uncertainty*. Knowledge as to when inputs will arrive at the work station. When the work environment is very complex and uncertain, work-flow uncertainty will be high.
2. *Task uncertainty*. Knowledge the employee has about how to actually complete the appropriate task.
3. *Task interdependence*. The extent to which an individual's job cannot be accomplished without the assistance and/or cooperation of others. For example, when two nurses assist a surgeon, a high degree of interdependence exists. Three forms of interdependence are sequential, reciprocal, and pooled.

The Slocum and Sims view of technology is similar to the Aston model in that mutually exclusive categories are not defined. Rather, technology in any organization can be characterized along the three dimensions of work-flow uncertainty, task uncertainty, and task interdependence.

Slocum and Sims suggest that work-flow predictability will be related to employee discretion. Specifically, when work-flow predictability is high, workers' jobs will be "programmed" to improve efficiency; programming, in turn, will have the effect of decreasing worker autonomy. Task predictability will generally be related to job specialization. That is, high job specialization can be achieved when there is little task uncertainty. Finally, job interdependence is generally associated with job groupings. Specifically, jobs that are highly interdependent will tend to be grouped together.

The basic objective of the Slocum and Sims model is to describe what changes in an organization's technology are necessary to change employees' perceptions of various task characteristics. The model itself is presented in Figure 6–5. Based on Hackman (1977), the model includes four techniques for redesigning tasks: (1) combining tasks, (2) forming natural work units, (3) establishing client relationships, and (4) vertical loading. These strategies are derived from Hackman and Oldham's (1976, 1980) job characteristics theory discussed in Chapter 3.

Slocum and Sims suggest that the implementation of any one of these strategies will have a direct impact on two or more objective technological dimensions and/or elements of organizational control. These objective changes, in turn, will cause employees to perceive changes in specific core task dimensions. For example, combining tasks serves to increase task uncertainty, decrease sequential interdependence (one form of job interdependence), and decrease systematized control (detailed procedures, rigid standards, and built-in monitoring devices). These objective changes are then expected to increase employee perceptions of task variety, identity, and autonomy.

The Slocum and Sims framework is the most complete model of interactions between technology and task design developed to date. While the model has not yet been empirically tested, it appears to hold much promise for helping to focus future task design research more specifically on the constraining and facilitating role of organizational technology. It is also possible to integrate concepts from each of the various technology frameworks to provide even more insights into the technology and task design relationship. First, however, we will look at a somewhat different theoretical orientation to technology, which also has implications for task design.

SOCIO-TECHNICAL SYSTEMS THEORY

Socio-technical systems theory represents a major philosophical, theoretical, and empirical attempt at applying the systems perspective to organizations. The general framework was initially developed and advanced by the Tavistock Institute of Human Relations in London.

As might be inferred from the term itself, socio-technical systems theory is composed of two basic elements: the *socio-* component refers to social and/or interpersonal processes, and the *technical* component means operational and/or mechanical processes. Socio-technical systems theory, then, represents a synthesis of two diametrically opposite viewpoints. One viewpoint is the scientific management/engineering/efficiency approach, while the other is the human relations/behavioral science school of thought.

Scientific Management

Scientific management (e.g., Taylor, 1911) was discussed in some detail in Chapter 2. At this point, we will simply re-emphasize the most salient aspects of Taylor's work as they relate to socio-technical systems theory. **113**

FIGURE 6–5   The Slocum and Sims Model of Technology and Task Design

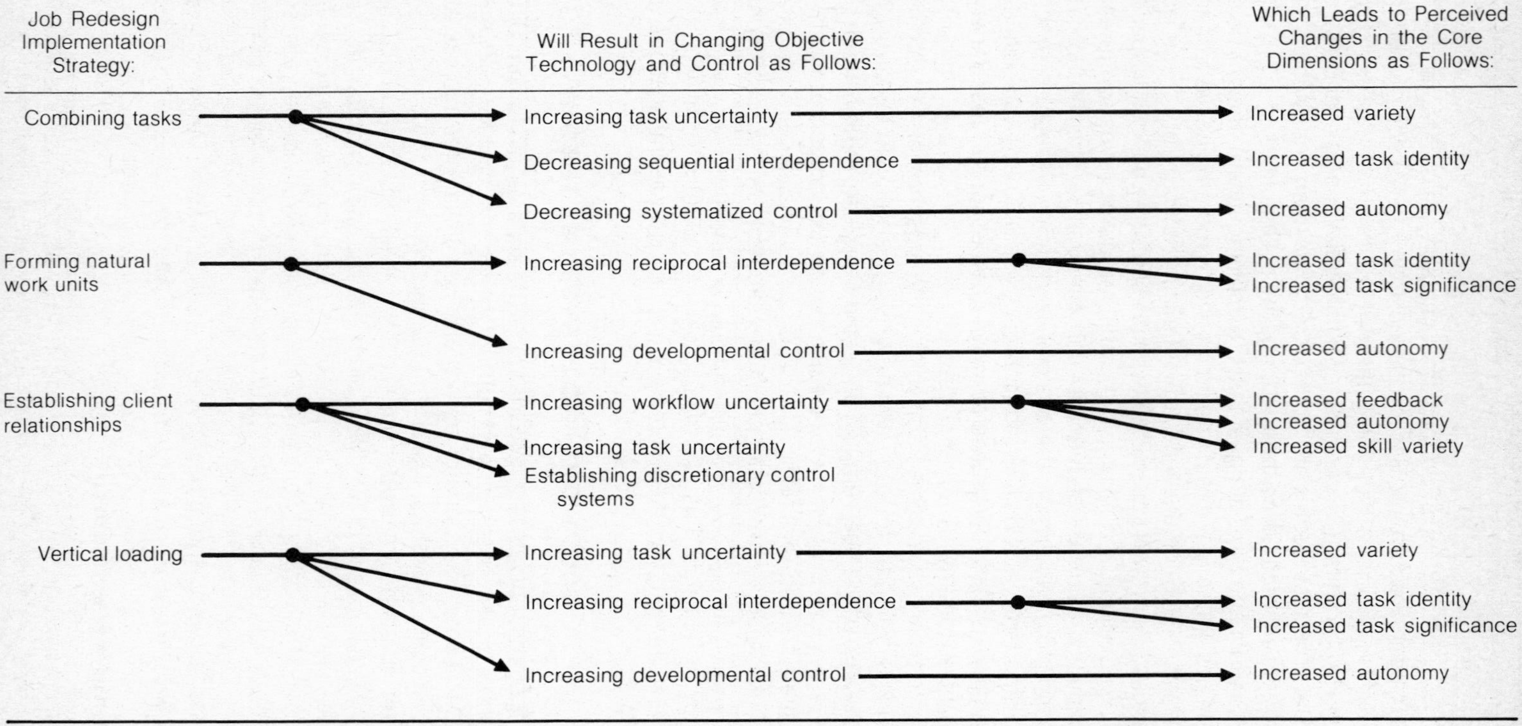

Job Redesign Implementation Strategy:	Will Result in Changing Objective Technology and Control as Follows:	Which Leads to Perceived Changes in the Core Dimensions as Follows:
Combining tasks	Increasing task uncertainty	Increased variety
	Decreasing sequential interdependence	Increased task identity
	Decreasing systematized control	Increased autonomy
Forming natural work units	Increasing reciprocal interdependence	Increased task identity / Increased task significance
	Increasing developmental control	Increased autonomy
Establishing client relationships	Increasing workflow uncertainty	Increased feedback
	Increasing task uncertainty	Increased autonomy
	Establishing discretionary control systems	Increased skill variety
Vertical loading	Increasing task uncertainty	Increased variety
	Increasing reciprocal interdependence	Increased task identity / Increased task significance
	Increasing developmental control	Increased autonomy

Source: J. W. Slocum, Jr., and H. P. Sims, Jr., "A Typology for Integrating Technology, Organization, and Job Design," *Human Relations* (Vol. 33, 1980), p. 205. Used by permission.

Recall that Taylor advocated the scientific study of tasks with the objective of maximizing efficiency and productivity. As a result of the widespread adoption of the scientific management approach, many organizations emphasized the technical aspects of production, with little or no regard for the human element. Hence, it might be argued that scientific management, by emphasizing the technical processes within organizations, attempted to optimize the technical subsystem at the expense of the social subsystem. As if in reaction to this extreme school of thought, an opposing approach to management evolved. This approach has come to be called the human relations movement and represents the other extreme included in socio-technical systems theory.

Human Relations

The human relations movement grew out of a now-famous series of studies at the Hawthorne plant of the Western Electric Company (Mayo, 1933; Roethlisberger and Dickson, 1939). While the specifics of the Hawthorne studies are beyond the scope of this discussion, a number of important generalizations from the studies were drawn by management theorists. These generalizations, which form the basic framework for the human relations school of thought, can be summarized as follows:

1. Employee satisfaction is primarily a function of the informal social work group.
2. Social control within a work group motivates members to produce at a rate not too far above or below the group's productivity norm.
3. Social factors, as opposed to technical factors, are the primary determinants of employee performance.

Thus , the human relations movement emphasized the human rather than the technical side of the organization.

The Tavistock Contribution

Two groundbreaking studies by researchers associated with the Tavistock Institute provide the basis for attempting to synthesize these opposing viewpoints. These studies will be briefly summarized in the following paragraphs.

The coal mining study.   Trist and Bamforth (1951) investigated the effects of a technological change in the coal mining operations in England on various social processes among the miners. Prior to the change, the miners worked in small groups and essentially worked the mines and gathered coal by hand. The group had considerable autonomy in a number of different areas of the work system. The technological change involved an assembly-line approach that focused on task specialization and routinization. This system failed, due to its lack of recognition of the importance of social processes in the workplace. Eventually, a composite system emerged, which provided a balance of technical and social processes. **115**

The textile mills study. Rice (1958) studied social and technical systems interactions in textile mills in Ahmedabad, India. These mills had recently installed new automatic looms, but had not realized the anticipated productivity increases. Tavistock researchers suggested the need to form autonomous work groups in order to facilitate commitment, communication, and positive social influence. Over a two-year period following the change, both production quality and quantity increased substantially.

These studies and others led the researchers at Tavistock to argue for the need to consider both the *technical* and *social* systems when planning and describing organizations. Since the two systems are obviously interdependent, it is imperative to optimize them jointly within the organizational context. That is, neither the extreme emphasis on the technical system by the scientific management school nor the extreme emphasis on the social system as advocated by the human relations school is entirely correct. Rather, it is necessary to achieve a balanced (i.e., jointly optimized) view.

To illustrate this deceivingly simple assumption, consider the example of two personnel specialists preparing job description manuals. Joint optimization would entail designing the total task to account for both the technical and social processes inherent in the situation. If the two individuals liked one another and enjoyed working together, perhaps the job should be set up so as to allow them to work as a team. Under this plan, the two people would each work on the same task at the same time. On the other hand, if the two workers did not like one another, teamwork might result in conflict. If this were the case, perhaps the specialists should work on separate projects, independently.

Managerial Implications

Following Miles (1980), we will now focus briefly on the managerial implications of socio-technical systems theory. Miller and Rice (1967) suggest that socio-technical systems theory offers management the opportunity to balance human needs, tasks, and organization within the context of an organizational system interacting with its environment.

The two primary subsystems, according to this framework, are the *task group* (i.e., the technical subsystem) and the *sentient group* (i.e., the social subsystem or informal group). As shown in Figure 6–6, these two types of groups may be virtually the same, or may have practically no overlap. The manager's primary responsibility is to ''regulate these boundaries in a manner consistent with the demands of the larger context'' (Miles, 1980, p. 114).

When the task is routine and not very motivating (i.e., low in scope), and when the larger context is stable, the task and sentient groups should be the same. In this case, the social processes of the sentient relationships can offset the dysfunctional aspects of the routine task. That is, social satisfactions may be sufficient to offset at least partially the probable lack of task-related satisfactions.

FIGURE 6-6   Task and Sentient Groups and Their Environment

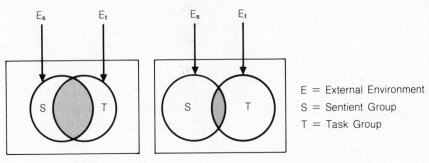

A. High Coincidence Condition   B. Low Coincidence Condition

E = External Environment
S = Sentient Group
T = Task Group

Source: R. H. Miles, *Macro Organizational Behavior* (Santa Monica, California: Goodyear Publishing Company, 1980) p. 114. Used by permission.

When the environment is changing, however, this balance may be difficult to maintain. In some cases, it may even detract from organizational effectiveness. For example, when the task is nonroutine and highly motivating (i.e., high in scope), and when the larger context is changing, the task and sentient groups may need to be different. Under such conditions, it may be necessary for the employee to focus specifically on the task itself. Behavioral and social processes within the sentient group, however, may distract the employee to such an extent that task performance is hampered. Hence, organizational effectiveness may be a function of the extent to which task group processes dominate sentient group processes.

TASK DESIGN AND TECHNOLOGY: AN INTEGRATIVE VIEW

In previous sections of this chapter, we have examined: (1) five different typologies or conceptualizations of organizational technologies, (2) how these various frameworks may relate to task design processes, and (3) the socio-technical systems view of organizations. In this section, we will attempt to integrate these various viewpoints into one general framework of technology and task design interactions.

Figure 6-7 graphically presents one view of how the various technological and task design variables and processes may be interrelated. Consistent with socio-technical systems theory, the framework includes two organizational systems that are of importance: the social system and the technical system. The social system, in turn, contains two basic elements.

One element of the social system is behavioral, group, and social processes that operate in the workplace. This element is similar to the sentient group described by socio-technical systems theorists. These processes will be explored in more depth in Chapter 9. The other component of the social system is the nature of the supervisor-subordinate relationship. It could be argued that since this relationship is structurally defined by **117** the organization, it is a part of the technical system. However, since both parties in such a relationship are characterized by basic behavioral, affective, and cognitive processes, and since the relationship itself is a social exchange, it seems more reasonable to include it in the social system of the organization. This aspect of the task design process will be more fully developed in Chapter 8.

The technical system of the organization is characterized by the five typologies or conceptualizations of technology summarized earlier in this chapter. As we move from the general to the specific, the first descriptive component of the technical system is represented by the Aston framework. Specifically, it can be assumed that operations, materials, and knowledge technologies are subsystems of the organization's technical system.

Next come the true typologies of technology. This component allows us to group or classify organizations into relatively discrete categories. Figure 6–7 includes only the four categories suggested by Perrow (1967). However, as we shall see later, the categories suggested by Thompson (1967) and Woodward (1965) are also implied in the framework.

The framework also suggests that different technological subsystems (knowledge, materials, and operations) may be placed in different categories. For example, geological and chemical laboratories may have employed fairly standard investigation and analysis procedures (i.e., few exceptions and analyzable search procedures in the operations-technology subsystem) in studying the first moon rocks (many exceptions and unanalyzable search procedures in the materials technology subsystem) returned by U.S. astronauts. Further, the scientists themselves may have been trained to approach their analyses in a highly programmed fashion (i.e., many exceptions but analyzable search for the knowledge-technology subsystem).

After categorizing the various technology subsystems of the organization, it is then possible to describe each of them in terms of the degrees of work-flow uncertainty, task uncertainty, and task interdependence inherent in the subsystems (e.g., Slocum and Sims, 1980). Within any category, operations, materials, and knowledge technologies can be represented along the three dimensions of work-flow and task uncertainty and job interdependence.

The two basic systems, technical and social, are then conceptualized as having a direct impact on the employee's task itself. As noted earlier, the impact of the social system on the task will be discussed in later chapters while the technical system–task design interface has been documented in this chapter.

The final element of the integrative framework is the view that just as technical and social factors influence task design processes, the task also influences the two systems themselves. This is perhaps best illustrated through an example of an organizational change. Suppose that a manager **118** read the first five chapters of this book and skipped the rest. Further,

FIGURE 6–7   An Integrative Framework of Technological Typologies, Socio-technical Systems Theory, and Task Design

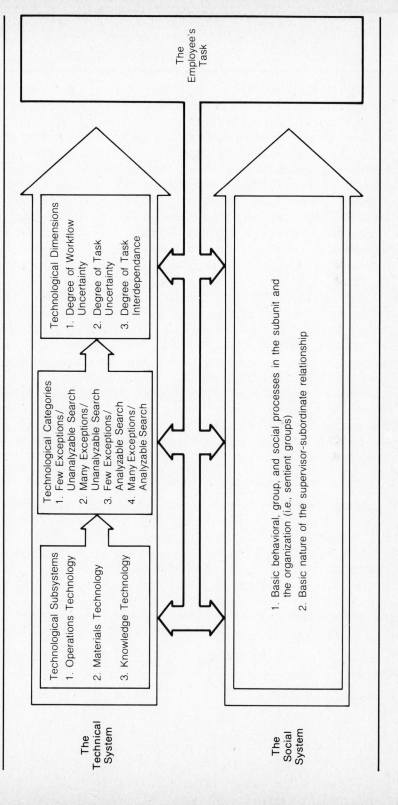

suppose the manager then initiated a task redesign effort in his or her organization with the intent of improving employee reactions to their jobs.

The change itself might initially involve a fairly straightforward modification in the degrees of work-flow uncertainty, task uncertainty, and task interdependence of the operations technology subsystem. This change, however, will probably also affect at least the knowledge technology subsystem and perhaps even the materials technology subsystem as well. Further, the task redesign effort will probably also affect existing social relationships and supervisor-subordinate dyads in the social system. Thus, a cyclical relationship probably exists among the technical and social systems of an organization and the task design variables and processes.

It is also interesting to speculate on some more precise interrelationships among task design variables and the technical system. One possible pattern of interrelationships is summarized in Table 6–2. Assume that we are focusing only on the operations subsystem of the organization. Column 1 of Table 6–2 summarizes the four technological types described by Perrow (1967). Also noted in Column 1 are corresponding categories from the typologies of Woodward (1965) and Thompson (1967): continuous process firms could be characterized by few exceptions and unanalyzable search processes, intensive technology by many exceptions and unanalyzable search processes, mass production and long-linked technologies by few exceptions and analyzable search processes, and small batch and mediating technologies by many exceptions and analyzable search processes. Of course, some of these match-ups are less than perfect and exceptions to each could be identified. The categories are, however, at least conceptually similar.

TABLE 6–2   The Technical System and Task Design

TECHNOLOGICAL TYPE	TECHNOLOGICAL PROFILE	PREDICTED LEVEL OF TASK SCOPE
1. Few exceptions Unanalyzable search (continuous process, for example)	Work-flow uncertainty: low Task uncertainty: moderate Task interdependance: low	Moderate to low
2. Many exceptions Unanalyzable search (intensive technology, for example)	Work-flow uncertainty: high Task uncertainty: high Task interdependance: high	High
3. Few exceptions Analyzable search (mass production/ long-linked technology)	Work-flow uncertainty: low Task uncertainty: low Task interdependance: low	Low
4. Many exceptions Analyzable search (small batch and mediating technology)	Work-flow uncertainty: high Task uncertainty: moderate Task interdependance: moderate	Moderate to high

Column 2 provides a potential technological profile for each category in terms of work-flow uncertainty, task uncertainty, and task interdependence. For example, technologies characterized by many exceptions and unanalyzable search processes will tend to have high work-flow uncertainty, high task uncertainty, and high task interdependence.

Finally, Column 3 provides a predicted level of task scope as a function of the technological profile in Column 2. For the example described above (situation 2), high levels of work-flow uncertainty, task uncertainty, and task interdependence will probably translate into high levels of perceived and objective task scope. Other predictions are offered for different technological profiles. Of course, as indicated earlier, all of these predictions are speculative. In fact, the entire framework is simply offered as one admittedly crude mechanism for drawing together different approaches to the study of technology and its impact on the design of work in organizations.

The preceding sections of this chapter have focused on past and present conceptualizations of organizational technologies. In a society subject to the rapid and unpredictable changes that characterize ours, however, these conceptualizations are likely to be inadequate in the future. In our next section, we will explore some predictions about future organizational technologies and outline some crucial concerns that will be important in understanding and describing these technologies.

FUTURE TECHNOLOGIES

Many of our examples in this book have been drawn from the automobile industry. The frame of reference for these examples has been the traditional assembly plant operated by, for instance, General Motors, Ford, or Chrysler. Imagine, however, a different kind of automobile assembly plant. Imagine a plant where robots assemble the cars. These robots weld the body parts together, bolt the doors on, and do most of the jobs normally assigned to humans in traditional plants.

Fantasy? No, this is an accurate description of Nissan Motor Company's existing plant in Zama, Japan. The facility averages more than 1,300 cars produced per day, yet the average number of employees on duty at any one time averages only 67. Further, most of these employees only monitor the automated work system and do little physical work themselves.

This example serves to point out the rate of technological change taking place in contemporary society. To many people, the auto plant described above is a vision of the future yet it is already in operation. The technologies of the future will no doubt stagger the imagination.

The nature of future technologies can be assessed on at least two levels.

First, it is useful to consider the nature of the societal context in the future, at least in the United States. At least three alternative futures can be described (Etzioni, 1979):

121

1. We may enter a period when we are "slower-paced, more content with pleasure and relaxation, less driven, less mobilized, less productive, less efficient, more corrupt, and more politicized."
2. We might move toward a reindustrialization. Such a period would be characterized by a "restoration in which old virtues, values, and taboos will be injected with new potency."
3. The United States might evolve into a quality-of-life society. This type of society would focus more on interacting with its ecological environment in a more positive fashion and on being more concerned with the quality, as opposed to the quantity, of work and output (Etzioni, 1979, p. 32).

The second level at which technological change can be considered is more micro in nature. Specifically, the issue relates to the *kinds* of industrial work to be performed in the future. This point has somewhat more focus to it, and can be dealt with in a more straightforward manner. Two particular dimensions of industrial work will probably reflect the greatest change:

1. There will probably be a continued move toward automation. The Nissan plant summarized earlier will become the rule rather than the exception. Already, the United States government grants a tax depreciation allowance to small and medium-sized firms that buy robots to perform dangerous jobs. It seems almost a certainty that more and more jobs will fall within the domain of automated systems of production. The workers themselves will become more a part of the control system.
2. Whatever kinds of jobs workers are doing will be done in a cleaner and safer environment. Government regulations (i.e., OSHA, etc.) have already forced a big step in this direction. The trend is also reinforced by such things as Walton's (1974) quality-of-work-life criteria summarized in Chapter 1.

Implications of future technologies for task design are difficult to identify. However, at least two points may be significant, one in a positive way and the other in a negative way. On the plus side, future technologies may virtually eliminate the routine, boring tasks created by the principles of scientific management. Hence, the worker may no longer be forced to connect wires in a hair dryer or put bolts in an engine mount all day.

On the other hand, one major dysfunction may occur. In effect, the automated work system forces the employee to become an observer, rather than a participant in the creation of a product or service. Over time, then, the employee may come to feel alienated from the work system itself. He or she will feel no sense of identity and may lose the feelings of responsibility and accomplishment that go along with doing many existing jobs.

Whatever the case, future managers and researchers need to consider the complex interrelationships among organizational technology and task design variables. Both of these organizational dimensions play an important role in influencing the quality of the employee's work experience.

SUMMARY

This chapter has looked at relationships among technology and task design variables in organizations. First, the nature of organizational technology was discussed. Next, we looked at how technology might constrain and/or facilitate task redesign or change efforts in various levels of situations. We then described five major conceptualizations of technology and related each to task design variables. Following a discussion of sociotechnical systems theory, we presented an integrative framework for analyzing technology and task design interactions. Finally, we offered some speculative comments on technologies of the future.

Clearly, the relationships between technology and task design are relatively strong and potentially quite important. A number of generalizations and predictions may be derived from the material presented in this chapter.

Most importantly, there appears to be a direct link between an organization's technology and the tasks its employees perform. While other intervening factors rule out a perfect linear relationship, in many ways an organization's technology is the sum of its tasks. This conclusion becomes even more important when the role of technology in contemporary society is considered. It is difficult to imagine an organization without a technology (although some technologies are clearly more abstract than others). If, in fact, an organization's technology is the sum of its tasks, then everyone that works is directly tied into one or more technological dimensions or processes. Given the rate of technological change currently being evidenced (i.e., by new products and services constantly being developed) and the increased attention likely to be directed at technology in the future (i.e., as a means to enhance productivity, etc.), it follows that the technology-task design interface is an extremely important component in organizational life to be considered, regardless of the assumed nature of future technologies one adopts.

At a more applied level, there are two additional important messages for management that emerge from this discussion. First, when contemplating or implementing a major technological change, the effects of the change on tasks within the organization should be considered. For a wide variety of reasons, an organization's technology (or technologies) may require some modification. It is important to recognize, however, that changing elements of technology will also likely change individual tasks.

Second, the manager must also take a broad perspective when initiating change from the micro side of the relationship. More precisely, when evaluating a potential task redesign effort, it is important to also look at the implications for the work flow and technology utilized by the organization. Even isolated task changes may affect a variety of technological processes.

In terms of research implications, it should be obvious that much remains to be done before the full extent and nature of the relationships among task design and technological variables are understood. It is hoped that this commentary has provided some useful insights and starting points. In Chapter 7, we turn our attention to another major contextual consideration for task design: the design of the overall organization.

7 TASK DESIGN AND ORGANIZATION DESIGN

Bill Adams and Jim Henderson were good friends when they attended State University. They both majored in marketing and, upon graduation, went to work as sales representatives for two different manufacturers of heavy equipment parts and supplies. A couple of years after graduation, they met again at a convention and spent one evening talking about their respective jobs. Bill said, "One thing that I don't like about my company is that they never let me make any decisions. For example, I have to call and get credit approval for any sale over $1,000, even for established accounts. I also have to get approval for quantity discounts, even though we have established decision rules. How much latitude do you have in making those kinds of decisions, Jim?"

Jim Henderson replied, "Well, I certainly don't have total control over what I can do, but I do seem to have more flexibility than you have. As long as a customer is ordering in the same general range as in the past, I can okay the sale, regardless of the amount. I can also extend credit to a new customer on my own, as long as I use what my sales manager calls 'reasonable judgment and common sense.' Quantity discounts are pretty standard, too, and we can set those up ourselves. You know, I'd bet part of our freedom has to do with our unit's size. We have 26 reps reporting to the sales manager. If she took the time to watch everything we did, she'd need a ten-day week."

"That may be part of the difference," said Bill. "My boss has only ten representatives to watch out for. Maybe he doesn't have enough to keep him busy, so he spends his time looking over our shoulders. It's almost like the company gives the sales managers fewer reps, just so they can watch us closer. That probably also accounts for all the reports he makes us write. I'll bet most of them end up in the circular file anyway."

"What kinds of reports?" asked Jim.

"All kinds of things. We submit reports on each customer we contact, whether we make a sale or not. The company outlines standard procedures we're supposed to follow, and the reports simply summarize each step in the procedure and how we addressed it. We also have to provide complete documentation on our expense reports. We even have to submit a weekly report projecting what we're going to do the next week. Two weeks later, we summarize what we did and did not do that was in the other report. I'd bet I spend 15 hours a week on paperwork. Don't you have to prepare any of those kinds of reports?"

"Oh, we have a few things like that," said Jim. "Our system is considerably less formal, however. We don't have to project our activities on a weekly basis or fill out customer contact summaries. In fact, I probably spend less than two hours per week on paperwork and reports."

Bill Adams and Jim Henderson do the same kind of work for two organizations in the same industry. Yet, they obviously see their respective jobs in quite different ways. Objective differences are also apparent between the two jobs. One major factor which accounts for these differences is that the two firms do not have the same form of organization structure and design. Bill's firm is relatively centralized and formalized, and his boss has a narrow span of control. Jim's firm, on the other hand, is considerably more decentralized and less formalized, while managers appear to have wider spans of control.

We saw in the last chapter that an organization's technology has an impact on the design of tasks within the organization. The preceding examples and the remainder of this chapter serves to illustrate interactions between task design variables and the organization's structure and design. Organization structure refers to the components, elements, and/or dimensions that can be used to characterize a firm. Elements of structure include decentralization, formalization, and span of control, as used earlier, and other elements that will be introduced later. Organization design is the manner in which the various structural elements are fitted together; the design of the organization is the overall configuration of the structural components.

At a general level, organization design and task design are natural complements. The organizing function of management is concerned with the arrangement and allocation of work within the organization. This arrangement and allocation of work for individual organizational members is essentially the process of task design; similarly, the aggregate arrangement and allocation of work across a number of employees is the process of organization design. A number of interrelationships, then, should exist.

The importance of relating the two concepts is also somewhat apparent. If the focus is on the macro level, the manager should be aware of the possible influences that various organization design configurations and/or changes may have on important task characteristics. From the **125** other perspective, it is also important to understand the potential implications for organization design if tasks are changed and/or rearranged. That is, the organization's design represents a major contextual element that may constrain and/or facilitate task design processes. These issues and others will be explored in this chapter.

The first section of the chapter will describe five basic dimensions of organization structure and relate each dimension to the task design process. The next section will focus on various models of organization design and the ways in which task design variables influence and are influenced by different designs. Next, we will present two models that attempt to tie together individual, task-design, and organization-design variables. Miscellaneous characteristics of organizations are then related to task design. The next section will briefly discuss potential interactions among organization design, technology, and task design. Finally, we will present conclusions and generalizations pertaining to task and organization design interactions.

ORGANIZATION STRUCTURE AND TASK DESIGN

A variety of structural components and dimensions have been identified and described by organization theorists. The components of organization structure most logically related to the design of tasks within the organization are: (1) decentralization, (2) specialization, (3) formalization, (4) span of control, and (5) line–staff roles. These characteristics are defined in Table 7–1. The following discussion of how these dimensions may relate to task design processes will be somewhat conjectural in places, since little research has been performed in this particular area. Further, it is important to remember that structural properties of organizations are likely to have their strongest impact on managers, as opposed to operating personnel. Hence, when we discuss task variety, for example, we are taking a broader, more general perspective than at previous points. That is, variety for a managerial job may relate less to specific numbers of activities and more to the number of *roles* the manager has. Further, autonomy may relate less to control over choice of work procedures and more to control over relevant decisions.

TABLE 7–1   Dimensions of Organization Structure

1. *Decentralization*. The extent to which decision-making power and authority are delegated to lower levels of an organization, as opposed to being retained at upper levels.
2. *Specialization*. The extent to which organizational tasks are highly subdivided into fractionalized components.
3. *Formalization*. The extent to which work-related activities and behaviors are regulated and defined by the organization.
4. *Span of Control*. The number of subordinates reporting directly to a particular manager.
5. *Line-Staff Roles*. The configuration of jobs directly related to the operating system (line) and jobs of an auxiliary, advisory, and/or support nature (staff).

Decentralization and Task Design

Decentralization refers to the extent to which power and authority in an organization are delegated to lower levels of the hierarchy. An organization that is decentralized, then, is one in which lower-level managers have control over their activities and can make a wide variety of decisions without the approval of upper-level management. Conversely, a centralized organization is characterized by little decision-making latitude for lower-level managers; most of the power and authority is retained at the upper levels of the hierarchy. In the examples used to introduce this chapter, Jim Henderson evidently works for a more decentralized firm, while Bill Adams' organization appears to be more centralized.

General Electric is a good example of a highly decentralized organization. Broken down into more than 100 operating product departments, the firm allows managers almost complete control over the design, manufacturing, pricing policies, and marketing of the unit's products. Decentralization is a primary element in GE's management philosophy (Gibson, Ivancevich, and Donnelly, 1979).

Since decentralization essentially pertains to decision making, its effects on task design will probably be seen most clearly in the jobs of managers, as explained earlier. Obviously, decentralization is likely to have its strongest impact on task autonomy. In the decentralized organization, the manager will have more control over decisions, and therefore should experience more task autonomy. Conversely, a manager in a more centralized firm will have less decision-making power, will consult his or her superior more frequently, and will probably perceive less task autonomy.

Feedback has also been shown to be related to decentralization (Read, 1962). This process is illustrated at GE. While a manager has almost total control over his or her unit, the manager is also accountable for the profitability of the unit. The manager receives frequent feedback from financial reports and from upper-level management as to how well the unit in general and the manager in particular are performing.

It seems reasonable to assume that decentralization will also be related to task significance. When managers have control over crucial decisions, they are likely to learn from experience the importance of their decisions. The GE manager, again, is able to realize how pricing decisions influence the income statement. Hence, the job itself will probably be seen as having a relatively high degree of significance.

At a slightly more abstract level, task identity may also be affected by decentralization. In the centralized firm, the manager may plan a course of action, but must seek permission before proceeding. That is, part of the total task is performed by the manager's supervisor. Decentralization, however, involves having the manager carrying through on the total project. More identity may be perceived as a result of this more complete process.

127

As indicated earlier, little empirical research exists in this area. Those studies that are available, however, tend to support a decentralization–task design interaction. Pierce and Dunham (1978b), for example, surveyed 155 insurance company employees and found negative relationships between a measure of organizational centralization and perceived task characteristics such as autonomy, feedback, variety, and identity. Moorhead (1981) also found a significant negative relationship between centralization and a summary index of task scope for a sample of resident physicians. Thus, the evidence tentatively indicates that employees will perceive higher levels of task scope in decentralized organizations than will employees in more centralized organizations.

Before proceeding, one final point is in order. The preceding discussion is not intended to imply that decentralization or centralization is a superior management strategy. In some instances, one technique may be most effective, while in other situations the alternative approach may work best. The intent is simply to illustrate potential task design and organization design interactions. We now turn our attention to another element of organization structure: specialization.

Specialization and Task Design

Specialization is the extent to which tasks are sub-divided into narrow components. Of all the organizational structure elements, specialization is probably most closely related to task design, especially for managers.

The rationale for high degrees of task specialization was first argued widely by Taylor (1911). As summarized back in Chapter 2, Taylor and his scientific management approach advocated a high degree of specialization. This specialization was assumed to facilitate high degrees of work proficiency and interchangeability among employees. A recent review concludes that specialization may have a positive impact on performance, but may simultaneously cause decreased satisfaction and increased turnover (Steers, 1977b). This conclusion is consistent with our critique of scientific management presented in Chapter 2.

The specialization—task characteristics linkages themselves are relatively simple and straightforward. High degrees of specialization are likely to be associated with low degrees of perceived variety, autonomy, feedback, identity, and significance. Conversely, low specialization probably will be related to high levels of these same attributes.

Interestingly, however, no data exists to actually support these predictions. The hospital study combined a measure of specialization with measures of formalization and standardization and found no relationship between this summary measure (called structuring of activities) and task scope (Moorhead, 1981). However, by combining the structural scores, simpler relationships may have been masked.

Formalization and Task Design

Formalization is the extent to which work activities are regulated or specified by organizational rules and procedures. Generally, formalization is assumed to have a negative impact on organizational performance due to the constraints it places on creativity and innovation for employees within the organization. The empirical evidence, however, is somewhat contradictory. It has been suggested that less formalization may be called for under conditions of unknown or unstable environmental conditions, while more formalization may be appropriate if the environment is more stable and predictable (Steers, 1977b).

Formalization–task design relationships are somewhat difficult to predict. Certainly, increased formalization should result in decreased autonomy for the employee, since the objective of formalization is to prescribe methods of task performance. However, it also seems logical that both more significant and less significant jobs could be formalized, as could highly specialized jobs (i.e., low variety) and jobs with little associated specialization (i.e., high variety). For example, a highly significant job, such as checking the life-support system for an astronaut, could be as easily formalized as the comparatively less significant job of reading residential water meters.

The insurance company study mentioned earlier, however, did find negative relationships between formalization and task variety, autonomy, feedback, and identity (Pierce and Dunham, 1978b). Hence, while there may be little conceptual rationale (except for task autonomy), the scant research evidence suggests that formalization will be inversely related to employee perceptions of task scope.

Span of Control and Task Design

Span of control is the number of employees who report directly to a manager: a span of control of 7 indicates that the manager has 7 immediate subordinates. The concept of span of control has been the subject of much discussion over the years (cf., Van Fleet and Bedeian, 1977). These discussions have generally focused on questions such as the optimum span of control, the effects of various spans on organization structure, and so forth. Figure 7–1 illustrates a general relationship between spans of control and organization design. As can be seen in the diagrams, wide spans of control are generally associated with "flat" organizations, whereas narrow spans of control are a characteristic of "tall" organizations. Flat structures are usually associated with increased levels of decentralization, whereas tall structures reflect higher degrees of centralization.

Since the span of control concept specifically includes both a superior and a set of subordinates, task design considerations should be described from both points of view. Further, while our previous sections have gener-

129

FIGURE 7–1   Spans of Control and Organization Design

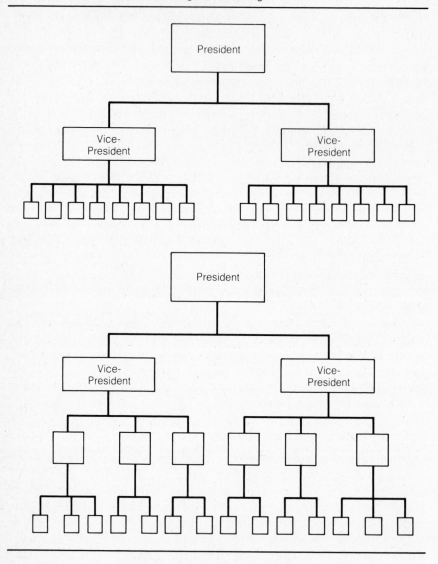

ally implied that various task characteristics will be influenced by elements of organization structure, there is likely to be more of an interactive relationship between span of control and task design.

For example, take the case of the subordinates. On the one hand, if their manager has a wide span, it follows that he or she will have less time to actively supervise any one of them. Therefore, their jobs may of necessity be designed to allow them more autonomy. Alternatively, some writers have suggested that the appropriate span of control in a particular organization should be a function of situational variables such as task structure. The rationale is that if tasks are highly structured (i.e., specialized and formalized), then the manager should be able to coordinate the activities of more employees than if the various tasks were less structured. Therefore, span of control and task design processes probably influence one another in an interactive fashion.

For the supervisor, the same kind of interaction probably occurs. The span of control that is dictated for the manager influences the design of his or her own task, since the span determines the amount of actual supervision time that will be required; the amount of supervisory work performed by the manager has an impact on other activities that will be a part of the managerial job. Hence, span of control influences the design of the manager's task.

The reciprocal process is demonstrated by what may occur when the span is initially developed. If the primary duty of the manager is supervision, then a wide span may be established. On the other hand, if the manager is expected to do other things such as paperwork, field work, etc., fewer subordinates may be assigned.

Line-Staff Roles

Most organizations reach a point where they must create auxiliary roles to support personnel directly involved with the organization's mission. These auxiliary roles are generally referred to as staff positions. A staff manager will have little direct authority in making decisions pertaining to the organization's day-to-day operations. Rather, the staff manager's job involves offering advice and suggestions, doing research work, and so forth. Positions with titles such as "Assistant to-" are generally staff jobs, as are many other jobs in personnel, marketing research, etc.

A line manager's job, on the other hand, is directly related to the organization's operations. Titles such as plant or production manager or sales manager are representative of line positions in organizations. These managers have the authority to make decisions, issue directives, and so forth, and are directly accountable for these decisions and directives.

In terms of task design variables, the line manager may experience more autonomy than the staff manager, since he or she can (and must) make more decisions. Similarly, the line manager may experience more task significance than the staff manager, since the latter's recommendations are subject to the approval of a line manager. On the other hand, the staff manager may enjoy some forms of feedback not available to the line manager. For example, a marketing researcher (staff) may recommend a certain marketing strategy to the marketing vice-president (line). The v.p. may report back to the researcher fairly quickly as to whether or not the recommendation has been accepted. The v.p., however, may then have to wait several months before he or she receives feedback from the marketplace as to the appropriateness of the decision. Of course, these examples **131** are simply offered to illustrate potential task design differences between line and staff roles; the true nature of such differences, if they exist at all, has not been explored by researchers.

Summary

This section has described potential interactions among dimensions of organization structure and task design variables. These potential interactions are summarized in Table 7–2. As mentioned earlier, most of these interactions are offered as tentative and conjectural patterns that may or may not exist. For example, the Pierce and Dunham (1978b) study used for support here was actually trying to demonstrate that *measures* of task structure and organization structure may overlap rather than be truly unique components of organizations. The interactions that were discussed, however, do seem to be reasonable explanations of how attributes of tasks and organizations may be related.

ORGANIZATION DESIGN AND TASK DESIGN

The preceding discussion has dealt with specific components or dimensions of organization structure. A more complete analysis of organizations, however, must focus on complex configurations of how the various

TABLE 7–2   Summary of Potential Structural Characteristics and Task Characteristics Interactions

1. *Decentralization* may have a (1) positive impact on autonomy
   (2) positive impact on feedback
   (3) positive impact on significance
   (4) positive impact on identity
   (5) positive impact on variety

2. *Specialization* may have a (1) negative impact on autonomy
   (2) negative impact on feedback
   (3) negative impact on significance
   (4) negative impact on identity
   (5) negative impact on variety

3. *Formalization* may have a (1) negative impact on autonomy
   (2) negative impact on variety
   (3) negative impact on identity
   (4) negative impact on feedback
   (5) unknown impact on significance

4. *Span of control* may be related to overall task structure in a reciprocal fashion such that: (1) wide spans may cause subordinate task autonomy
   (2) overall task structure may dictate appropriate spans
   (3) the supervisor's own task may dictate appropriate spans

5a. *Line role* may have (1) more autonomy
   (2) more significance
   (3) variable degrees of variety, identity, and feedback

5b. *Staff role* may have (1) little autonomy
   (2) moderate significance
   (3) more feedback
   (4) variable degrees of variety and identity

structural dimensions are combined to form an overall framework. This framework is called organization design and is the unique combination of decentralization, standardization, etc., which an organization adopts. In this section, we will look at potential interactions between a variety of organization design alternatives and task design variables. Two points, however, should be made first: (1) since little empirical research exists in this area, the discussion will, of necessity, be speculative at times, and (2) a variety of task design configurations are likely to exist in any organization; the patterns we will discuss are simply most likely to be predominant.

Mechanistic and Organic Organizations

One framework for describing patterns of organization design is the mechanistic-organic continuum developed by Burns and Stalker (1961). These researchers surveyed 20 British industrial organizations in an attempt to discover relationships among characteristics of the external environment and managerial practice. Environmental characteristics studied included the rate of change in relevant technology and rate of change in the marketplace.

Results of the study indicated that two quite different types of management systems could be described. The extent to which one type of system was utilized over the other was seen to be a function of environmental stability. One system was called the *mechanistic* form of organization design and was suggested to be most appropriate in conditions of relative environmental stability. The other system was the *organic* design and was suggested for conditions of relative instability.

Characteristics of the two types of systems are summarized in Table 7–3. Clearly, tasks in a mechanistic organization will tend to be primarily low scope in nature. Attributes such as "specialized," "rigidly defined," "specific role definition," "hierarchic . . . control," and "decisions issued by superiors" tend to suggest a task with very little variety, autonomy, feedback, etc.

Alternatively, an organic system, characterized by "generalized role definition," "tasks . . . continually adjusted," and "leader not assumed to be omniscient" is generally descriptive of more challenging, complex tasks (i.e., tasks high in scope). Hence, the manner in which tasks are structured may indirectly be a function of environmental instability. That is, conditions of the environment may dictate certain forms of organization design that, in turn, may have important task design implications. Other models of environment-organization design interactions (e.g., Chandler, 1962; Lawrence and Lorsch, 1967; Osborn and Hunt, 1974) beyond the scope of this discussion may have similar implications. The pattern of potential interactions, however, would be redundant with what has already been presented in this discussion. Hence, we will now direct our attention at other alternative views of organization design. **133**

TABLE 7–3   Mechanistic and Organic Organizations

MECHANISTIC	ORGANIC
1. Tasks are highly fractionated and specialized; little regard paid to clarifying relationship between tasks and organizational objectives.	1. Tasks are more interdependent; emphasis on relevance of tasks and organizational objectives.
2. Tasks tend to remain rigidly defined unless altered formally by top management.	2. Tasks are continually adjusted and redefined through interaction of organizational members.
3. Specific role definition (rights, obligations, and technical methods prescribed for each member).	3. Generalized role definition (members accept general responsibility for task accomplishment beyond individual role definition).
4. Hierarchic structure of control, authority, and communication. Sanctions derive from employment contract between employee and organization.	4. Network structure of control authority and communication. Sanctions derive more from community of interest than from contractual relationship.
5. Information relevant to situation and operations of the organization formally assumed to rest with chief executive.	5. Leader not assumed to be omniscient; knowledge centers identified where located throughout organization.
6. Communication is primarily vertical between superior and subordinate.	6. Communication is both vertical and horizontal, depending upon where needed information resides.
7. Communications primarily take form of instructions and decisions issued by superiors, of information and requests for decisions supplied by inferiors.	7. Communications primarily take form of information and advice.
8. Insistence on loyalty to organization and obedience to superiors.	8. Commitment to organization's tasks and goals more highly valued than loyalty or obedience.
9. Importance and prestige attached to identification with organization and its members.	9. Importance and prestige attached to affiliations and expertise in external environment.

Source: Adapted from T. Burns and G. M. Stalker, *The Management of Innovations* (London: Tavistock, 1961), pp. 119–22. Used by permission.

The Mintzberg Framework

In a recent groundbreaking book, Henry Mintzberg (1979) proposes a framework that includes five basic structural configurations, or forms of organization design. These five configurations, summarized in Table 7–4, are termed Simple Structure, Machine Bureaucracy, Professional Bureaucracy, Divisionalized Form, and Adhocracy. The five forms are differentiated along three dimensions: (1) the prime coordinating mechanism adopted by the organization, (2) the key part of the organization, and (3) the type of decentralization utilized by the organization.

The following sections will describe each form of organization design and the types of task designs likely to exist within each.

TABLE 7–4 Mintzberg's Five Designs

STRUCTURAL CONFIGURATION	PRIME COORDINATING MECHANISM	KEY PART OF ORGANIZATION	TYPE OF DECENTRALIZATION
Simple structure	Direct supervision	Strategic apex	Vertical and horizontal centralization
Machine Bureaucracy	Standardization of work processes	Technostructure	Limited horizontal decentralization
Professional Bureaucracy	Standardization of skills	Operating core	Vertical and horizontal decentralization
Divisionalized Form	Standardization of outputs	Middle line	Limited vertical decentralization
Adhocracy	Mutual adjustment	Support staff	Selective decentralization

Source: Henry Mintzberg, *The Structuring of Organizations: A Synthesis of the Research*, © 1979, p. 301. Reprinted by permission of Prentice-Hall, Inc., Englewood Cliffs, New Jersey.

Simple Structure

Essentially, the Simple Structure is a form of organization design based on direct supervision as its primary coordinating mechanism, with the strategic apex (upper-level management) as its most important part, and utilizing vertical and horizontal centralization. Mintzberg (1979) suggests that middle-sized retail stores, a new government department, and a fairly small corporation controlled by an aggressive entrepreneur would be examples of Simple Structure organizations.

Organizations characterized by Simple Structure tend to be quite young. Organizations in a period of crisis also tend to maintain or adopt the Simple Structure. A final determinant of the use of Simple Structure (actually, a factor generally associated with young organizations) is the case of the owner-manager (i.e., an entrepreneur). Other general characteristics of the Simple Structure include informal communication networks, decision-making power residing with the CEO, strong employee loyalty and identification, few levels in the hierarchy, and little task specialization.

Overall, then, tasks within the Simple Structure organization would tend toward the complex, nonroutine form. Employees are likely to perform a variety of activities (due to the low level of specialization), and will probably feel that their jobs are quite significant (perhaps a function of their loyalty and identification with the organization). The informal communication network and direct supervision would probably also indicate a reasonable degree of feedback.

The autonomy dimension will be more complex, however. Lower-level managers and employees are likely to experience a relatively high level of autonomy in making routine, day-to-day decisions. This follows from the informal communication system and low level of specialization. However, middle-level managers will have considerably less autonomy in their ac- **135** tivities. Power in the Simple Structure is at the top. Hence, policy considerations and other key decisions will be made by the CEO (more than likely the owner-manager). Overall, then, task scope in the Simple Structure will tend to be quite high, although those managers directly underneath the CEO may have considerably less autonomy than they might desire.

Machine Bureaucracy

The Machine Bureaucracy is characterized by standardization of work processes as the prime coordinating mechanism, the technostructure (the process of standardization) as its most crucial part, and limited horizontal decentralization. Examples of Machine Bureaucracy forms of organization design include a steel company, an automobile manufacturer, and an airline.

Machine Bureaucracies typically emphasize high degrees of formalization and vertical and horizontal task specialization. This type of organization typically operates in a simple and stable environment and is relatively mature (both in size and age). The firm has a regulated technical system, focuses a great deal of attention on how to control activities within the organization, and has efficiency as a primary managerial objective. Other characteristics of the Machine Bureaucracy include a very formal system of communication, rigid patterns of authority, and a very high level of division of labor. Finally, this form of organization tends to have a relatively high level of intra-organizational conflict.

Tasks within the Machine Bureaucracy, obviously, will be the antithesis of those within the Simple Structure. Our previous discussions have suggested that high degrees of formalization and specialization, characteristics of the Machine Bureaucracy, will tend to be associated with low overall task scope in general and low levels of variety and identity in particular. With respect to autonomy, "managers of the middle line are relatively weak, and the workers of the operating core have hardly any power at all" (Mintzberg, 1979, p. 322). Significance of various tasks would probably also be seen as being virtually non-existent.

Professional Bureaucracy

The Professional Bureaucracy utilizes the standardization of skills as its prime coordinating mechanism, has the operating core (where the work is actually done) as the most important part of the organization, and is decentralized along both vertical and horizontal dimensions. The organization focuses on horizontal task specialization among skilled professionals. Examples of Professional Bureaucracies include universities, public accounting firms, and general hospitals.

A primary objective of this form of organization design is to develop internalized norms on the part of its professionals, such that their goals are congruent with the goals of the organization itself. Power is typically a function of expertise, as opposed to hierarchical position. The professional task itself involves diagnosing a problem and then choosing any of several predetermined and predefined methods for dealing with the situation. Other characteristics of the Professional Bureaucracy include relatively few middle-level managers, members' allegiance to the profession rather than the organization, occasional problems in coordination, and a certain degree of rigidity, which, in turn, constrains innovation.

The basic task within the Professional Bureaucracy appears to have extremes of both high and low scope elements. Clearly, the professional has an extremely high degree of autonomy. The professor can decide how to teach a class and the surgeon can decide what surgical procedure to use in a given situation. Indeed, professional autonomy is a primary dimension of this form of organization. Significance would also tend to be very high. An educator transmitting knowledge, a surgeon saving a life, and an accountant auditing the books of a major corporation will all perceive the importance of their work. Finally, feedback would also be apparent in most professional jobs (i.e., patient recovery, student learning, etc.).

At the same time, other task elements such as variety and identity may be at a somewhat lower level. The surgical specialist, for example, may perform the same operation repeatedly. The circumstances may vary and the characteristics of the patients may not be uniform, but the basic procedure itself is the same. Similarly, the professor typically encounters a student for one class out of 40–50 the student may take during a degree program. Hence, the professor may not know the background of the student, the student's overall academic framework, or what happens to the student after the semester is over. The result may be a relatively low level of identity.

Certainly, the professional task has more variety and identity than most other jobs, however. The autonomy of the professional task itself allows the individual the opportunity to create the variety and/or identity that may be lacking. The point is that variety and identity may simply be present to a lesser degree than other relevant task attributes.

Divisionalized Form

The Divisionalized Form of organization design is described in terms of standardization of output as a prime coordinating mechanism, the middle line (i.e., the interface between the strategic apex and the operating core) as the key part of the organization, and the adoption of limited vertical decentralization. Most large corporations utilize this form of organization design. The basic nature of the Divisionalized Form is to create a number of quasi-autonomous organizations-within-the-organization. These units are then coordinated by a central administrative structure.

The Divisionalized Form delegates much power from the strategic apex to the upper levels of the middle line (i.e., from headquarters to the upper **137** levels of each division or subunit); however, the power is generally retained at this level and not delegated further down the organizational hierarchy. Further, there is fairly strong pressure within the Divisionalized Form for each unit or division to take on the characteristics of the Machine Bureaucracy. The market environment of the Divisionalized Form is quite diverse. Further, increases in both age and size seem to cause an organization to move toward this mode of organization design.

In terms of task design processes, since the subunits adopt fairly independent structures, tasks within each subunit will tend to take on the same configurations as in the corresponding form of organization design. That is, if a particular subunit is structured as a Machine Bureaucracy, tasks within the subunit will tend to resemble tasks that might develop within an autonomous organization of the same design. Moreover, while the Machine Bureaucracy will tend to predominate (Mintzberg, 1979, p. 385), the subunits may also take on characteristics of the Simple Structure, the Professional Bureaucracy, and/or the Adhocracy. Tasks within the subunit, then, will tend to follow the same patterns.

The one consistency across Divisionalized Forms relates to the managerial jobs at the upper level in each subunit. According to Mintzberg (1979), these managers will be given "close to full autonomy to make their own decisions" (p. 383). Hence, these managers should perceive a great deal of autonomy in performing their duties.

Adhocracy

The Adhocracy form of organization design utilizes mutual adjustment (informal communication) as a means of coordination, has as its most important component the support staff, and maintains selective patterns of decentralization. Examples of Adhocracies include Texas Instruments and other electronics firms, NASA, and many aircraft manufacturers.

Adhocracies tend to avoid characteristics of bureaucratic forms of organization design, especially specialization, formalization, and unity of command. Power tends to be based on expertise, just as it is in the Professional Bureaucracy. However, as noted in our discussion of that design, coordination within the Professional Bureaucracy is achieved by standardization. The Adhocracy, on the other hand, strives toward innovation and avoids standardization.

Strong emphasis within the Adhocracy is placed on liaison devices. Further, whatever decision-making power is needed in a particular situation is generally granted by the organization (hence the term selective decentralization). The Adhocracy structure develops under conditions of environmental complexity and rapid change. Finally, this form of design tends to be relatively inefficient due to its high communication costs and frequent change.

138   To use the task design nomenclature, tasks within the Adhocracy would tend to be relatively high in scope. Managers and operating employees would tend to be given much autonomy in making decisions, allowed to engage in a variety of activities, and so forth. Probably more than any other form of organization design, then, tasks within the Adhocracy will tend to conform to current prescriptions for enhancing employee quality of working life.

Summary

The preceding sections have summarized five basic formulations of organization design configurations. Each section included a description of probable forms of task design likely to be found within that type of structure. These descriptions are summarized in Table 7–5. Admittedly, some of the linkages are more obvious than others, and many could be developed from alternative points of view with equal justification. However, our objective at this point is simply to identify potential patterns of organization design–task design interactions. The patterns described here may prove to be a basis for further understanding, or may be displaced by alternative formulations. We now direct our attention to more precise frameworks, which propose complex relationships among organization, task, and individual variables.

MODELS OF ORGANIZATION, TASK, AND INDIVIDUAL CONGRUENCE

In recent years, two models have been developed and tested that propose complex interactions among the form of design adopted by the organization, the nature of the task, and characteristics of the individual. The models have two things in common: they use the mechanistic-organic framework of Burns and Stalker (1961) summarized earlier in this chapter, and both assume that individual differences such as growth need strength (e.g., Hackman and Oldham, 1976, 1980; also see Chapter 3) play a role in determining employee reactions to their tasks. These models differ from our previous discussions in that on the one hand they are more complete and developed theoretical formulations, but at the same time they are more general in nature.

Porter, Lawler, and Hackman Model

The Porter, Lawler, and Hackman (1975) model of organization design, task design, and individual difference interactions is presented in Figure 7–2. The model describes organization design as being either mechanistic or organic, task design as being either simple or complex, and employee growth need strength as being either high or low. The model, then, is a 2 × 2 × 2 table predicting employee reactions to the various combinations of variables. The predictions are derived from expected congruency relationships among the variables. Specifically, satisfaction and perfor- **139**

TABLE 7–5   Summary of Mintzberg's Organization Designs
with Corresponding Task Designs

ORGANIZATION DESIGN	PROBABLE TASK DESIGN(S)

1. Simple Structure	1. Specific Attributes:
	  a. Low autonomy for middle-to-upper managers below the CEO
	  b. High autonomy for others
	  c. High degree of feedback, variety, identity, and significance
	2. General Configuration: Complex, non-routine, generally quite challenging; perhaps frustrating for ambitious managers below the CEO

2. Machine Bureaucracy	1. Specific Attributes: Low autonomy, feedback, variety, identity, and significance 2. General Configuration: Routine, simple, boring, generally not very challenging or stimulating

3. Professional Bureaucracy	1. Specific Attributes:
	  a. High autonomy, feedback, and significance
	  b. Moderate variety and identity
	2. General Configuration: Complex, challenging; professionals have enough autonomy to actually vary other elements of their work themselves

4. Divisionalized Form	1. Specific Attributes:
	  a. High autonomy for division-level managers
	  b. Low autonomy for lower-level managers
	  c. Variety, identity, feedback, and significance vary as a function of subunit form
	2. General Configuration: Varies as a function of subunit form; may be similar to tasks within the Simple Structure, Machine Bureaucracy, Professional Bureaucracy, or Adhocracy

5. Adhocracy	1. Specific Attributes: High autonomy, feedback, variety, identity, and significance 2. General Configuration: Complex, nonroutine, very challenging

mance are viewed as being influenced by levels of individual, task design, and organization design congruence.

Modifications to this original framework have recently been suggested and tested by Pierce, Dunham, and Blackburn (1979). In part, the refinement of the model is based on evidence accumulated since the original presentation in 1975. The modification hinges on the growth need strength (GNS) variable. At the time of the original model, it was felt that high GNS individuals would respond favorably to a complex task and unfavorably to a routine task; it was also assumed by some that a low GNS person would respond favorably to a routine task and unfavorably to a complex task. Hence, the original model was based partially on this premise.

Pierce, et al. (1979), however, note that while several studies have documented GNS moderating effects, both high and low GNS individuals respond most favorably to a complex, high scope task. More specifically,

FIGURE 7-2   Porter, Lawler, and Hackman Model

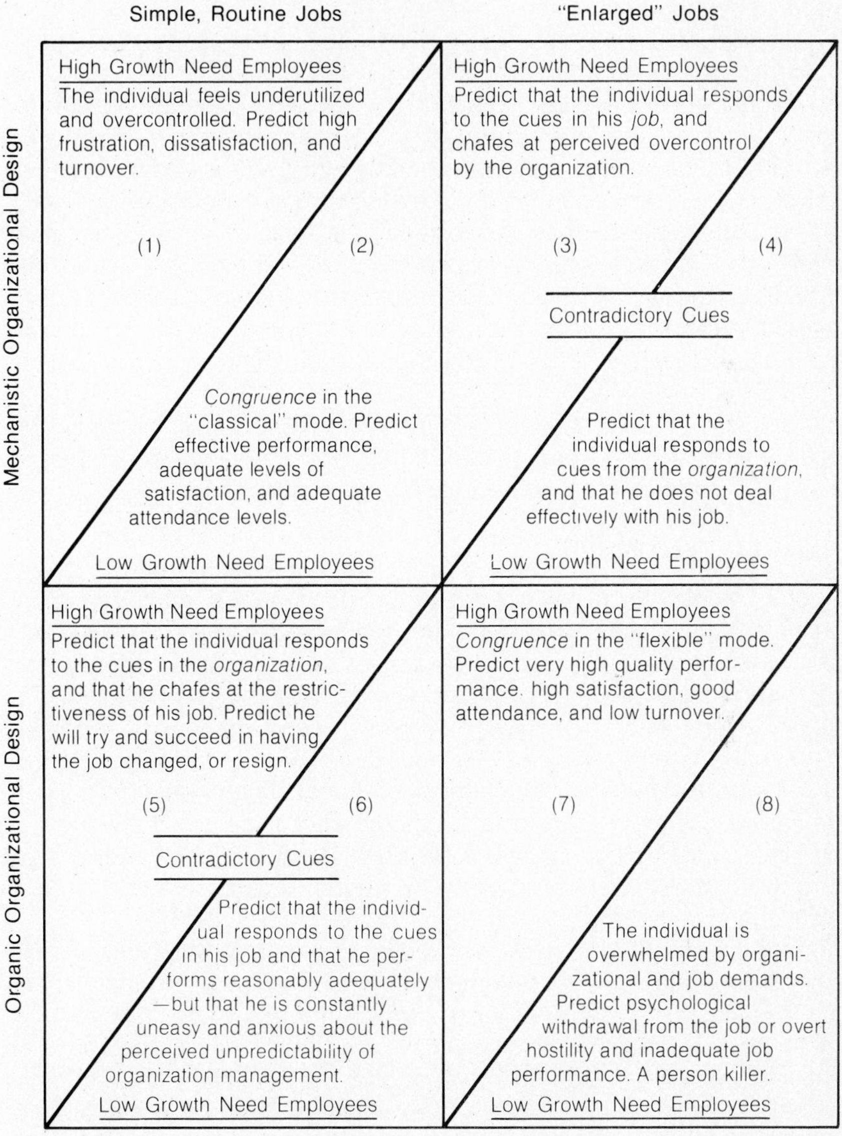

	Simple, Routine Jobs	"Enlarged" Jobs

Mechanistic Organizational Design

High Growth Need Employees
The individual feels underutilized and overcontrolled. Predict high frustration, dissatisfaction, and turnover.

(1)   (2)

Congruence in the "classical" mode. Predict effective performance, adequate levels of satisfaction, and adequate attendance levels.

Low Growth Need Employees

High Growth Need Employees
Predict that the individual responds to the cues in his *job*, and chafes at perceived overcontrol by the organization.

(3)   (4)

Contradictory Cues

Predict that the individual responds to cues from the *organization*, and that he does not deal effectively with his job.

Low Growth Need Employees

Organic Organizational Design

High Growth Need Employees
Predict that the individual responds to the cues in the *organization*, and that he chafes at the restrictiveness of his job. Predict he will try and succeed in having the job changed, or resign.

(5)   (6)

Contradictory Cues

Predict that the individual responds to the cues in his job and that he performs reasonably adequately —but that he is constantly uneasy and anxious about the perceived unpredictability of organization management.

Low Growth Need Employees

High Growth Need Employees
Congruence in the "flexible" mode. Predict very high quality performance, high satisfaction, good attendance, and low turnover.

(7)   (8)

The individual is overwhelmed by organizational and job demands. Predict psychological withdrawal from the job or overt hostility and inadequate job performance. A person killer.

Low Growth Need Employees

Source: From *Behavior in Organizations* by L. W. Porter, E. E. Lawler, and J. R. Hackman. Copyright © 1975, McGraw-Hill Book Company. Used with the permission of McGraw-Hill Book Company.

many researchers now believe that both high and low GNS employees will prefer a high scope, complex task; the high GNS individuals may simply have a stronger preference.

The reformulation also included one other refinement. The original model assumed that when task and organization combinations were contradictory, employees would respond to whichever was most consistent with their own needs. The reformulation, however, argues that since the job is closer to the worker, primary reactions will be to the task itself. The design of the organization is felt to be of secondary importance.

The reformulated model was tested on a sample of insurance company employees. Table 7–6 summarizes predictions of the original model, predictions of the revised model, and results of the study. As indicated, the revised model received considerably more support than did the original predictions. Clearly, these findings suggest rather important relationships among elements of the social system (i.e., the organization), the nature of the task, and characteristics of the employee. This is also consistent with a basic theme of this chapter: to consider either the organization or the task without regard for the other is a critical over-simplification.

Nemiroff-Ford Model

Another model of relationships among individual, task design, and organization design variables has been proposed by Nemiroff and Ford (1976a). This model utilizes the mechanistic-organic continuum to represent organization design, a predictable/simple–uncertain/complex continuum to describe task design variables, and growth need strength as a primary individual difference variable. One additional individual variable, however, is also included: bureaucratic orientation. Bureaucratic orientation refers to an individual's preference for a structured environment in the workplace and is assumed to be matched most effectively with a mechanistic structure. Alternatively, individuals with a low degree of bureaucratic orientation would be more appropriately matched with an organic design.

The Nemiroff-Ford model is depicted in Figure 7–3. Essentially, this framework simply predicts that the three sets of variables will interact and influence task effectiveness (general task performance) and human fulfillment (acquisition of psychological rewards such as satisfaction). The specific predictions made by the Nemiroff-Ford model are similar to those made by Porter, et al. (1975). For example, high levels of overall congruence (i.e., mechanistic structure, simple task, low GNS, high bureaucratic orientation; organic structure, complex task, high GNS, low bureaucratic orientation) are expected to produce high levels of task effectiveness and human fulfillment. Similarly, high incongruence leads to low levels of each outcome variable, and intermediate levels of congruence/incongruence lead to moderate levels of each outcome variable.

142   To date, the model had received one empirical test (Nemiroff and Ford,

TABLE 7–6   Interactions among Organization Design, Task Design, and Individual Differences

SOCIAL SYSTEM STRUCTURE	JOB DESIGN	GROWTH NEED LEVEL	PORTER ET AL. PREDICTED LEVEL OF SATISFACTION AND PERFORMANCE	RANK ORDER PREDICTED BY PORTER ET AL.	RANK ORDER PREDICTED BY PIERCE DUNHAM & BLACKBURN	SUMMARY OF ACTUAL RANK ORDER
Organic	Complex	High	Highest	1	1	1
Mechanistic	Simple	Low	High	2	7	6
Organic	Simple	High	Intermediate	4.5	5	7
Mechanistic	Complex	High	Intermediate	4.5	2	3
Organic	Simple	Low	Intermediate	4.5	6	5
Mechanistic	Complex	Low	Intermediate	4.5	4	4
Organic	Complex	Low	Lowest	7	3	2
Mechanistic	Simple	High	Lowest	8	8	8

Source: Adapted from J. L. Pierce, R. B. Dunham, and R. S. Blackburn. "Social Systems Structure, Job Design, and Growth Need Strength: A Test of a Congruency Model." *Academy of Management Journal*, 1979, 22, p. 224. Used by permission.

FIGURE 7-3   The Nemiroff-Ford Model

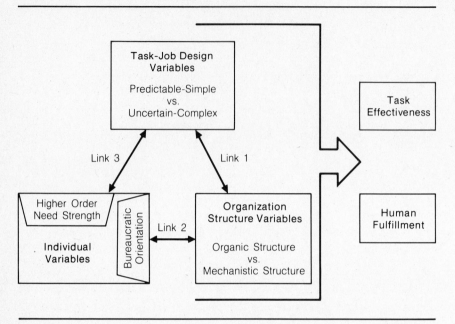

Source: P. M. Nemiroff and D. L. Ford, Jr. "Task Effectiveness and Human Fulfillment in Organizations: A Review and Development of a Conceptual Contingency Model," *Academy of Management Review*, 1976, *1*, p. 70. Used by permission.

1976b). Results obtained from two food processing plants in the Midwest, both of which were essentially mechanistic, generally supported the model's predictions (the organic predictions, however, were untestable since the organization was mechanistic in nature). Consistent with the logic behind the reformulated Porter, et al. (1975) model, the incongruent relationships involving GNS were not as strongly supported as were other aspects of the model.

In summary, then, it seems that certain patterns of configurations of task design, organization design, and individual variables appear to be more desirable than others. That is, some combinations result in more favorable levels of satisfaction, motivation, and perhaps performance than do other combinations. While the individual component is still subject to debate, organic design–complex, high scope tasks and mechanistic design–simple, low scope tasks appear to be reasonable combinations. We now turn our attention to how task design processes may be related to other elements or dimensions of organizations.

TASK DESIGN AND OTHER ORGANIZATIONAL VARIABLES

In previous sections, we have explored interrelationships among specific structural dimensions (i.e., decentralization, standardization, etc.) and design configurations (i.e., mechanistic-organic, etc.) and task design processes. We have also looked at models of individual-task-organization congruence. In this section, we will briefly look at how task design processes may influence and/or be influenced by three other organizational subsystems: organizational climate, the status subsystem, and the communication subsystem.

Task Design and Organizational Climate

Organizational climate has been defined as "the perceived properties or characteristics found in the work environment that result largely from actions taken consciously or unconsciously by an organization and that presumably affect subsequent behavior" (Steers, 1977b, p. 101). Operationally, climate is generally considered to consist of a variety of dimensions, including task structure, decision centralization, and feedback (cf., Campbell and Beatty, 1971). While climate is usually assumed to be an individual- or group-level variable, for the sake of parsimony, we will describe it at the aggregate level. It should be kept in mind, however, that we are really talking about how the individual or group perceives the organization.

It seems reasonable to suggest that task design variables affect perceptions of organization climate, and that organizational climate may influence task design processes in both a direct and an indirect fashion. The first suggested relationship seems fairly obvious. Since the task itself is so close to the employee, in an abstract sense, it follows that the manner in which the employee perceives and reacts to the task will influence how the overall organization is perceived. For example, if the employee has a boring, routine task, and if the employee is dissatisfied with the job because of these attributes, it follows that the employee will perceive the overall organization in a generally negative fashion. Similarly, if the employee is enjoying a challenging and complex task, he or she may have an overall positive image of the organization.

In a direct sense, organizational climate may also influence how the task is perceived by the employee. If the organization has an image of being trusting, open, and responsible, if the reward system is generous and fair, if promotion policies are favorable, and if the supervisor and co-workers are pleasant people to work with, the employee may see the job in a more positive way than might be the case under other circumstances. If, for example, a new general manager comes in and starts making undesirable changes (from the employee's perspective) in personnel and the reward and promotion policies of the organization, this may cause the employee to focus on previously unnoticed and/or unimportant, negative attributes of the task, eventually altering the employee's perceptions of the total task.

Climate may also influence objective task design in an indirect fashion. Simply stated, an organization characterized by a participative, forward-looking, and socially concerned management philosophy (or climate) may **145** be more attuned to the current interest in quality-of-work-life issues. This organization may be more apt to experiment with various task redesign alternatives aimed at improving jobs. On the other hand, an organization with an authoritative, traditional, and classical management outlook may be more likely to cling to task specialization approaches and move more slowly toward work redesign strategies. Essentially, then, organizational climate may influence the extent to which an organization is willing to modify existing task design arrangements.

Task Design and the Status Subsystem

Another organizational characteristic that influences task design processes is the concept of status. Certainly, objective status differences exist among hierarchical levels in an organization. Our concern at this point, however, is status differences within hierarchical levels and across occupational groupings. For the sake of illustration, we will briefly describe three different situations in which status differences may affect task perceptions and evaluations.

From a managerial perspective, most organizations are characterized by different levels of status across functional areas. In a customer-oriented firm such as Proctor and Gamble, a marketing job may carry more status than a job at the same organizational level but in the finance department. While this is slowly changing, the personnel department in most organizations has often been accorded less status than other departments. It follows, then, that a manager in a lower status area may perceive and react to his or her job in a generally less favorable manner than would a manager in a higher status area within the same organization.

An analogy can be drawn for operating employees. In a retail department store such as Sears, an employee in the jewelry department probably has more status than a person in the hardware department who, in turn, probably has more status than an employee in the coffee shop. It seems likely, then, that these people will perceive their jobs differently and, as a direct result, will probably exhibit varying degrees of satisfaction, turnover, and so forth.

From a somewhat different viewpoint, status differences clearly exist across occupational groups such as doctors, lawyers, and executives, as opposed to cab drivers, garbage collectors, and dish washers. Certainly, significant objective differences exist among these jobs. However, some of the "higher status" jobs can actually be described in generally negative terms. A probate attorney, for example, may spend long periods of time poring over legal documents, law books, etc., but will still describe the job in positive terms. At the other extreme, the job of cab driving may exhibit several of the characteristics generally ascribed to "good" jobs (i.e., autonomy over working hours, feedback from tips, etc.), but receive a generally negative description. Some jobs have even had their titles changed for the specific purpose of enhancing status. For example, garbage collectors are frequently referred to as sanitation engineers. Further, many people in these "lower status" jobs go to great lengths to add to the meaningfulness of their task by creating games, concentrating on social interaction, etc. (cf., Walsh, 1974).

In summary, there appears to be a potentially important relationship between the status a particular job has and how the employee perceives and reacts to the task. While few generalizations about this relationship can be drawn at this point, the manager should be aware that status differences within organizational levels may be an important element to consider in task design decisions.

Task Design and the Communication Subsystem

The final organizational subsystem to be related to task design is the formal communication network (the informal communication processes in organizations will be addressed in Chapter 9). Some researchers have suggested that the appropriate form of communication network within the organization is a function of task complexity. For example, if a task is very complex, it follows that information needed to accomplish the task is not likely to be available to any one person. Hence, a great deal of horizontal communication among group members, vertical communication between group members and the supervisor, and diagonal communication between group members and staff specialists may be needed to perform the task effectively (cf., Connolly, 1977).

On the other hand, if the task is relatively routine, simple, and straightforward, few information-processing requirements will exist. Accordingly, communication can effectively be accomplished via standard operating procedures, policy manuals, etc., and with less emphasis on formalized interpersonal communication (O'Reilly, 1977).

The same type of argument could be developed for varying degrees of task interdependence. Since high levels of task interdependence dictate coordination and joint problem-solving, communication systems must be developed to facilitate these processes. To the extent that little task interdependence exists, there will be less need for the development of sophisticated communication networks. In summary, then, it seems logical that task complexity and task interdependence may have significant implications for designing organizational communication subsystems. Finally, communication processes in organizations may also influence task design perceptions and reactions. This operates primarily through the informal communication subsystem, however, and will be addressed in a later chapter.

147

ORGANIZATION DESIGN, TASK DESIGN, AND TECHNOLOGY

The focus of Chapter 6 was on task design and technology inter-relationships, while this chapter has dealt with task design and organization design interrelationships. Since a considerable amount of research has also examined organization design and technology interactions, it now seems appropriate to briefly consider potential relationships among all three areas of concern.

Most of the technology typologies discussed in Chapter 6 were derived from attempts to link technology and organization design (e.g., Woodward, 1965; Thompson, 1967; Hickson et al., 1969). The most explicit linkages are made by Woodward and will be the basis for this discussion. Recall that Woodward suggested three basic forms of technology: small batch, mass production, and continuous process. Her research indicated that, at a very general level, organizations using small batch and continuous process technologies were designed in a manner similar to an organic structure (Burns and Stalker, 1961). Specifically, they tended to be nonspecialized and decentralized, with wide spans of control and so forth. Mass production firms, on the other hand, were similar in form to a mechanistic system; they were more specialized and centralized, and had narrower spans of control, etc.

In our discussion of technology, we predicted a high degree of task complexity and scope for small batch technologies, a low level of task complexity and scope for mass production technologies, and a moderately high level of task complexity and scope for continuous process technologies. In a previous section of this chapter, it was also predicted that high scope tasks would be associated with organic organization designs, while simpler low scope tasks would be characteristic of mechanistic organization designs. Hence, predictions of task design–technology and task design–organization design relationships are generally consistent with the technology–organization design predictions made by Woodward and others.

Similar but redundant logic could be used to develop predictions from other technology typologies. At a basic level, relationships among these important organizational characteristics can be summarized as in Figure 7–4. Figure 7–4 predicts that an organization's technology will exert a causal influence on its design. Further, both technology and organization design may influence and be influenced by task design. Managers should recognize these potential interactions when considering a change in either technology, organization design, and/or task design. Further, researchers should begin to focus on expanded frameworks such as this to better understand contextual influences on task design processes.

SUMMARY AND CONCLUSIONS

148   This chapter has investigated potential interactions among task design,

FIGURE 7–4   Technology, Organization Design, and Task Design

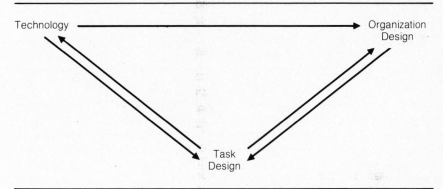

organization design, and, in some cases, individual variables. First, we looked at how five structural components of organization structure may influence objective and/or perceived elements of task design. We then described task design configurations that may exist in various forms of organization design. Integrative frameworks of individual, task, and organization design variables were then discussed. We next looked at other organizational variables and task design. Finally, more complex considerations were addressed.

At the end of our previous chapter ("Task Design and Technology"), we were able to develop an integrative framework to characterize the various topics of interest. Considering the speculative nature of many of the relationships discussed in this chapter, however, it doesn't seem reasonable to offer such a framework for task and organization design variables. More specifically, our limited knowledge base constrains theoretical development to the point that any framework we might offer would be subject to so many alternative explanations as to be of little practical value. We can, however, derive some potentially worthwhile conclusions and generalizations that may be of some importance to managers contemplating work redesign efforts and to researchers in the field.

First, it seems likely that specific structural components of organizations influence elements of task design. Decentralization, specialization, formalization, span of control, and line-staff roles all determine objective and/or perceived attributes of tasks within a firm. Decentralization, specialization, and formalization probably exert the most direct and observable force; the effects of span of control and line-staff roles are probably more ambiguous and indirect.

Second, task design elements may influence characteristics of the organization. Although influence in this direction is probably less pronounced, some structural elements are partially a function of task design processes. For example, span of control for some managers, especially   **149** first-line supervisors, may be strongly affected by the degree of structure inherent in subordinates' tasks.

Third, other organizational variables influence and are influenced by task design processes. In particular, organizational climate, the communication subsystem, and the status subsystem may be important variables to consider. The status subsystem, especially, may offer a great deal of potential for increased understanding of the task design process.

These three conclusions lead to an important generalization. Managers must be aware of these reciprocal relationships when planning and/or implementing a change in either area. Many contemporary organizations undergo a myriad of changes, including changes in departmentalization, the addition and/or deletion of subunits, changes in structural relationships, and so forth. It follows that these changes may introduce other unintended changes in task design processes. For example, an organization may adopt a policy of increased centralization due to a poor economic condition. Top management may feel that potentially important decisions require their review. As a result, however, talented managers at lower levels in the organization may begin to feel frustrated due to a lack of autonomy and leave the organization.

Further, if a manager decides to introduce a work redesign program in the firm, structural properties of the organization may either change as a direct result, or else may require future modification. The new task configurations, for example, may dictate less formalization, a different communication subsystem, and so forth. These points will be further developed in Chapter 10.

Another conclusion to be reached is that patterns of task design probably vary systematically across different forms of organization design. Whether one adopts a fairly simple framework, such as the mechanistic-organic distinctions, or a more complex view, such as Mintzberg's five forms of design, different types of tasks probably characterize each type of organization. Thus, when describing, analyzing, and/or studying tasks, it is important to consider the organizational context.

The most important generalization to be drawn from this point is that various forms of organization design probably constrain and/or facilitate task design processes. In organizations with organic designs, for example, tasks are probably designed in such a way as to enhance employee quality of work life. Further, if the organization wanted to make tasks even more challenging, motivating, meaningful, and so forth, the nature of the organization would probably facilitate the required changes. On the other hand, a mechanistic organization is probably characterized by less challenging and motivating jobs. If for some reason a manager in the organization wanted to introduce a work redesign effort, he or she would probably find that the mechanistic design constrained the available alternatives. More specifically, the organization itself would probably serve as a barrier to the effective redesign of tasks within it.

In summary, it appears that significant relationships may exist among organization design and task design processes. It is important to consider these relationships when dealing with either area. Otherwise, unintended consequences may accrue to both the organization and its participants.

8 TASK DESIGN AND LEADER BEHAVIOR

Sally Williams has just been hired as an accounting clerk for the distribution center of a national retailer. On her first day at work, she is told to report to Betty Hanson, her supervisor. Betty spends several hours with her, explaining what her duties are and providing information about the organization in general and the nature of Sally's job in particular. For the first several days, Betty has to spend quite a bit of time working with Sally. As time passes, Sally becomes more and more proficient, requiring less of Betty's time. In the course of a normal working day, however, any of the ten accounting clerks is likely to encounter some problem that he or she can't handle. When this happens, they call Betty, who decides what to do.

Within the work unit, there are essentially three jobs that are performed. Incoming invoices must first be verified to insure that prices correspond with contractual agreements, that quantity discounts have been granted, and so forth. Next, the order number must be cross-checked with an inventory number to make sure that the merchandise has arrived with no shortages or damage. Finally, the invoice must be posted and a pay-out authorization prepared and forwarded to the disbursement department. Some of the accounting clerks prefer to spend all of their time doing one task, such as invoice verification, while others prefer to take one set of invoices through all three operations. Since Betty has considerable say over how the work is distributed, she tries to accommodate individual preferences.

Occasionally, someone makes an error that is detected either by the disbursement department or the warehouse. The mistake is pointed out to Betty, who in turn explains the problem to the individual responsible for making the error. Betty also keeps a mental tally of who hasn't made an error for several days and compliments that person on his or her work. In a formal appraisal every six months, Betty talks with Sally and the others about their work. She reviews both the quality and quantity of their output, their attendance, their attitude, and their overall contribution to the organization. She then recommends some level of salary increase for each of the clerks.

In this scenario, not unlike many real work settings, there are significant relationships among the nature of the task, the nature of the employee, and the nature of the leader. In a very large number of organizations, leaders are responsible for training, problem solving, assigning work, providing feedback, evaluating performance, and distributing rewards. That is, they facilitate and complement the individual's task accomplishment process.

The importance of leader behavior in a discussion of task design again relates to the context in which jobs are performed. As indicated above, employees tend to look first to their leader when a task-related problem develops. Further, a task change effort is likely to be influenced by the extent to which the supervisory role facilitates or hampers the intended change. Finally, the supervisor himself or herself may play a dominant role in actually defining the task itself.

As briefly mentioned in Chapter 6, leader or supervisor behavior is also an important element in the social system of the organization. Further, the supervisor-subordinate relationship is one of the most complex in any organization. Technology and organization design variables are essentially objective, even though different individuals may not perceive them in the same way. Group and social variables, to be discussed in the next chapter, are certainly less objective than technology and organization design, but the individual interacts with group members and other co-workers as peers and colleagues. Although social power may influence peer relationships, formal power and authority are not generally important among organizational equals.

The supervisor, however, is different. The supervisor is an organizationally designated person responsible for assigning work, monitoring the work, evaluating performance, and so forth. Hence, the supervisory role is a "given" in much the same way as technology and organization design. That is, it exists on its own merits, regardless of the individuals concerned. Yet, while the role itself is supposedly defined by the organization, any one supervisor brings to the role a unique combination of needs, behaviors, personality traits, and so forth. Further, each supervisor-subordinate dyad is also unique, since the subordinates themselves are all different. For these reasons, the relationship between a supervisor and a subordinate is extremely difficult to understand and explain, but at the same time is very important in describing organizational behavior in general and task design processes in particular.

The task that an individual performs and the person to whom the individual is responsible are probably the two most basic points of contact **153** that employees have in the organization. Further, it seems reasonable to assume that the manner in which a person perceives and reacts to either of these factors will influence how the person perceives and reacts to the other. A logical framework for describing how the variables interact is presented in Figure 8–1.

This framework is composed of three sets of variables, three direct relationships, and three indirect relationships. The individual component of the framework, in turn, consists of a variety of factors, including both affective and behavioral outcomes (such as satisfaction and performance) and individual differences (such as growth need strength and need for achievement). Task scope represents the extent to which task attributes such as variety, autonomy, etc. are present in a particular job. Leader behavior refers to the set of behaviors (i.e., directive, supportive, etc.) that may be used to characterize leaders or supervisors in various settings.

The framework suggests that there are direct or main effects between each pair of variable categories. The framework also suggests that each variable category intervenes between or moderates the direct relationship between the other two categories. The main effects between task scope and individual variables, including the role of individual differences, have been covered in Chapters 3 and 4. A discussion of the main effects between leader behavior and individual variables is not directly relevant at this point, but the interested reader should consult Stogdill (1974). Our primary in-

FIGURE 8–1   A Framework for Describing Interactions among Individual, Task Design, and Leader Behavior Variables

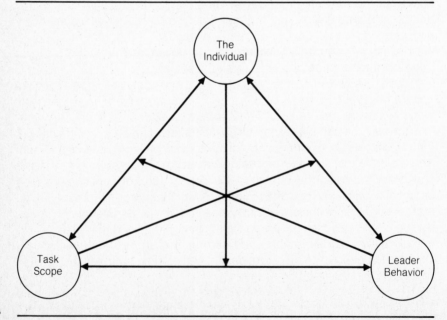

terests are with the remaining areas of the framework: the intervention of task scope between leader behavior and the individual, the intervention of leader behavior between task scope and the individual, and, finally, main effects between scope and leader behavior and the intervention of individual variables between the two.

THE LEADER BEHAVIOR PERSPECTIVE

Leader behavior has been one of the most widely researched and studied areas in the field of organizational behavior (cf., Stogdill, 1974). In recent years, the trend has been toward the development of situational theories of leadership. As a group, situational theories are characterized by the description of appropriate forms of leader behavior (i.e., behavior capable of enhancing employee satisfaction, motivation, and/or performance) for various situations and the specification of factors that systematically vary the situation. At a general level, then, the objective of situational theories of leader behavior is to be able to predict, given a certain situation described by a set of designated variables, that specific forms of leader behavior will be related to employee effectiveness. Two of the most well known and widely referenced situational theories suggest that task design variables are a major element in the determination of appropriate leader behavior. Hence, these theories focus on the intervention of task design variables in the relationships between leader behavior and individual variables.

Contingency Model of Leadership

The contingency model of leadership (Fiedler, 1967) was the first situational theory to be advanced. Fiedler's model suggests that group performance is a function of the interaction between leadership style and the favorableness of the situation. Leadership style refers to specific forms of leader behavior, while situational favorableness refers to the extent to which the situation allows the leader to utilize influence and power.

Situational favorableness. The favorableness of the situation is determined by three factors: task structure, leader-member relations, and leader position power. Task structure, in turn, is described by four components: (1) goal-path multiplicity, (2) decision verifiability, (3) decision specificity, and (4) goal clarity. Fiedler summarizes these four dimensions and classifies tasks as either being structured (low multiplicity, high verifiability, high specificity, and high clarity) or unstructured (high multiplicity, low verifiability, low specificity, and low clarity). Leader-member relations refers to the degree of trust, confidence, and respect subordinates have in the leader. Fiedler classifies leader-member relations as being either good (when there is respect and trust in the leader) or poor (when trust and respect in the leader are low). Finally, position power is the power inherent **155**

in the leader's role itself. Fiedler classifies leader position power as being either strong or weak.

These three situational variables, task structure, leader-member relations, and position power, determine the favorableness of the situation from the vantage point of the leader. By dichotomizing each variable, as described in the preceding paragraph, eight distinct situations are defined. According to Fiedler's model, the most favorable situation is the one in which task structure is high, leader-member relations are good, and position power is strong. Conversely, the least favorable situation is one in which task structure is low, leader-member relations are poor, and position power is weak. The other six situations describe varying intermediate levels of favorableness. Fiedler suggests that different forms of leader behavior will be most appropriate for different degrees of favorableness.

Leader behavior. Two specific forms of leader behavior are described by the contingency model. A *task-oriented* leader is one who derives satisfaction primarily from task performance, whereas a *relationship-oriented* leader is more interested in successful interpersonal relationships.

The theory's predictions. Over a 20-year period, Fiedler and his associates have conducted many studies in a variety of settings to determine the relationships among leader behavior, situational favorableness, and group performance. In general, these results suggest that a task-oriented leader will perform best in situations that are very favorable or very unfavorable. Further, it is suggested that relationship-oriented leaders will be most effective in the intermediate situations.

Research evidence. A number of criticisms have been levied at the contingency model. Graen, et al. (1970), for example, have suggested that the data and statistical tests used by Fiedler are inappropriate. The fact that the theory was developed inductively, rather then deductively, has also been criticized (Graen, et al., 1970; McMahon, 1972). In the concluding comments of their review, Schriesheim and Kerr (1977, p. 13) state that,

> The contingency theory of leadership is probably the most widely known of all situational leadership theories and has done far more than any other to stimulate thought about the importance of situational moderators. Today, however, it is obvious that the theory suffers from several major shortcomings and problems which are sufficient to seriously impair its usefulness.

At this point, suffice it to say that the contingency model is still the subject of much debate. The bulk of the empirical evidence is generally not supportive of the theory in one or more ways. Nevertheless, Fiedler's model has had a substantial impact on both academic research and managerial practice over the past several years. Even though most evidence is negative, the contingency model does describe one interesting way in which task variables may intervene in the leader-subordinate relationship. A second theory that also takes this viewpoint is the path-goal theory.

Path-Goal Theory of Leadership

The path-goal theory of leader effectiveness was advanced by Evans (1970) and expanded by House (1971) and House and Mitchell (1974). Our discussion will be based on the most current statement of the theory. The basic assumption of path-goal theory is that a leader's functions are to enhance employee motivation to perform, satisfaction with the job, and acceptance of the leader. The basic propositions of the theory are as follows:

1. Leader behavior is acceptable and satisfying to subordinates to the extent that the subordinates see such behavior as either an immediate source of satisfaction or as instrumental to future satisfaction.
2. The leader's behavior will be motivational (i.e., increase effort) to the extent that (1) such behavior makes satisfaction of subordinates' needs contingent on effective performance and (2) such behavior complements the environments of subordinates by providing the coaching, guidance, support, and rewards necessary for effective performance.

Specifically, the theory suggests that two classes of moderating or situational variables intervene between leader behaviors and outcome variables.

Situational variables. One category of situational variables is personal characteristics of the subordinates. One of these personal characteristics is locus of control. Locus of control refers to the extent to which people attribute what happens to them to their own behavior rather than to chance or luck. Research indicates that individuals who attribute outcomes to their own behavior are more satisfied with a participative leader, whereas individuals who attribute outcomes to chance respond more favorably to a directive leader (Mitchell, 1973). The second personal characteristic specified by path-goal theory is subordinates' perceptions of their own ability with respect to their task. Path-goal theory suggests that the higher the degree of perceived ability, the less subordinates will view leader directiveness and coaching as acceptable.

The second category of situational variables is the work environment. Aspects of the work environment include the task itself, the formal authority system of the organization, and the primary work group. The theory asserts that leader behavior will be motivational to the extent that it helps subordinates cope with environmental uncertainty created by these factors. Since most empirical research has focused on the moderating effects of the task, a separate section will summarize the research in this area. First, however, the types of leader behavior included in path-goal theory will be described.

157

Leader behavior. Path-goal theory originally described two forms of leader behavior: directive and supportive. In 1974, participative leader behavior was added (House and Dessler). Finally, House and Mitchell (1974) describe four types of leader behavior to be included in the theory:

> *Directive leadership.* Characterized by a leader who lets subordinates know what is expected of them, gives specific guidance as to what should be done and how it should be done, makes his or her part in the group understood, schedules work to be done, maintains definite standards of performance, and asks that group members follow standard rules and regulations.
>
> *Supportive leadership.* Characterized by a leader who is friendly and approachable, who shows concern for the status, well-being, and needs of subordinates, does things to make the work more pleasant, and treats members as equals.
>
> *Participative leadership.* Characterized by a leader who consults with subordinates, solicits their suggestions, and takes these suggestions into consideration before making a decision.
>
> *Achievement-oriented leadership.* Characterized by a leader who sets challenging goals. expects subordinates to perform at their highest level, continuously seeks improvement in performance, and shows a high degree of confidence that the subordinates will assume responsibility, put forth effort, and accomplish challenging goals.

House and Mitchell (1974) provide a thorough review of the empirical research on each of these dimensions within the context of path-goal theory.

The theory's predictions. Fiedler's contingency model is a very precise theory. The model specifies exactly how variables will interact to influence performance. Path-goal theory, on the other hand, is comparatively ambiguous and vague. Figure 8–2 depicts the path-goal view of how leader behavior and situational variables interact to influence subordinate attitudes and behavior. Obviously, the relationships presented in Figure 8–2 are very general.

This lack of precision, however, is by design. House and Mitchell indicate that "the theory, in its present stage, is a tentative explanation of the effects of leader behavior—it is incomplete because it does not explain other kinds of leader behavior and does not explain the effects of the leader on factors other than subordinate acceptance, satisfaction, and expectations." The theory is stated in such a way as to allow modification and refinement in light of subsequent empirical findings.

Task structure as a moderator. As noted by Evans (1979), the most frequently examined aspect of path-goal theory has been the moderating effects of task structure on the relationships between leader behavior and motivation/satisfaction/performance. Further, since these effects are the primary concern of this discussion, the research evidence will be examined closely. House and Mitchell (1974) summarize the expected relationships as follows:

> 1. Directive leader behavior will be positively related to satisfaction and expectancies for subordinates engaged in ambiguous, unstructured [i.e., high scope] tasks and nega-

FIGURE 8-2   Summary of Path-Goal Relationships

LEADER BEHAVIOR AND CONTINGENCY FACTORS		CAUSE	SUBORDINATE ATTITUDES AND BEHAVIOR
1 Directive	1 Subordinate Characteristics Authoritarianism Locus of Control Ability	Influence > Personal Perceptions	1 Job Satisfaction Job→Rewards
2 Supportive			2 Acceptance of Leader Leader→Rewards
3 Achievement-Oriented	2 Environmental Factors Task Formal Authority System Primary Work Group	Influence > Motivational Stimuli Constraints Rewards	3 Motivational Behavior Effort→Performance Performance→Rewards
4 Participative			

Source: Robert House and Terence Mitchell. "Path-Goal Theory of Leadership." *Journal of Contemporary Business*, Autumn, 1974. Used by permission.

tively related to satisfaction and expectancies for subordinates engaged in clear, structured [i.e., low scope] tasks.

2. Supportive leader behavior will have its most positive influence on subordinate satisfaction for those working on frustrating, stressful, or dissatisfying tasks [while frustrating, stressful, or dissatisfying do not necessarily describe a low scope task, the manner in which House has operationalized such tasks indicates that that is the intended interpretation].

House and Dessler (1974) tested these suggested relationships on two samples. Task structure, or scope, was measured by a ten-item scale interpreted as the extent to which the task stimuli, execution rules, and procedures were repetitive, simple, and unambiguous. Individuals in the upper and lower third of the distribution were classified as having structured and unstructured (i.e., low and high scope) tasks. For individuals with structured tasks, directive leader behavior was negatively correlated with satisfaction; for individuals with unstructured tasks, directive leader behavior was positively correlated with satisfaction. Further, for individuals with structured tasks, supportive leader behavior was positively correlated with satisfaction; for individuals with unstructured tasks, there was no relationship between supportive behavior and satisfaction. These findings are consistent with predictions of the path-goal theory.

Recognizing that the ten-item measure of task structure utilized by House and Dessler (1974) might represent an unrealistically narrow description of tasks, Johns (1978) replicated their study using a more direct measure of task scope, the Job Rating Form developed by Hackman and Oldham (1974). This instrument is a complement to the Job Diagnostic Survey. Rather than look at just a summary index of task scope or structure, **159**

Johns utilized task variety, identity, significance, autonomy, and feedback, plus the motivating potential score as indices of task structure. The study was conducted on an industrial sample of 362 first-line employees. For directive leader behavior, 16 of the 20 hypothesized differences were in the predicted direction, although only 5 of the differences were statistically significant. For supportive leader behavior, 14 of the 20 differences were in the predicted direction, with 5 differences significant. Although the *pattern* of relationships found by Johns (1978) supports path-goal theory, the *magnitude* of the relationships is suspect. As one explanation for the findings, Johns notes that his sample was drawn only from one organizational level, and therefore range restriction problems may have masked true relationships.

Results conflicting with path-goal theory predictions have also been obtained. Downey, Sheridan, and Slocum (1976), for example, found opposite moderating effects for the predicted directive leader behavior relationships. These researchers measured task structure with the House and Dessler (1974) instrument. They concluded that the moderating effects of task structure may be more complex than specified by the theory.

In a more descriptive sense, real-world examples and cases have also provided a certain amount of support for path-goal predictions. Each of the following situations took place in real job situations:

Incident 1: Automated Data Systems, a small midwestern computer services company, does a large amount of keypunching for its clients. The company employs four full-time keypunch clerks and a keypunch supervisor. The previous supervisor had had a serious morale problem and eventually left the company. The manager of ADS indicated that the supervisor had insisted on explaining each job to the clerks, even when it was simple and straightforward. The supervisor had also practiced very close supervision. The clerks resented the supervisor because she treated them as though they were incompetent. The new supervisor, however, fits in much better. He assumes that the clerks can handle routine assignments and is described as being much more friendly and concerned.

Clearly, in this example, directive supervision was inappropriate due to the low level of task scope present in the keypunch clerk's job. When a more supportive and less directive leader was matched with the group, however, an improved situation developed. Appropriate leader behavior did seem to be at least partially a function of task design at ADS.

Incident 2: Ajax Packers is a manufacturing company located in Houston. They utilize a very complex work flow arrangement system. Essentially a large machine shop, Ajax turns out a fairly constant flow of parts for its own inventory. The parts are later assembled into packers (complex oil well finishing components). The shop also does small batch jobs for other companies. At any one time, a machinist may have a backlog of work for inventory plus two or three outside jobs.

At Ajax, the supervisor is primarily a scheduler and coordinator. The machinist generally has no way of knowing how low inventory levels of a given component might be, nor how urgent an outside job is. The supervisor, then, plays a large role in directing work activities. He or she usually tells the machinist which job to start on next and often must interrupt one job to get another one back in sequence.

In this situation, then, directive leader behavior is both appropriate and necessary. The complex work flow arrangement dictates a fairly structured orientation by the supervisor. Further, this directive behavior is not perceived as being redundant, since the task is relatively unstructured. The plant manager even indicated that less directive and more "people-oriented" (i.e., supportive) supervisors were generally not effective at Ajax.

Incident 3: Jack Young, a recent college graduate, was hired as a first-line supervisor in a large plant of an electronics firm. Initially, his boss took a fairly directive approach to training and developing Jack as a manager. He told him how things were to be done, when they were to be done, and so forth.

As time passed, however, the boss gradually began to handle things differently. He would frequently ask Jack's opinion of a situation or a problem. He began to include Jack in meetings and would delegate some fairly important decisions to him. Jack eventually realized that the behavior of his boss had not really changed. Actually, he himself had changed. He had become a knowledgeable supervisor capable of and motivated to handle additional responsibility. Jack's boss was generally a participative leader, and he was simply allowing Jack to participate in more and more situations. Again, appropriate leader behavior appears to have been a function of task design. The managerial task is assumed to be motivating and ego-involving. While a certain degree of directiveness was initially necessary, participative leader behavior was eventually optimal.

Path-Goal Theory: Summary and Conclusions

At a general level, the path-goal theory of leadership has been fairly well supported in the literature. There are still some problems associated with the theory, particularly in terms of measurement deficiencies, but the framework appears to be generally sound.

The preceding illustrations also serve to reinforce the contention that leader behavior and task design are interrelated. Each situation, based on real people and real organizations, illustrates that the design of an individual's task is an important consideration when describing appropriate leader behavior. In summary, the empirical evidence and selected examples of managerial practice indicate the potential usefulness of the path-goal theory of leadership. In our next section, we consider an alternative but complementary viewpoint of task design–leader behavior interactions.   **161**

THE TASK DESIGN PERSPECTIVE

The path-goal theory reviewed in the previous section assumes that the leader-individual relationship is most crucial, with task and other variables as moderators. It assumes that some portion of variance in employee satisfaction, motivation, and/or performance can be explained by leader behavior, and that by also taking into account task variables, an additional but incrementally smaller portion of variance can be explained.

An alternative formulation of variable interrelationships would involve reversing the relative impact of leader behavior and task variables. More specifically, it can be postulated that task variables have a direct impact on employee attitudes and behaviors, and that taking into account leader behavior variables, the prediction of outcome variables can be improved.

Recently, Griffin (1979) has advanced a model derived from this perspective. The model is based on three assumptions:

1. The individual-task interface is the most basic relationship within organizations. Since most of an individual's time in an organization is spent performing one or more tasks, it follows that individuals will evaluate the quality of their work experience to a significant extent on how they perceive their tasks and on how closely this perception matches their preferences.
2. Different individuals will respond to task stimuli in different ways. Some individuals will respond very favorably to a high scope, complex task; some individuals will respond in a neutral or slightly favorable manner to a high scope task; finally, a few individuals may respond unfavorably to a high scope task. This variation may be attributable to motivational variables such as growth need strength (which the model assumes), demographic variables such as age and experience, and/or an unknown set of other variables.
3. The primary purpose of the leader as supervisor is to facilitate and complement subordinates in the performance of their tasks; that is, the leader's role is supplemental in nature. To the extent possible, a leader should tailor her or his behavior to correspond with the degree of individual-task congruence present in the work place.

The model assumes that the moderating effects of individual growth need strength discussed in Chapter 3 do, in fact, exist.

As indicated previously, task scope may be operationalized in a number of different ways. Conceptually, this model views tasks as varying along a high scope–low scope continuum. A high scope task is defined as a job characterized by large degrees of appropriate task dimensions. Conversely, a low scope task can be described as having low levels of these same dimensions. The growth need strength literature indicates that individuals with high growth need strength will respond favorably to high scope tasks. Further, individuals with low growth need strength will respond less favorably to high scope tasks. While it should be stressed that low growth need strength individuals will probably not react negatively to high scope tasks, their reaction may be indifference or only a mildly favorable response. Since all organizations will have some low scope and some high scope tasks, it follows that optimal conditions would match **162** individuals with high growth need strength with high scope tasks.

Individual-task congruence. The model describes four forms of individual-task congruence, or compatibility. Individual-task congruence exists when the needs of the individual match the motivational character- istics of the task being performed. One combination of variables is to have a high growth need strength person performing a high scope task. This combination is assumed to be congruent and is termed Cell 1. Another possibility is that low growth need strength individuals will be assigned to high scope tasks; this combination is assumed to be less congruent and is called Cell 2. Cell 3 of the model is also less congruent and represents the situation where a high growth need strength individual performs a low scope task. Finally, when a low growth need strength person performs a low scope task, the match is described as congruent and is termed Cell 4. Again, however, it should be stressed that the congruence con- cept is relative, and the classification of Cell 4 as congruent is simply to ac- knowledge that a low scope task may be more optimally performed by a low growth need strength individual than by a high growth need strength individual.

Congruence and leader behavior. As described earlier, the model assumes that appropriate forms of leader behavior will be a function of individual-task congruence. The specific forms of leader behavior in- cluded in the model are derived from path-goal theory. The rationale for the use of path-goal theory is twofold: (1) path-goal theory acknowledges the importance of task structure, and (2) the previously described flexibility in path-goal theory allows the necessary modifications for inclusion in the model.

Employees in the Cell 1 situation are described as highly motivated and having a strong desire for higher-order need satisfaction. These employees will tend to expect some degree of this need satisfaction to derive from the performance of a complex, nonstructured, high scope task for which they feel responsible, perceive as significant, and have an awareness of ex- pected performance. The job described by the Cell 1 situation presumably allows these feelings. Hence, the individual will tend to derive intrinsic satisfaction from the task itself and tend to become ego-involved in the performance of the task.

Two forms of leader behavior from path-goal theory appear to be ap- propriate for this situation. First, achievement-oriented leader behavior is expected to motivate employees to strive for higher levels of productivity and to have more confidence in their ability to meet the challenging de- mands of their job. It follows, then, that this form of leader behavior may be appropriate for the Cell 1 situation. Further, participative leader behavior would also be appropriate. Mitchell (1973) suggests that such behavior should serve to clarify organizational contingencies. It should allow sub- ordinates to select goals that are personally meaningful, allow them more control over the task, and facilitate their ego-involvement. **163**

The Cell 2 situation is characterized by subordinates who are performing high scope tasks and who, because of lack of motivation, may not be able to cope psychologically with such an ambiguous situation by structuring their own activities. The function of the leader here would appear to be to provide task structure by planning, organizing, coordinating, directing, and controlling the work of subordinates. Such behavior is analogous to directive leadership. The model predicts that this form of behavior by the leader in the Cell 2 situation would lead to favorable outcomes.

In the Cell 3 situation employees with high growth need strength are performing low scope, simple, and routine tasks. These individuals will tend to look to their job as one source of need satisfaction, but will find these needs unfulfilled due to the nature of their task. Their reaction will probably be frustration and dissatisfaction. Research evidence (House and Mitchell, 1974) suggests that employees who perform this type of frustrating and dissatisfying work will respond favorably to supportive leader behavior.

Supportive leader behavior focuses on the leader being friendly and approachable and exhibiting concern for the well-being of subordinates. This supportive behavior will probably not eliminate feelings of frustration and dissatisfaction; however, the dysfunctional consequences of these feelings can, perhaps, be minimized.

In the Cell 4 situation, a low growth need strength employee is performing a low scope task. Directive leader behavior will probably be inappropriate for this situation, since the employee will not need to have the job structured. Similarly, supportive behavior will also be unnecessary, since the employee is not particularly likely to be frustrated or dissatisfied. Participative and achievement-oriented leader behaviors are advocated when the employee is ego-involved with the task and is deriving intrinsic satisfaction from it. Since these characteristics are not descriptive of the Cell 4 situation, these forms of leader behavior would be inappropriate.

Since directive, supportive, participative, and achievement-oriented leader behaviors are all unnecessary in this situation, an alternate form of leader behavior may be appropriate. One implicit assumption of the path-goal theory (and most other widely recognized leadership models as well) is that the various forms of leader behavior described by the theory are collectively exhaustive. That is, the theory assumes that a leader must behave in either a directive, supportive, participative, or achievement-oriented manner. This common characteristic of most leadership models has also been noted by Schriesheim and Kerr (1977).

The Cell 4 task is of a routine nature, and there is a lack of negative consequences for the employee as a result of this routineness. Because of the low level of ego-involvement on the part of the subordinate in the Cell 4 situation, none of the leader behaviors suggested by path-goal theory are conceptually appropriate. What may be appropriate, though, is a form of minimum-interference leader behavior, whereby the leader monitors performance but doesn't actively supervise the employee. Little or no interaction between the leader and subordinate would be required as long as adequate levels of performance are maintained. This form of behavior might be termed maintenance leader behavior.

Maintenance leader behavior is similar to the concept of "substitutes for leadership" (Kerr, 1976), discussed in the next section. Kerr argues that, for a number of reasons, a subordinate may be able to perform independently of the leader and, therefore, not require supervision. Factors accounting for this independence may include intrinsic task satisfaction, policies and procedures, education, and experience. The concept is also somewhat similar to "laissez-faire behavior" (Lewin, Lippitt and White, 1939), which describes a leader who is essentially a nonparticipant.

Maintenance behavior, however, is an independent construct with unique features distinguishing it from both substitutes for leadership and laissez-faire leadership. It is not a lack of leadership. On a direct basis, a subordinate in the Cell 4 situation will probably not require directive, supportive, participative, or achievement-oriented behavior on the part of his or her leader. This does not mean, however, that no supervision is required. Rather, the leader in this situation may find it appropriate to maintain a low level of involvement with subordinates. If performance and/or satisfaction problems arise, the leader may, however, intervene in a directive and/or supportive fashion to solve the problem.

Once the problem has been corrected, the leader reverts to maintenance behavior. This form of leader behavior appears to be conceptually appropriate for the Cell 4 situation. This alternative, along with other leader behaviors, is depicted graphically in Figure 8–3.

Empirical evidence. To date, the model has received one empirical test (Griffin, 1980). A longitudinal field study was conducted in a manufacturing organization. Subjects were categorized as Cell 1, 2, 3, or 4 based on their perceptions of their tasks and their level of growth need strength. Within each cell, measures of leader behavior were correlated with productivity, overall satisfaction, satisfaction with job, and satisfaction with supervisor. Results provided reasonable support for the model in terms of satisfaction, but little support for performance as an appropriate outcome variable. The fact that the study was based primarily on perceptual data and that a restricted sample was used serves to further temper the results. Enough support was found, however, to warrant additional modification and research aimed at determining what advantages, if any, the model may have over alternative formulations.

Summary. This section has explored one approach to the study of individual-task-leader interactions. In contrast to path-goal theory, the model just discussed suggests that the impact of leader behavior on individuals will be secondary in nature and dependent upon the relationship **165**

FIGURE 8-3   Relationships among Individual, Task Design, and Leader Behavior

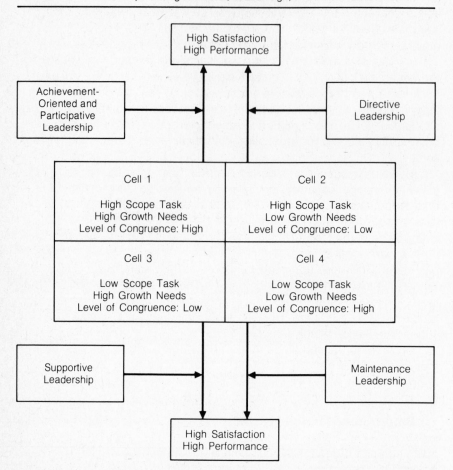

High Satisfaction
High Performance

Achievement-
Oriented and
Participative
Leadership

Directive
Leadership

Cell 1	Cell 2
High Scope Task High Growth Needs Level of Congruence: High	High Scope Task Low Growth Needs Level of Congruence: Low
Cell 3	Cell 4
Low Scope Task High Growth Needs Level of Congruence: Low	Low Scope Task Low Growth Needs Level of Congruence: High

Supportive
Leadership

Maintenance
Leadership

High Satisfaction
High Performance

Source: Adapted from R. W. Griffin, "Task Design Determinants of Effective Leader Behavior," *Academy of Management Review*, 1979, *4*, p. 221. Used by permission.

between the subordinate and the task. Since the model is a comparatively new approach, the empirical evidence is not sufficient to assess accurately the model's validity.

TASK DESIGN AND LEADER BEHAVIOR INTERACTIONS

The previous discussions have focused on ways in which task and leader behavior variables may interact to influence subordinate outcomes. More specifically, individual satisfaction, performance, and/or motivation were viewed as the primary dependent variables of interest. A final point of view relevant to our discussion is the interactive process among the task and leader behavior variables themselves. That is, how do task variables, including the job holder, affect the leader and, conversely, how does leader behavior affect the task? The little research that exists pertaining to these issues is sketchy at best, and there is no theoretical framework for analysis. Hence, our discussion will be at a more general level than in the previous sections. There are at least three types of relationships within the general framework that are of interest at this point: (1) the impact of the job on leader behavior, (2) the nature of the job as a substitute for supervision, and (3) the impact of leader behavior on subordinate perceptions of the job. Each of these areas will be discussed separately.

Impact of the Task on Leader Behavior

At a conceptual level, it seems obvious that the manner in which a particular task is designed will affect how a leader will behave with respect to an employee performing that task. For example, if a task is designed such that the incumbent is allowed little decision-making latitude and most decisions are to be made by the supervisor, it follows that the leader's behavior will be different than when the job incumbent is given a great deal of autonomy and control in the decision-making process. The tasks described at the beginning of this chapter, for example, were structured in such a way that the supervisor could vary the design of individual tasks to accommodate individual preferences. The nature of the work system dictated that the supervisor make certain decisions about the assignments. Unfortunately, there is little research evidence available for documenting and describing how these processes occur.

Some insights, however, may be gained by examining selected task-change studies that have appeared in the literature. If task characteristics influence leader behavior, a change in the task should probably result in a change in the leader's behavior. There are at least two factors that could account for the latter change. First, a change in a person's work environment should tend to cause the person to become more aware of that environment. As time passes, supervisors will tend fo form a mental set of their work environment, including the nature of their subordinates' tasks. When these tasks are changed, however, the change may act as a stimulus, causing supervisors to alter their mental set. This alteration, in turn, may modify the supervisors' behavior toward the subordinates performing the task.

A second factor which may cause a change in supervisory behavior concerns the interrelationship between the subordinate's job and the supervisor's job. (A discussion of the impact of task design factors on the supervisor's role itself is found in the next section. Our immediate concerns are with supervisory behavior, but some aspects of the discussion will, of necessity, refer to the supervisor's role.) Both the job enrichment approach (Herzberg et al., 1959) and the job characteristics approach (Hackman and **167**

Oldham, 1980) to task redesign involve giving the subordinate a portion of the supervisor's job. Herzberg (1968), for example, speaks of vertical job loading. Vertical job loading includes, among other things, the granting of additional authority and freedom and the provision of relevant information directly to the worker rather than to the leader. Further, Hackman et al. (1975) advocate giving the worker freedom, independence, and discretion in scheduling work and deciding how it will be done. It follows that by "taking away" a portion of the leader's job, the organization may change the manner in which the leader behaves with respect to the person who "took over" that part of his or her job. Three studies provide helpful insights into this process.

Friedman (1961) describes the results of an industrial job enlargement program. After the job change, first-line supervisors changed the way in which they related to their subordinates and began to discuss their problems directly and openly with the people they supervised. As a result, the prestige and status of the workers involved also increased. Other studies, however, have indicated negative consequences in terms of supervisory behavior.

Whyte (1955) reports on a job enlargement study in which female employees were allowed to control the speed of their assembly line. The workers themselves indicated increased satisfaction as a result of the change. However, considerable conflict arose among supervisory personnel and the enlargement program was abandoned.

A more rigorous field experiment in job redesign and its impact on supervisory behavior has been reported by Lawler, Hackman, and Kaufman (1973). This study involved changing the jobs of a group of telephone operators by, among other things, having the operators perform some functions previously performed by their supervisors. The researchers note that interpersonal relations among operators and supervisors were severely disrupted. In particular, supervisors were described as experiencing less job security and more free time, resulting in operators feeling "oversupervised" and complaining that their supervisors were spending too much time looking over their shoulders. Lawler et al. (1973, p. 61) conclude that "any positive motivational effects that might have accrued as a result of the increases in variety and autonomy in the directory assistance job were more than counteracted by the negative effects the changes had on the attitudes and behavior of the [supervisors]."

Hence, it appears that task changes may result in changes in the behavior of the task supervisor. Further, the scant research evidence suggests that the supervisory changes may well be negative. As noted by Hackman (1977), task design changes may dictate other organizational changes. It follows that one specific change needed may be training programs aimed at better preparing supervisors for the effects the task design change will have on their own jobs. This issue will be more fully discussed in Chapter 10.

The Job as a Leadership Substitute

Recently, Kerr (1976) has suggested that in some circumstances a variety of individual and organizational factors may serve as substitutes for leadership. That is, these factors may act to reduce or eliminate the subordinate's dependency on the leader. One potential substitute for leadership is task structure.

It may be possible to impose sufficient structure on a job so as to eliminate most instances of decision uncertainty and the necessity for problem solving. If this can be done, it may then be possible to describe the job in detail in policy manuals, job descriptions, rules statements, and so forth. Hence, the employee will encounter a situation requiring a decision only infrequently and even then will have a set procedure for answering relevant questions. While it may still be necessary to maintain a hierarchical leader for administrative purposes (i.e., performance appraisal, reward distribution, etc.), the supervisory process may be all but eliminated. Of course, this process will not be desirable in most cases for two primary reasons: (1) many jobs may not be amenable to such high, rigid structure, and (2) such high structure is analogous to extreme job specialization, which may have dysfunctional consequences (see Chapter 2).

Kerr (1976) specifies four task characteristics that may serve as leadership substitutes, three of which are structural, with the other being attitudinal. Kerr suggests that if a task is unambiguous and routine, methodologically invariant, and/or provides its own feedback, there may be little need for task-oriented or job-centered leadership. Further, if the task is intrinsically satisfying, the need for supportive or considerate leadership will be neutralized.

A recent study by Kerr and Jermier (1978) indicates that the leadership substitutes concept (including additional factors such as experience, training, etc.) may have considerable utility for future research. This approach may be useful from both a practical and a theoretical perspective in terms of better understanding the complex leadership process. Finally, as mentioned previously, the leadership substitutes concept is similar to maintenance leader behavior (Griffin, 1979), but the two concepts are distinct constructs. The primary difference is that leadership substitutes are offered as alternatives to hierarchical leadership, while maintenance leadership is a form of leader behavior, albeit behavior characterized by limited interaction between leader and subordinate.

Impact of Leader Behavior on Task Variables

A final point to be considered in this section is the influence of leader behavior on subordinate perceptions of task variables. As described in Chapter 6, leader behavior is a part of the social system in an organization. In conjunction with other social system elements, the technical system, and organization design variables, leader behavior (both formal and informal) **169** may have a substantial impact on both the objective and perceived task of an employee. Leadership theorists have generally recognized that some aspects of leader behavior are oriented or directed toward the task being supervised. In early studies, researchers at Ohio State (Stogdill and Coons, 1957) and the University of Michigan (Likert, 1967) described two forms of leader behavior, termed *initiating structure* and *job-centered*, which focus on assigning work, meeting schedules, and evaluating performance.

The situational theories discussed earlier also include forms of leader behavior directed at structuring the task. Fiedler's (1967) *task-oriented* behavior and House and Mitchell's (1974) *directive* behavior are both concerned with planning and organizing subordinate activities. Until recently, though, there have been no attempts to relate leader behaviors to employee perceptions of specific task characteristics within a task design framework. Two studies, however, have recently been conducted specifically to investigate this issue.

Griffin (1981a) has suggested that in some job settings supervisors may have considerable discretion and latitude in assigning tasks to employees. The jobs described at the beginning of this chapter would fall into this category. One supervisor may feel that by assigning several different tasks to the same individual, he or she may be preventing mental fatigue and boredom. Alternatively, a different supervisor may assume that by continually assigning the same tasks to the same individuals he or she is increasing efficiency through familiarity and reducing role stress and ambiguity through high role clarity and high predictability. It follows that subordinates of one supervisor should perceive their jobs differently from subordinates of the other supervisor.

This supposition was tested in an industrial setting. Twenty-nine first-line supervisors were asked, via structured interviews, the extent to which they assigned work to their subordinates in such a way as to provide variety, autonomy, feedback, and identity. One month later, two subordinates of each supervisor were randomly selected and asked to complete the Job Characteristic Inventory (Sims et al., 1976), a perceptual measure of the amount of variety, autonomy, feedback, and identity inherent in one's job. (This instrument was described in Chapter 5.)

Correlations between the extent to which supervisors tried to provide these various task dimensions and the extent to which subordinates actually perceived these same dimensions were all very high. In that setting, at least, supervisors seemed to have considerable ability to alter the tasks of their subordinates.

The other study (Griffin, 1981b) combined two different tests to investigate the indirect effects of leader behavior on both employee perceptions of and reactions to their tasks. The conceptual framework utilized was the Social Information Processing approach (Salancik and Pfeffer, 1977, 1978). This viewpoint was briefly introduced in Chapter 3 and will be described in somewhat more detail in Chapter 9. Essentially, the concern in this study was with the extent to which supervisory comments and verbal cues about employee tasks actually influenced perceptions of and reactions to those tasks.

First, effects were tested in a laboratory setting. Twenty subjects, working alone, wired electric lamp sockets for 30 minutes. Another twenty subjects did the same task, but in the presence of a "supervisor." During the task, the supervisor (actually, the experimenter) made several comments referring to the high degree of task variety, autonomy, feedback, and identity in the job. After completion of the task, the subjects filled out the Job Characteristic Inventory and a measure of satisfaction. Subjects who received the verbal cues perceived significantly higher levels of all task characteristics and also indicated more satisfaction than those who received no cues, even though both groups performed the same task.

Next, the same effects were compared against "real" task effects in a field experiment. One group of approximately 80 manufacturing employees received no treatment (i.e., they received no manipulation or experimental change) and therefore constituted a control group. Another group received increased verbal cues about their jobs from their supervisors (the supervisors participated in a two-day training program designed to teach them when and how to offer meaningful and relevant comments emphasizing positive attributes of their employees' tasks). A third group of employees had their jobs objectively changed in accordance with Hackman and Oldham's (1980) job characteristics theory. A fourth group received both treatments: their jobs were redesigned and their supervisors also began to offer verbal cues.

All employees completed the JCI and a satisfaction measure prior to the change and again approximately four months after the change. Results indicated that the verbal cues (Group 2) and the objective changes (Group 3) each enhanced perceptions and satisfaction to about the same extent. The combined effects (Group 4) were significantly greater than either single effect. That is, verbal cues alone and objective task changes alone caused employees to perceive significantly higher levels of core task characteristics in their jobs and also to express greater satisfaction with their jobs. The combined effects of cues and changes caused an even greater increase in perceptions and satisfaction.

It seems reasonable to conclude that supervisory behavior may have a significant impact on task design. Perhaps of all the potential leader behavior–task design interaction perspectives presented in this chapter, this one holds the most promise for both future research and managerial practice.

A FINAL POINT: THE LEADER'S TASK

Before concluding our discussion of leader behavior–task design interrelationships, an important related issue warrants attention: the design of **171** the leader's task. Our previous discussions have focused on the relationships between a leader's behavior and the task of a subordinate.

Most of the task design research to date has been concerned with jobs of operating employees, clerical workers, and so forth. Attention has been focused primarily on the operational characteristics of these jobs, such as variety, feedback, and so forth. Even though early formulations (e.g., Hackman and Lawler, 1971) included interpersonal dimensions such as friendship opportunities and dealing with others, these have been largely ignored by contemporary researchers.

The manager's job, however, may consist to a large extent of interpersonal relationships, such as dealing with others in the workplace. As shown in Figure 8–4, the manager or leader must interact with his or her own superior, a group of peers, and a group of subordinates. The interpersonal characteristics of the leader's task may be as important or more important than content attributes such as task variety, identity, etc.

Indeed, describing the manager's job may require a higher level of abstraction than describing an operating employee's job. Variety, for ex-

FIGURE 8–4 Interpersonal Nature of the Leader's Task

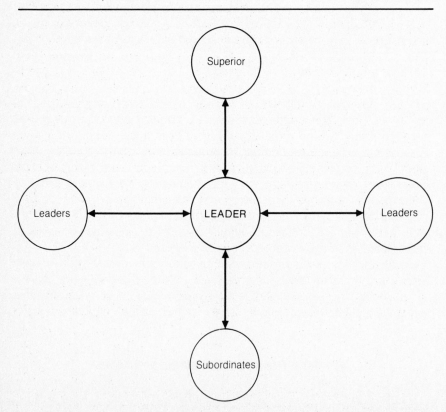

ample, may be better represented as the number of role relationships inherent in the leader's job, while autonomy may be more closely related to the leader's flexibility in moving from one role to another. Further, it may also be true that one role relationship is more motivating than another. Hence, the leader's task may be properly designed along some lines, but less effectively designed along others. Unfortunately, these concepts and suggestions are offered only as speculation at this time. More empirical research and better insights from management practice are needed to fully characterize and understand the leader's task.

SUMMARY

This chapter has focused on possible relationships among individual, task design, and leader behavior variables. These interrelationships seem particularly important since they are primary variables in the employee's work environment. A general framework used as a basis for discussion suggests that there are direct relationships between each pair of variable categories and that each category also intervenes between the direct relationship of the other two categories.

This framework was used to categorize the available literature and relate it to the task design area. A number of deficiencies and several inconsistencies in the literature were also noted. The evidence indicates that much previous research may have been too narrow in its approach. More specifically, rather than focusing on how task design *or* leader behavior variables influence employee attitudes and behaviors, a more reasonable approach might be to investigate more fully how task design *and* leader behavior variables influence each other and how they interactively influence and are influenced by characteristics of the subordinate.

Overall, the leader behavior–task design relationships seem to be highly important as an avenue of increased understanding of task design processes. As with technology and organization design, leader behavior is a crucial contextual element in the workplace that influences and is influenced by the design of jobs. A change in either leader behavior or task design may purposefully or inadvertently alter the other. The point, again, is that tasks are not performed in a vacuum; other factors *must* be considered when attending to task design issues. In the next chapter, we describe another primary contextual variable of considerable importance: group processes.

9 TASK DESIGN AND GROUP PROCESSES

In previous chapters, we have examined how technology, organization design, and leader behaviors may influence and be influenced by task design variables and processes. We now direct our attention at how task design may be related to a final major aspect of organizations: group and social processes. Group and social processes are also major contextual variables that may influence and be influenced by task design processes. Very few jobs are performed in isolation. Many jobs require that the job-holder regularly interact with other people, both inside and outside of the organization. Even jobs that do not require interaction are usually performed in the presence of other people. Given the basic social nature of most people, then, group and social processes will almost invariably come into play.

As we shall see, a number of group-related processes and characteristics may both objectively and subjectively affect individual employees and their jobs. These variables and concepts are relevant when discussing task design in organizations. For our purposes, we will define a group as a set of two or more interdependent people who interact in order to achieve a common goal.

Essentially, there are three types of groups that may be identified in organizations. A *functional* group is one that is created by organization design processes. These formal groups have indefinite time horizons and include most functional departments in a firm. *Task* or *project* groups are also created and specified by the organization, but generally have a specific task and a more limited time horizon. Examples include special task forces, project planning teams, and committees. Finally, an *interest* or *friendship* group is one that is created by the members themselves. The interest or friendship group may be either formal or informal. Examples include people who gather for lunch every day in the company cafeteria, social groups, and, in some cases, trade unions.

Obviously, there may be varying degrees of overlap between the organization-created and the member-created groups. For example, a work group of five people may also be a friendship group: they may eat lunch together, talk a lot among themselves, and socialize on the weekends. A different scenario, however, may also describe a work group that is not a friendship group: the members may work together for eight hours every day, but may each eat lunch alone (or with other groups), have little conversation not related to work, and never see one another after work. As we shall see, both organization-created and member-created groups may exert considerable influence on task design processes.

This chapter consists of four major sections. First, we will discuss a recently developed major topic relevant to task design: the role that social and informational cues may play in determining employee task perceptions and reactions. This approach to task design was briefly introduced in Chapter 3, and was directly and indirectly referred to in our preceding three chapters. In this chapter, we will present a more complete description of the topic. Next, we will look at basic characteristics of groups. Wherever possible, we will relate these to task design considerations. Our primary purpose in discussing the characteristics, however, is to provide some theoretical insights for the following sections. In our third section, we will describe how organizations often use groups as a basis for organizing work activities. Our focus will be on designing jobs for groups. Finally, we will present three case studies of successful and less-than-successful interactions among task design and group processes in organizations.

Our first topic, again, is the social information processing approach to task design. The rationale for discussing this topic at the beginning of the chapter is that it is the only available theoretical framework for describing and explaining how social processes interact with task design variables. Specifically, an initial understanding and appreciation of this viewpoint will make topics covered in later sections of the book more salient and relevant to the reader.

THE SOCIAL INFORMATION PROCESSING FRAMEWORK

As indicated above, the social information processing framework has had a significant impact on the field of task design in recent years. In this section, we will briefly examine the theoretical background of the framework, describe the framework itself, summarize relevant research, and offer some managerial implications of this viewpoint on task design processes.

Theoretical Background

Over the years, a number of writers have postulated that individuals and/or groups influence the manner in which they themselves perceive their environment. One early example of this assumption is found in March and Simon (1958), where it is suggested that information from the environment influences the decisions and behaviors of people within the organization. The most widely referenced approach, however, is the work of Karl Weick.

Weick (1969, 1977) has developed a concept termed "environmental enactment." Environmental enactment suggests that phenomenon cannot become a part of an individual's environment without the individual participating in the creation (i.e., the enactment) of that environment. Stated in simpler terms, this viewpoint suggests that an individual's perception of the environment is partially determined by those elements and characteristics of the environment the individual chooses to include. Hence, a manager's behavior in his or her job becomes his or her perception of the job.

Social Information Processing Framework

Using the work of Weick (1969, 1977) and others as a basis, Salancik and Pfeffer (1978) have developed what they call a social information processing (SIP) approach to job attitudes and task design. The model is presented in Figure 9–1. The part of the model most relevant to our discussion is the box termed "Job or Task Environmental Characteristics." Specifically, the SIP framework predicts that individual perceptions of their jobs are a function of social information. Further, social reality construction processes intervene between this social information and task perceptions.

Operationally, this viewpoint suggests that people may perceive their tasks not in an objective sense, but in terms of informational cues they receive from the work environment. This process may manifest itself in a number of different ways:

1. When participative techniques are used to plan and implement work design changes, the representatives (and those who elected them), through their involvement and commitment to the project, may become more satisfied as a result of the process itself, aside from any real changes.
2. By completing a pre-change assessment questionnaire such as the Job Diagnostic Survey, workers focus their attention on those factors included in the questionnaire. Hence, they come to perceive their jobs in terms of variety, autonomy, and so forth.
3. Job changes may be real or only constructed through managed social processes (Salancik and Pfeffer, 1978).

We now direct our attention at briefly reviewing relevant research dealing directly or indirectly with the SIP framework.

Research Evidence

176 At a general level, the SIP framework attempts to explain variations in

FIGURE 9–1 Social Information Processing Approach to Job Attitudes and Task Design

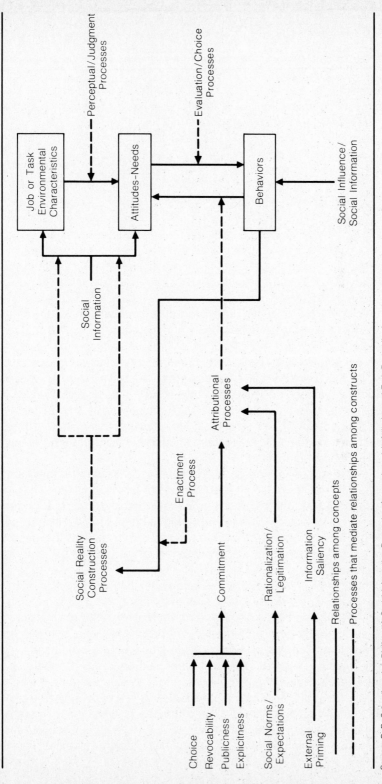

Source: G. R. Salancik and J. Pfeffer, "A Social Information Processing Approach to Job Attitudes and Task Design," *Administrative Science Quarterly*, 1978, 23, p. 227. Used by permission.

employee task perceptions. Specifically, if two employees perform the same task, but describe it in different terms (which will usually be the case), some factor or set of factors must account for the variations. The SIP framework suggests that social information and social reality construction processes are the primary factors to be considered.

Recently, a number of studies have tested ways in which this process may occur. In two different laboratory studies, people were assigned to perform tasks that were different in an objective sense (O'Reilly and Caldwell, 1979; White and Mitchell, 1979). In both cases, informational cues in the form of written evaluations by "previous workers" (actually written and manipulated by the researchers) or verbal comments by a "co-worker" (really an experimenter confederate) were structured so as to provide either positive cues (i.e., that the task was high in scope) or negative cues (i.e., that the task was low in scope). Results indicated that in both studies, "employee" task perceptions and satisfaction were significantly influenced by these informational cues.

A study of public health nurses found task perceptions to be influenced by individuals' frames of reference and general job attitudes (O'Reilly, Parlette, and Bloom, 1980). Another laboratory study found that observing other workers express positive attitudes about a task caused subjects to describe the task as higher in scope than subjects who were not exposed to the positive attitudes (Weiss and Shaw, 1979). Finally, a study of 658 heterogeneous employees found that the complexity of jobs performed by significant others in the immediate work environment had a substantial impact on how an employee reacted to characteristics of his or her own job (Oldham and Miller, 1979).

A common characteristic of all of these studies is that they assumed that social and informational cues stem from other co-workers in the work environment. As was discussed in the last chapter, important and meaningful cues may also come from the jobholder's supervisor (e.g., Griffin, 1981b). Due to the power of the supervisor with respect to the subordinate's task, this process may have even more potential as a source of perceptual variation.

In summary, the research evidence seems to offer strong support for the contention that social and/or informational cues about a job influence how an employee perceives and reacts to that job. Obviously, this is not to suggest that objective properties of the task don't influence perceptions and reactions. Indeed, several of these studies found significant relationships between both objective task attributes and informational cues and employee perceptions and reactions (e.g., Weiss and Shaw, 1979; White and Mitchell, 1979). Hence, the evidence fairly clearly indicates that both objective and social/informational attributes of tasks influence how employees perceive and react to those tasks. A remaining question, however, is the extent to which one set of stimuli has greater impact than the other;

that is, which set is the primary determinant of task design perceptions and reactions.

Managerial Implications

Since the SIP framework is relatively new, little is known about how the various processes may operate in organizations. Since most task design interventions, however, take place in group settings (i.e., in a group-based design or in an individual-based design in the context of a group of co-workers), the issues raised by the SIP framework are extremely important.

Until more is known, the managers should simply note that social factors may be important determinants of the success or failure of any task redesign effort. The basic group factors and processes discussed in the remainder of this chapter and the SIP framework in particular indicate that social processes may be powerful determinants of how the individual will perceive and react to a task. Hence, in order for a task redesign attempt to be successful, necessary antecedent conditions may include:

1. Commitment and open communication channels from those in charge of the change: this will facilitate employee interest in the impending change and serve to focus attention on the positive attributes of the change.
2. The enhancement of work-group cohesiveness and performance norms and the minimization of role dynamics difficulties: this will foster a more generally positive atmosphere for the change and should serve to focus attention on and enhance interpersonal discussion of salient aspects of the task changes.
3. Diffusion of the task change effort throughout the organizational system: this will serve to reinforce and maintain patterns of interpersonal discussion among all relevant employees, thereby increasing the likelihood of a successful task redesign change.

Of course, these suggestions are merely generalizations from our existing knowledge base. It is hoped that managers and researchers will continue to explore the important role that group and social factors play in task design processes.

As an intermediate step, attention should perhaps be focused on less abstract and more observable group processes. Condition 2 above makes reference to cohesiveness, norms, and rules. These traditional group characteristics may be of particular value when considering the group context of task design. The next section will consider these primary group characteristics and their potential impact on task design.

BASIC CHARACTERISTICS OF GROUPS

Group theorists have identified and described a number of basic characteristics that exist in groups. The most commonly described characteristics include norms, leadership, roles, cohesiveness, and status systems. Leadership was the primary topic of Chapter 8, while status sys- **179** tems were briefly discussed in Chapter 7. Accordingly, we will now focus our attention on potential interactions among cohesiveness, norms, and roles and task design processes.

Group Cohesiveness

Group cohesiveness is the extent to which members of the group are attracted to each other and the extent to which members are motivated to maintain the integrity of the group. A variety of factors may serve to enhance group cohesiveness, including:

1. *Inter-group competition.* When a group competes with another group, the result is likely to be an increase in cohesiveness within both groups.
2. *Personal attraction.* Assuming that a certain level of trust already exists in a group, cohesion will be enhanced if members are attracted to one another.
3. *Favorable evaluation.* Cohesiveness is likely to increase if the group is favorably evaluated (i.e., if the group receives some form of recognition or positive feedback).
4. *Agreement on group goals.* To the extent that group members agree on the purposes and objectives of the group, cohesion will be increased.
5. *Frequency of interaction.* When group members interact frequently, cohesiveness will tend to be enhanced.

Similarly, certain factors also may result in decreased cohesiveness within groups. For example:

1. *Group size.* In general, the larger a group becomes, the greater the tendency for cohesion to decline.
2. *Disagreement on goals.* Just as agreement in goals fosters cohesion, disagreement in goals of the group may cause cohesiveness to decrease.
3. *Intra-group competition.* Competition among individual group members, either formal or informal in nature, will have an adverse impact on cohesion.
4. *Domination.* When one or more group members attempt to dominate the group, cohesion will decline.
5. *Unpleasant experiences with the group.* When members are not attracted to one another, when trust is low, or when bad things happen to the group (i.e., an athletic team losing several games), there is a tendency for cohesion to decline (Szilagyi and Wallace, 1980).

There also tend to be reasonably strong relationships between cohesion and group goal accomplishment. The reason for this is that in a highly cohesive group, the group has more influence over its members, thereby fostering behaviors aimed at goal accomplishment. Of course, the goals of the group may or may not be congruent with the goals of the organization. The important contingency variable in this relationship, as we shall see in the next section, is the performance norms of the group.

At this point, two suppositions are offered. Their importance will be apparent later in the discussion. First, group cohesion will be a crucial determinant of the success of autonomous work groups in organizations. Second, the level of group cohesion may be an important variable to consider when describing and evaluating the social information processing view of task design. That is, as indicated earlier, a high degree of group cohesion may enhance (from the organization's perspective) the kinds of social cues workers pass among themselves.

Group Norms

Norms refer to standards of behavior for individuals within groups. Specifically, norms provide boundaries between acceptable and unacceptable behaviors. For example, some academic departments have norms pertaining to appropriate dress for teaching. In some departments, this norm might be that male instructors will wear coats and ties. If a member violates this norm by wearing jeans one day, he will be "punished" by group members through remarks such as "Don't we pay you enough money to buy a suit?," "Gee, George, you look just like one of the students," and so forth.

In another department, the norms might be exactly the opposite, with more formal attire being undesirable. A faculty member who shows up one day in a new suit may be greeted by remarks like "Look at 'Fancy Dan'," "He's just trying to impress the Dean," etc.

It is also useful to note that norms vary within the group for different individuals. Using the faculty example again, it may be perfectly acceptable for younger assistant professors to dress informally. More senior faculty, however, and especially the department head, may be expected to dress somewhat more formally.

As opposed to group cohesiveness, group norms do have specific relevance for task design processes. This relevance takes on varying degrees of formality. For example, many groups have norms that new group members (i.e., the least senior member) will perform some task or set of tasks that is unappealing, or else gets in the way of effective task performance. These "duties" might include things like:

1. Making the first pot of coffee in the morning (in an office).
2. Accompanying the cashier to the bank every evening (in a small retail store).
3. Dealing with certain kinds of problem customers; i.e., those that complain a lot (in a large department store).
4. Serving customers seated the farthest distance from the kitchen (in a restaurant).
5. Working the "full-service" pumps while a more senior employee collects money from the "self-service" customers (at a gas station).
6. Being assigned the low-commission line of merchandise (in a sales department).
7. Typing tables and figures while others do text (in a secretarial pool).

Similar examples of norm-directed behaviors could be developed for more senior members of a group. For example, the senior members of an academic department may be expected to handle larger classes. As time passes, many of these informal task requirements may become institutionalized. While they may not be a written part of an individual's job description, and while they may not be detected by objective task measurement techniques (as described in Chapter 5), they do nonetheless become a part of the employee's job. Hence, differential work norms within **181** the group may be important for attaining a better understanding of task design processes in organizations.

One specific category of norms alluded to earlier was the performance norms of the group. Performance norms are expected levels of performance to be attained by the group and/or its members. Some groups may have high performance norms; they work hard at achieving a high level of output. Individuals who produce too far below the norm are sanctioned. Other groups may have low performance norms; in this case, the group attempts to restrict output at a point close to the minimum level acceptable by the organization. Members may be sanctioned by producing at a rate too far above *or* below the norm in this case.

Table 9–1 presents relationships among group cohesiveness, group performance norms, and actual group performance. As indicated, the highest level of performance results from high cohesion and high performance norms. Conversely, low cohesion and low performance norms lead to low performance. When confronted with this latter situation, the manager can only hope to enhance norms and cohesion through strategies such as emphasizing task accomplishment, utilizing participative management, stimulating intergroup competition, or, as a last resort, disbanding the group (Szilagyi and Wallace, 1980).

Role Dynamics

The final group characteristic to be discussed in this section is the concept

TABLE 9–1   Relationships among Group Cohesiveness, Group Performance Norms, and Performance

		Cohesiveness	
		High	Low
Performance Norms	High	High Performance	Medium Performance
	Low	Low Performance	Low Performance

Source: A. D. Szilagyi and M. J. Wallace, *Organizational Behavior and Performance*, 2nd ed. (Santa Monica, California: Goodyear Publishing, 1980), p. 223. Used by permission.

of *role dynamics*. A role is the behavior expected of the occupant of a given position in a group by other group members (Shaw, 1976). At one level of analysis, an individual fills a variety of roles as a result of memberships in an organization, a family, fraternal groups, social and recreational groups, religious groups, and so forth. At a more micro level of analysis, the individual also has a number of roles within the organization, including supervisor, subordinate, team member, committee(s) member, union member, and so forth. It is with this set of roles that we are concerned.

One important aspect of role dynamics is the *expected role*. The expected role refers to the role as perceived and/or determined by the organization and other group members. Hence, the formal components of task design processes are elements of the expected role. The informal norm-directed components of the job, described in the previous section, are also parts of the expected role, albeit less observable and more subjective.

The individual employee senses these expectations in the form of the *perceived role*. The perceived role, then, is what the employee believes that he or she should do. For a variety of reasons (e.g., different frames of reference, attitudes, situational variables, etc.), there may be a difference in the expected and perceived roles. The employee's perception of task attributes (i.e., variety, autonomy, etc.) are components of the perceived role.

Finally, the manner in which the employee operationalizes the perceived role is the *enacted role*. That is, the enacted role is the set of behaviors actually engaged in by the employee. Due to differences in skills and abilities, motives, and so forth, the enacted role may differ from the perceived role.

Hence, the expected sequence of events is the expected role, the perceived role, followed by the enacted role. To the extent that significant differences exist among these three elements, any or all of these outcomes may result: role conflict, role ambiguity, and/or role overload.

Role conflict generally relates to the perceived role-enacted role linkage and is characterized by multiple demands from one or more members of the group (i.e., peers and/or leader), which in turn create uncertainty for the worker. *Inter-role conflict* occurs when discrepancies arise between roles. For example, an employee may be a functional member of a work group and also a member of an important committee. At times, there may be strong demands on the employee's time from both groups. Hence, conflict exists between the two roles of operating employee and committee member.

Intra-role conflict is the situation where the employee perceives conflicting expectations from two different constituencies within the context of one role. The classic example of intra-role conflict is that likely to be experienced by first-line supervisors. The operating employees may see the supervisor as "one of them," particularly if he or she was promoted from their ranks. They may expect less pressure, more overtime, etc. Manage-

183

ment, however, sees the first-line supervisor as now being "one of them." Accordingly, the supervisor may be expected to pressure subordinates to increase output, impose and enforce strict rules, etc.

Finally, a less frequent form of role conflict is *intra-sender conflict*. This occurs when one person, probably the supervisor, sends contradictory expectations to the employee. For example, on Monday the boss may tell an employee that overtime has been running too high and that, from now on, everyone *must* leave at 5:00. On Wednesday, however, the boss tells the employee not to leave until a certain project is completed, regardless of how long it takes. The employee is faced with two very clear but mutually exclusive task demands.

When differences exist between the expected and perceived role, *role ambiguity* may develop. Role ambiguity, as the term implies, is uncertainty as to what should be done within the context of a particular role. Determinants of role ambiguity include things like a poor job description, high complexity in jobs (i.e., different occupational levels), and/or personality traits of the individual (i.e., some people have higher tolerances for ambiguity and/or a lower need for clarity than do other people; therefore, what is role ambiguity to one person may not be role ambiguity to another).

A final potential consequence of incongruencies among expected, perceived, and enacted roles is *role overload*. Role overload occurs when there are so many demands made on a person's time that he or she cannot adequately cope with them, or when the person is given or assumes so many roles that none of them are effectively performed. An example might be the person who is "stretched too thin" across multiple roles (i.e., committee assignments, task or project groups, a functional group, etc.), to the point where none of the jobs are being done adequately. In response to role overload, the employee may withdraw from the situation, simply ignore some of the role demands, and/or request assistance from others.

A number of fairly obvious and straightforward generalizations and two somewhat more complex arguments can now be advanced regarding interactions among task design and role variables. The basic relationships can be summarized as follows:

1. As task scope increases, the possibility for role ambiguity and/or conflict increases.
2. An increase in task scope (i.e., a work redesign program) is likely to be followed by immediate increases in role ambiguity and conflict until employees familiarize themselves with new task procedures and until flaws in the new work system are corrected.
3. If task scope is increased too much, role overload may result.
4. If role ambiguity and/or overload exist, the employee may adopt various techniques for bringing about a desired degree of task structure.

Two other observations which are less obvious warrant additional discussion. First, role conflict and ambiguity may stem from incongruent cues from the organizational context. Recall that the Porter, Lawler and Hackman (1975) model of organizations, task designs, and individuals (described in Chapter 7) predicted that if organization and task design variables were incongruent, the employee would focus on that element closest to his or her own need structure. Another possibility is that incongruent organization and task designs may result in role conflict and/or ambiguity. For example, an organic organizational system may result in a certain set of expected role elements, while a simple, routine task within that system may convey a different set of expectations. The likely consequence, then, would be role conflict, and perhaps ambiguity, for the employee. This reasoning has been empirically supported in a study of public utility employees (Schuler, 1977).

A second implication of role dynamics for task design processes relates to the concept of multiple roles. Throughout this book, and in other treatments of the topic, we speak of the employee's "job," redesigning the "task," the amount of variety, autonomy, feedback, identity, and significance inherent in the employee's "work," and so forth. Yet many employees have several "jobs" and "tasks." Most managers, for example, have at least the two roles (i.e., tasks): performing work for their superiors and directing the efforts of subordinates. In addition, many managers have the additional roles (i.e., tasks) of committee memberships and so forth.

It is thus possible to characterize task design elements at two different levels of understanding. First, we can describe the nature of a task (i.e., its scope, its relevant attributes, etc.) *within* roles. The supervisory role of a manager may have a certain level of scope, complexity, and/or challenge, whereas the operational role may have a quite different nature altogether. Further, the various support and service roles, such as committee and/or task force memberships, may have still other levels of scope.

Second, it is also possible to describe the nature of many jobs *across* roles. Indeed, managerial task variety could be reflected as the number of different roles that the manager has within the organization. Similarly, one element of managerial task autonomy may be the freedom the manager has to shift from one role to another as opposed to having role changes dictated by the organization. Certainly, this two-level idea is somewhat conjectural, but it does seem to be a reasonable approach to understanding task design processes for many managerial jobs.

The preceding discussion has focused on three basic characteristics of groups: cohesiveness, norms, and role dynamics. These characteristics will be integrated as appropriate in our discussions of other group-related aspects of task design. One such area of growing importance to organizations—designing jobs for groups as opposed to individuals—is discussed in our next section.

DESIGNING JOBS FOR GROUPS

The rationale for using groups as a basis for organizing work generally stems from any or all of three overlapping perspectives. First, the organization may be attempting to be consistent with socio-technical systems **185** theory. Recall that socio-technical systems theory (discussed in Chapter 6) argues for the importance of integrating the technical and social systems of the organization. The general method for enhancing the social system, in turn, has been to facilitate social interaction and development by placing employees in groups and then giving these groups considerable control over their activities. This form of group is called the *autonomous work group* and is characterized by the following general dimensions:

1. The group is assigned a whole task, in which the mission of the group is sufficiently identifiable and significant so that members find the work of the group meaningful.
2. Workers in the group each have a number of the skills required for completion of the group task, and so the flexibility of the group in carrying out the task is increased. When individuals do not have a robust repertoire of skills initially, procedures are developed to encourage cross-training among members.
3. The group is given autonomy to make decisions about the methods by which the work is carried out, the scheduling of various activities, the assignment of different individuals to different tasks, and (sometimes) the selection of new group members.
4. Compensation is based on the performance of the group as a whole rather than on the contributions of individual group members (Hackman, 1977, p. 141).

It should be carefully noted that these descriptions do *not* represent normative guidelines or principles; rather, they are simply descriptive generalizations about the nature of many autonomous work groups.

A second reason that work may be organized at the group level is simply that the nature of the task may be such that a group effort is more efficient and/or effective than a series of individual efforts. For example, employees in an automated plant (i.e., a continuous process facility) may have tasks that are so highly interdependent that individual task performance is virtually impossible. Similarly, the maintenance crew for an airline may perform the task of servicing a 747 more efficiently working as a group rather than as a collection of individuals. This type of group, which we will call an *operative work group*, might be described by the following characteristics:

1. The group is assigned a complete task, in which the goals and objectives of the group are identifiable and the task has a moderate degree of significance, such that the members may see it as meaningful.
2. Workers in the group generally have a fairly narrow repertoire of skills to the extent that each member has an identifiable and relatively constant role in the group. While some informal job rotation may occur, it is usually not sanctioned by the organization.
3. The group is generally given little autonomy as to how the task is to be performed, the scheduling of activities is usually performed by the group's supervisor, and the group seldom has a voice in selecting new members.
4. Compensation is usually based on individual performance and/or seniority, although special rewards (i.e., bonuses, awards, etc.) may be granted at the group level.

As with the case of autonomous work groups, these generalizations regarding operative work groups are descriptive of common characteristics. In practice, a considerable number of variations may occur.

186 A final reason for creating work groups is to allow the organization to function as a matrix. A matrix organization is one that superimposes a product/service arrangement over a functional structure. That is, the firm is departmentalized along traditional functional (i.e., marketing, production, and finance) lines. Next, horizontal groups are created to work on specific projects. An example of a matrix organization is found in Figure 9–2. As indicated, the firm uses a functional structure. However, a new product task force has also been created by selecting one member from each department.

The departments themselves are functional groups, as defined earlier in this chapter, and were not specifically created to work as groups. Rather, they are a convenient and efficient way to structure the organization on a permanent basis. The task force, however, represents a specific organizational attempt to utilize a work group for task accomplishment. The factors dictating the need for such a task force might include increased environmental complexity and/or the desire to bring together experts to work together on all phases of a major project. For example, General Motors created task forces such as this to develop its so-called X-cars (Chevrolet Citation, etc.) in the mid- to late-1970s.

FIGURE 9–2   Matrix Organization Design

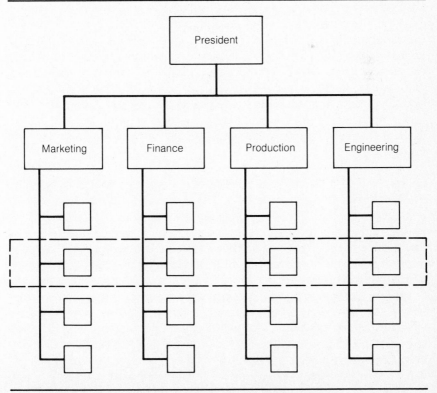

This type of work group will be called a *team* and can be described by the following generalizations:

1. The group is given a complete and meaningful task with an identifiable goal.
2. Workers in the group have specialized skills based on their functional areas of expertise. As the project moves through its various stages of development, different roles will take on more importance.
3. The group is given a reasonable degree of autonomy about the process of attaining its goal. The scheduling of activities, however, is somewhat constrained in that group members have obligations to their permanent functional groups and also to other teams to which they may have been assigned. The group may have a voice in requesting certain new members to augment and/or supplement existing members. In less frequent instances, the group may request that a member be removed from the group.
4. Compensation is a function of performance appraisals by the functional supervisor and, in many cases, relevant team leaders.

Characteristics of Work Groups

Using the group characteristics discussed earlier in this chapter, cohesiveness, norms, and role dynamics, it is possible to construct a likely profile of each type of work group. It should be noted that these profiles are intended to be descriptive as opposed to prescriptive, and represent general patterns as opposed to universal arrangements.

First, the autonomous work group is likely to exhibit a high degree of cohesiveness. Indeed, it has even been suggested that a high initial level of cohesiveness is a necessary condition for establishing this form of work group (Hackman, 1977). Simply stated, the overall nature of the autonomous work group is such that high levels of cohesiveness are fostered. For example, the members are likely to agree on the group's goals and to have a high frequency of interaction. Further, when the group is given the autonomy to select its own members, personal attraction is also likely to be high.

The autonomous work group is also likely to have high performance norms. By giving the group a considerable degree of control over its activities and rewarding members for overall group performance, the likely result will be a high level of commitment to the group. Specifically, since rewards are granted as a function of group performance, it follows that members will develop an attitude of interdependence such that each member will exert a high degree of task-related effort. High performance norms should emerge.

In terms of role dynamics, group members may experience a moderate level of role ambiguity, conflict, and/or overload. That is, since roles are varied by the group itself, it follows that any one member may perceive unclear, conflicting, or too many task-related cues from the other members. Unclear cues may lead to role ambiguity, conflicting cues to role conflict, and excess cues to role overload. On the other hand, the member also has some control, such that he or she can clarify the cues. For these reasons, then, conflict, ambiguity, and/or overload may be of moderate concern to the group and also to the manager to whom the group is responsible.

The operative work group will probably be characterized by a moderate level of cohesiveness. There will probably be a basic agreement on the group's goals. Since the members are each responsible for a specific function, however, the frequency of interaction may not be as great as for the autonomous work group. Further, since rewards will probably be individually based, a certain degree of intra-group competition may be perceived. For these reasons, cohesiveness will tend to be moderate.

Performance norms will also tend to be moderate. Since group performance probably has no effect on rewards, and may not even be assessed, the group climate is simply such that high performance norms will not be fostered. This process is also influenced by the lack of interaction among group members.

Finally, operative group members are not likely to experience significant levels of role conflict, ambiguity, or overload. Each member has a specific function in the group, thereby minimizing role conflict. Since the role is also reasonably well-defined by the organization, role ambiguity will probably not develop. Finally, while role overload may be a problem in specific instances, the general nature of the expected role in operative work groups is probably such that overload will be minimized.

The third type of work group, the team, will also tend to exhibit a moderate degree of cohesiveness. The members may not always agree on goals, the possibility of domination exists, interaction may be sporadic, and personal attractiveness may not always be favorable. On the other hand, matrix organizations may tend to stimulate a certain degree of intergroup competition among the various teams.

Performance norms of the team will tend to be quite high, however. Since members initially enter the group from different functional areas, they may feel a certain degree of responsibility for demonstrating the competence of their respective departments. The representative from marketing, for example, may feel, "I've got to show these people that we're not a bunch of door-to-door salesmen." Hence, individual pride and motivation may serve to enhance the performance norms of the group.

Finally, role dynamics may tend to be problematic for team members. Since each member has a responsibility to and a role in multiple groups, the probability of role conflict is increased. For example, a member of two different teams may be assigned specific tasks by each team. Unfortunately, time commitments to the employee's functional group may preclude the completion of both tasks on schedule. Role ambiguity may also result from unclear and ambiguous directions from team leaders. Role overload is also a potential problem, due to the number of team memberships the individual may have.

In summary, group cohesiveness will tend to be high in autonomous **189** work groups and moderate in operative work groups and teams. Performance norms will most likely be high in autonomous work groups and teams and moderate in operative work groups. Finally, the probable incidence of role dynamics problems is moderate in autonomous work groups, low in operative work groups, and high in teams. These profiles are summarized in Table 9–2.

We now turn our attention to some general guidelines for creating these various forms of work groups. The guidelines may serve to enhance cohesiveness and performance norms and minimize role dynamics problems, and also to influence the overall effectiveness of the group.

How to Design Work Groups

Of the three types of work groups under discussion, managerial practice is most understood with respect to the creation of autonomous work groups and teams. The reason for this is fairly obvious: such groups generally emerge because someone made a specific decision to create a work group. On the other hand, the operative group is seen more as a means to an end. That is, creating a group is not really an objective; rather, the manager simply realizes that using a group will be an efficient way to get a job done. For these reasons, fairly clearcut procedures for designing autonomous work groups and teams have been developed. In the following sections, we will summarize a series of guidelines for developing each of these types of groups and offer some general comments on creating operative work groups.

Designing autonomous work groups. In creating an autonomous work group, the focus is on the group itself: how to facilitate the

TABLE 9–2 Group Characteristics and Work Groups

	Autonomous Work Group	Operative Work Group	Matrix Organization Team
Probable Level of Cohesiveness	High	Moderate	Moderate
Probable Level of Performance Norms	High	Moderate	High
Probable Incidence of Role Conflict, Ambiguity, and/or Overload	Moderate	Low	High

emergence of high performance norms, minimize conflict, satisfy interpersonal needs, and so forth. Such a group may be an entirely new organizational unit, or it may be developed around an existing operative work group. The following procedures and guidelines for designing autonomous work groups have been suggested:

1. The group should be relatively small (perhaps fewer than fifteen members) so that group membership may be psychologically meaningful.
2. Pure group process interventions (i.e., sensitivity training) focusing solely on interpersonal relations or the group's social climate should be avoided, since such efforts have generally not enhanced (and occasionally have diminished) group task-effectiveness.
3. The pay system should be structured such that individual pay is determined by group performance.
4. The role of the first-line supervisor should be changed from group decision-maker to liaison with higher management and other work groups.
5. The group should be given the authority to plan, organize, and control a defined piece of work and be responsible for both the quality and quantity of its performance (Hackman, 1977).

Of course, these guidelines should be interpreted as general suggestions, not ironclad rules. The use of these guidelines does not guarantee success. The manager must diagnose the existing work system, determine if the use of autonomous work groups is warranted, assess the relevant organizational factors, and then modify, delete, and/or expand upon these guidelines as need be.

Designing teams. In designing a work team, the emphasis should be on integrating the group into the organizational system: balancing the multiple role requirements of the group members, facilitating inter-group communication and coordination, etc. The suggested guidelines for creating teams are:

1. A reasonably large proportion of the team's membership should consist of the line managers who will be responsible for the implementation of the team's output.
2. Team members must have all relevant information made available to them.
3. A team member should have the power to commit his or her department to a course of action relevant to the team's mission.
4. The team must utilize an influence system based on expertise.
5. Lateral organization processes (i.e., teams) should be integrated into vertical organizational processes (i.e., functional departments).
6. Team members should be selected based on dual qualifications: task-relevant expertise and interpersonal skills (Galbraith, 1977).

At this point, a caveat is in order. Many of the preceding guidelines and other points in our discussion of teams may be somewhat unclear to the reader who is not familiar with matrix organizations. Unfortunately, we are faced with a Catch-22 situation. On the one hand, a discussion of group-based task design processes would be incomplete without an analysis of teams or project groups. On the other hand, an in-depth discussion of matrix organizations was clearly beyond the scope of this book. We have **191** attempted to offer a balanced treatment, and hope that the reader has benefited. For more information on matrix organizations, the interested reader should consult Galbraith (1971) and/or Davis and Lawrence (1977).

Designing operative work groups. As indicated earlier, relatively little attention has been focused on proper techniques for designing operative work groups. As a result, general guidelines do not exist. The manager responsible for such a group, however, might be advised to consider the following suggestions:

1. The group should be designed in such a way as to facilitate and enhance group cohesiveness (i.e., avoid intra-group competition, encourage interaction, etc.).
2. The group should be designed in such a way as to foster the emergence of high performance norms (i.e., reward group performance if possible, assign highly productive employees to the group, etc.).
3. The group should be designed so as to minimize the likelihood of role conflict, ambiguity, and/or overload (i.e., create well-defined roles, etc.).

The bulk of this chapter to this point has been concerned with general characteristics of groups and the nature of various types of work groups. It might also be useful to look now at how task design considerations and group processes have operated in real organizations. Our next section summarizes three examples of how real organizations have, with varying degrees of success, managed task design and group process interactions.

TASK DESIGN AND GROUP PROCESSES: CASE STUDIES

The three cases below were selected to provide representative insights into managerial practice vis-a-vis task design and group processes. The cases provide examples of successful, moderately successful, and unsuccessful interactions between these two important sets of variables.

Volvo Kalmar Plant

The Volvo plant at Kalmar, Sweden, briefly summarized in Chapter 3, began production in 1971. In response to extremely high levels of turnover and absenteeism and numerous wildcat strikes, Volvo management, led by Pehr Gyllenhammar, designed the Kalmar plant so as to offset many of the negative factors associated with traditional assembly-line work. Using results obtained from two preliminary studies, one in the upholstery department of an automobile plant and the other in a truck assembly plant, the Kalmar facility was designed to integrate the technical and social systems (see Chapter 6 for a discussion of socio-technical systems theory) of the plant through the use of autonomous work groups.

A cross-sectional diagram of part of the plant is presented in Figure 9–3. Specific characteristics of the plant can be summarized as follows:

FIGURE 9–3   Volvo Kalmar Plant

1. Stores.
2. Body buffers.
3. Material intake by electric trucks.
4. Preassembly.
5. Materials.
6. Bodies (on the left, stationary; on the right, moving).
7. Pause area.
8. Toilets, etc.
9. Changing rooms.

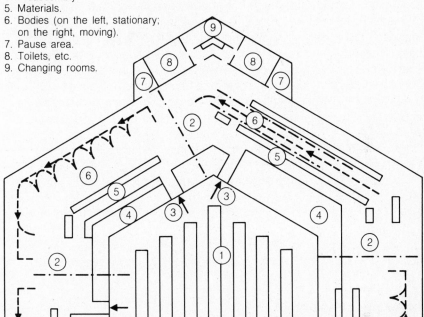

1. Each production bay is designed to provide the feeling of being in a small workshop. For example, large windows along the outer walls provide natural light, and each bay has separate lounge and rest facilities.
2. Automobiles being assembled are mounted on computer-controlled trolleys that roll along the floor. If problems arise, an automobile can be pulled out of the production flow for more work. The trolley can also be tilted in order to facilitate work underneath the automobile.
3. The work is performed by autonomous work groups ranging in size from 15 to 25 members. Each group has a general set of tasks, such as upholstery, wiring, etc. The group itself determines which members will perform which tasks and can pause or speed up their work pace as long as they keep up with the general production flow.
4. Computers display hourly productivity rates onto display screens. Hence, the groups receive almost instant feedback.

Results of this arrangement have been generally favorable, although some negative factors also emerged. For example, the plant itself cost more to construct and has lower capacity than a conventional plant. Volvo management, however, argues that the benefits far outweigh the costs. **193**

Further, the production system is actually quite consistent with the company's high-cost / low-volume marketing strategy.

In summary, the Volvo experience is essentially a success. The organization, via the use of autonomous work groups, took advantage of primary group processes to facilitate overall effectiveness. Highly cohesive groups with high performance norms and (apparently) few role dynamics problems have been developed and maintained. It can also be speculated that such favorable conditions probably result in group members continually reinforcing the positive attributes of the situation for other group members. That is, from the SIP perspective, group members probably provide and receive favorable social and informational cues regarding their task situation. Overall, then, Volvo structured contextual variables so as to accomplish the organization's objectives. Technology, organization, design, leader behavior, and group processes were all managed so as to facilitate both the objective structuring of jobs and the informal network of interpersonal processes.

While some evidence exists that work arrangements that are appropriate in one country may not be appropriate in another (cf., Foy and Gadon, 1976), this company has recorded an impressive development in matching task design and group processes. As we shall see, not all experiments have been as successful (this section is based on Dowling, 1973; Gibson, 1973; Gyllenhammar, 1977; and Szilagyi and Wallace, 1980).

Topeka Pet Food Plant

In January 1971, General Foods Corporation opened a Gaines Pet Food plant in Topeka, Kansas. The plant had been in the design and construction phases since 1968. General Foods managers had wanted to create a plant which would not be characterized by the same levels of worker alienation and dissatisfaction found in existing plants (i.e., they had the same goals as Volvo). With the assistance of behavioral consultant Richard E. Walton, they established a number of innovative design characteristics for the new plant, including:

1. *Autonomous Work Groups*. Work groups consisting of from seven to fourteen employees and a team leader were established as a basis for organizing work. Each group was given responsibility for a large segment of the production system. The group decided which members would perform which tasks. Finally, the group as a whole selected new members when someone left and took responsibility for developing the capabilities of both new and old members.
2. *Challenging Job Assignments*. Each group task was designed so as to provide a number of challenging, stimulating jobs, although certain nonchallenging jobs (i.e., the forklift operation) could not be eliminated.
3. *Job Mobility and Rewards for Learning*. The pay system was designed so that employees were rewarded for learning other jobs within the group and then other jobs outside of the group. Group members were, in effect, rewarded for learning more and more elements of the plant's overall operations.

4. *Facilitative Leadership*. The role of first-line supervisors was to facilitate group development and decision-making processes.
5. *Self-Government*. Instead of developing an initial set of rules and regulations, plant management allowed only the most necessary guidelines to emerge as needed.
6. *Status Symbols and Physical Environment*. Common status systems such as preferential parking for managers, plush offices, and segregated rest areas were not utilized. Further, the plant itself was laid out so as to facilitate and encourage ad hoc gatherings for both social interaction and also work coordination.
7. *Information Availability*. All relevant economic information and managerial decision guidelines were made available to all appropriate operating employees. This facilitated a high degree of decentralization within the plant (Walton, 1972).

In addition to these specific design characteristics, other elements of the overall process also facilitated this innovative production system. For example, employee hiring decisions were based primarily on factors such as a history of initiative, decision-making ability, and the ability to work as a group member. Further, the plant was not unionized. Finally, the plant was small, new, and geographically isolated, allowing new procedures to be implemented with relatively little difficulty.

After some initial adjustments, the operation at Topeka began to compile a generally favorable economic record. For example, plant fixed overhead was 33% lower than traditional plants, quality rejects were reduced by 92%, morale was good and absenteeism was low, and both the plant's safety record and its turnover rate were excellent.

Over the years, however, a number of problems began to creep into the system. One basic reason that this happened was that the plant was not congruent with the total organizational system. In a sense, the Topeka operation was a round peg among a group of square pegs and square holes. As new employees entered the system and as managers were transferred in and out of the plant, they were not adequately integrated into the existing social network. Group cohesiveness began to decline, as did performance norms. Role conflict and ambiguity became more common.

A substantial portion of the autonomy of the work groups was eliminated. So, too, were the self-government and self-development systems. The existing conditions in the plant have been referred to as a "Steady State with Traces of Erosion" (Walton, 1978). The present situation seems to lie somewhere in between a true autonomous work group arrangement (which was the original situation) and a collection of operative work groups.

From another point of view, the SIP framework also helps explain the declines at Topeka. As previously provided responsibilities and privileges such as autonomy, self-development, and so forth were eliminated, morale problems probably arose. As workers began to discuss and criticize these events, they evidently reinforced their own diminished satisfaction. That is, rather than enhancing the work situation, social and informational cues here may have been oriented primarily toward undesirable attributes of the situation, with the result being perceptions slightly less positive than was the case initially.

195

In summary, then, the Topeka plant represents a moderately successful integration of task design and group process elements. Although the system has moved somewhat away from its original arrangement and philosophy, a generally positive situation still exists. We now turn our attention to our final case, one characterized by much greater incongruence between task design characteristics and group processes (this section was developed from Walton, 1972, 1975; Schrank, 1974).

Lordstown Vega Plant

The Lordstown plant of General Motors Corporation was designed to be the most efficient automobile assembly facility in the world. The plant covers over fifty acres, has eighteen miles of conveyor belts, and can turn out over 100 new cars per hour (in contrast to an industry average of 50 to 60 per hour). The labor force averages between 24 and 25 years of age, making it the youngest of any GM facility. Specific aspects of the plant were designed to improve normal working conditions in automobile plants. For example, many of the most difficult jobs were automated.

Yet, rather than being a productivity showplace, Lordstown has been the scene of strikes and sabotage, and problems at the plant have been documented in *The New York Times* and *Playboy*. Near-riots have occurred and millions of General Motors dollars have disappeared in lost production. The factors contributing to these problems are at the same time simple and complex, and the task design–group process interactions are somewhat subtle.

The Lordstown plant is operated by GM's Assembly Division (GMAD), recognized for its emphasis on efficiency and productivity. Over the years since the plant was opened, management has tried to boost output by cutting the number of people on the assembly line and increasing the number of operations the individual was responsible for (it should be noted that these efforts were not aimed at increasing task variety; rather, the worker was simply expected to insert twenty bolts rather than ten, and so forth).

The Walker and Guest (1952) study found automobile workers to be essentially satisfied with factors such as pay and benefits, but very dissatisfied with the nature of their jobs. Twenty years later, Lordstown workers expressed the same sentiments, only more vocally.

Workers at the plant rebelled because of a number of factors: (1) they claimed to be more motivated than older auto workers; hence, they wanted different treatment, (2) they felt that GM was breaking agreements by setting specific production levels and then raising them after they were met, and (3) they felt that the high pace of production virtually eliminated social interaction, freedom to leave the line even for a moment, and so forth. Their reactions to these complaints, as indicated earlier, included strikes and sabotage. Also, the workers developed an informal group-oriented approach to work, which forms the specific basis for our discussion of task design and group process interactions at Lordstown.

This group approach to work probably began by accident. A likely scenario involves one worker doing his own job and also covering for the co-worker beside him while that person went to the bathroom. Afterward, the second employee did both tasks while the other took a short break. The system evolved into a fairly standard procedure, which the workers named "doubling."

In its fully developed form, doubling involves a number of workers, typically four, creating an informal work group. For a certain period of time, normally 15 to 30 minutes, two of the workers work at a very rapid pace and perform *all* of the tasks assigned to the four individuals. Meanwhile, the other two workers are free to rest, talk, make phone calls, and so forth. When the designated time has elapsed, the workers switch roles. Hence, during a normal day, a given worker may work four hours at an extremely fast pace and have four hours of leisure time.

The workers themselves claim that performance does not suffer because of doubling. Specifically, they argue that the two members of the group who are working at any particular time must pay more attention to the various tasks. As a result, quality does not suffer and may even improve. Quality, as well as morale, was also felt to be improved as a result of the increased flexibility and social interaction.

GMAD, on the other hand, strongly opposed the concept of doubling. They felt that a worker getting paid should be working and not socializing. Further, it was argued that the increased effort when a group member was doing the work of two employees was sufficiently great as to hurt performance by the end of the day due to fatigue. Workers who were caught doubling were generally given disciplinary layoffs.

The basic implication to be drawn from the Lordstown plant relates to the clash between the technical and social systems of an organization. The plant was evidently designed to maximize the potential of the technical system with little thought for the social system. Forces within the social system, however, emerged in the form of informal work groups attempting to meet the technical requirements of the organization while simultaneously attending to the social needs of the workers. When the technical system, represented by GMAD, attempted to eliminate or constrain the social system, major conflicts arose. It seems that management, then, had failed to anticipate the potential power generated by groups within the organization and had also failed to capitalize on this power.

In summary, it should be noted that the Lordstown situation was extremely complex and that a variety of interpretations have been offered. We have focused primarily on one small segment of the overall problem because this one segment is relevant for understanding task design and group and social processes in organizations (this section was based on Miles, 1980; Kreman, 1973).

Summary and Conclusions

The preceding sections have summarized how task design and group processes have operated in harmony and conflict in three different organizational settings. Two factors prohibit the situations from being directly comparable. First, General Foods and Volvo created work for groups in order to balance the technical and social systems, while General Motors created work for individuals and attempted to ignore the social system in general and group processes in particular. Second, the fact that the Volvo plant is in another country precludes us from having as much relevant information as might be desired.

Three conclusions, however, do seem to be appropriate. First, the use of groups as a basis for organizing work (i.e., autonomous or operative work groups) appears to be a reasonable and effective alternative in some settings. While technology may somewhat constrain what an organization can do, the Volvo case illustrates that even in a capital-intensive industry such as automobile manufacturing, task design arrangements can be improved. (One could argue that it was easy for Volvo to adopt this approach because it was building a new plant. However, another Swedish firm, Saab-Scandia, successfully introduced the autonomous work group concept into an existing facility.)

Second, in order to be truly effective, the work group arrangement must be integrated into the *total* organizational system. The problems arising at Topeka, for example, were generally brought about by an incompatible work group system (the plant) and organization structure (General Foods). The organization must focus not only on designing tasks for groups, but also on either designing the organization structure to accommodate the work group arrangements or else designing the groups to function within the constraints of the existing organization. Chapter 7 provides more information on organization and task design considerations.

Finally, even when the organization cannot and/or will not use groups as a basis for organizing work, it must not ignore the role that basic social needs and general group characteristics such as cohesiveness, norms, and role dynamics play in the workplace. General Motors has learned this lesson all too well. The organization must attempt to balance the economic needs of the technical system with the interpersonal needs of the social system.

SUMMARY

This chapter has described interrelationships among task design and group and social process variables. First, we discussed the social information processing framework of task design. We then described the basic group characteristics of cohesiveness, norms, and role dynamics. Next, we summarized three methods for organizing work at the group level: autonomous work groups, operative work groups, and matrix organization teams. Finally, we analyzed three examples of how organizations, with varying degrees of success, have dealt with task design–group process interactions.

In general, the SIP framework appears to be of considerable importance in task design. The framework is well developed conceptually and consistently supported by research. Unfortunately, it is also somewhat abstract; therefore, managerial implications and potential uses of the approach are still somewhat limited. The more observable and better understood characteristics of cohesion, norms, and roles may be of more immediate value in actually utilizing task design techniques in group settings.

In the last five chapters, we have discussed a number of techniques for measuring relevant task properties and have attempted to integrate task design processes with four major categories of organizational variables: technology, organization structure and design, leader behavior, and group processes. In our next chapter, we focus on the more applied issues of actually planning, implementing, and evaluating task redesign programs in organizations. The framework to be developed suggests the importance of evaluating and understanding how and why the various measurement techniques and aspects of technology, structure, leaders, and groups must be considered by organizations if redesign programs are to be more generally successful.

10 IMPLEMENTING TASK REDESIGN

At various times throughout this book, we have referred to managers redesigning jobs within their organizations. Usually, these references were rather cursory in nature. The primary reason why the actual redesign process has been treated at such a general level is the author's belief that task redesign efforts must be framed in an appropriate organizational context. That is, task redesign processes influence and are influenced by a complex network of organizational factors, including the task itself, the employee, the organization's technology, the organization's structure and design, leader behaviors, and group and social processes. A manager who one day decides to introduce task redesign in his or her organization, wants to start the next day, and anticipates being finished the following day is likely to be in for several surprises.

Before meaningful task changes can be developed, contextual variables must be considered. The last several chapters have helped provide an understanding as to how task design variables interact with primary contextual elements. At this point, then, we are ready to focus on the more complex issue of how task design and redesign processes relate to this complete network.

First, we will describe the general organization change perspective. We will then discuss an implementation procedure derived from the job characteristics theory (Hackman and Oldham, 1976, 1980). Finally, a more complete implementation framework, developed from the integrative material presented in the last several chapters, will be presented and described in detail.

AN ORGANIZATION CHANGE PERSPECTIVE

This section will outline the general nature of planned organizational change. We will briefly examine the primary factors or elements that cause organizations and managers to contemplate change, general approaches to planned change, the basic steps which should be followed in most planned change efforts, and common factors that cause problems in many change attempts.

Reasons for Change

Six basic factors serve to stimulate most planned organizational change attempts. It should be noted that some overlap may exist among these various stimuli, but each can also be a unique factor to consider. The following paragraphs outline the six factors.

Changing technology. As discussed in Chapter 6, technology refers to the conversion process which organizations utilize to transform inputs into outputs. In order to remain effective, many organizations find it necessary to maintain state-of-the-art transformation processes. That is, as new and more efficient production methods are developed, organizations are inclined to change from outdated procedures to the newer methods. For example, as the number of ways in which plastic parts can be used increases, firms that previously made products from metal, wood, and/or glass may find it useful to convert to plastics. Production with plastics, however, generally involves different production processes and, therefore, a change in technology.

Changing environment. Another primary stimulus for organizational change is environmental change. New competitors, shifts in the economy, and/or changes in consumer preferences may all bring about organizational change. For example, when K-Mart demonstrated in the early 1960s that discounting was a viable retailing strategy, other merchants such as Woolworth, Wards, Sears, and Penneys were forced to shift their own positions. Hence, a change in the environment may dictate organizational change.

Quality of work life. Quality of work life, as discussed in Chapter 1, refers to the quality of an individual's experiences within an organization. Organizations, labor unions, and the federal government all seem to be concerned about the potential problems associated with widespread worker alienation. Therefore, managers are occasionally motivated to change organizational practices simply to enhance the quality of employee work life for the purpose of minimizing alienation.

Organizational problems. A related situation that may stimulate organization change is some sort of problem that the organization must **201**

deal with. Many such problems seem to be behavioral in nature. Examples include declining morale, increased turnover and/or absenteeism, increased conflict, poor communication, and decreased productivity. Of course, these situations are generally the result of some other problem, but it is these factors (actually, symptoms of the larger problem) that catch the manager's attention. Hence, it may be felt that a change is necessary to rectify the situation.

Changing work force.   Changes in the work force from which the organization draws its human resources may also bring about organization change. The most obvious example of this process is the influx of women into previously male-dominated occupations. Organizations must react to this either directly or indirectly by modifying selection criteria, reward systems, and socialization processes. Even physical facilities such as the "executive washroom" may require change.

Government.   A final major stimulus for organizational change is the government. As the government, through its legislative, executive, and judicial branches, enacts new laws and modifies existing ones, affected organizations must react. The usual reaction is change. For example, when the Occupational Safety and Health Act was passed, most large manufacturing firms found it necessary to change a number of existing work procedures and create a system to deal with the corresponding paperwork.

Approaches to Change

Managers and behavioral scientists have developed a variety of planned change approaches and techniques. At a general level, these approaches can be categorized as focusing on the individuals within organizations, on organizational structures and systems, and on organizational climate and interpersonal dynamics (Porter, Lawler, and Hackman, 1975).

People-oriented change.   One way to change people in organizations is to physically substitute one individual or group for another. For example, selection criteria can be modified such that people with different skills and abilities are brought into the organization. At the same time, existing members of the organization may be phased out by termination, transfer, and/or attrition. Skills and abilities of existing employees can also be changed through training and development activities. Finally, attempts can be made at changing employee motives such as need for achievement (McClelland, 1965).

Structure and systems change.   Structure and systems changes refer to modifications to either the design of the organization itself and/or to major systems within the organization. Structural changes might include a move toward increased decentralization, adopting a matrix form of organization, and so forth. Primary systems that may be the focus of a change effort are the technical system (technology), the work system (task redesign), the reward system, and/or the control system.

Climate and interpersonal change.   Climate and interpersonal change efforts generally attempt to modify such things as communication processes, conflict resolution strategies, and other behavioral variables. Examples of techniques with these objectives include survey feedback, transactional analysis, sensitivity training, and team building.

Steps in the Change Process

Regardless of the type of planned change technique being utilized, the implementation process itself is very important. The actual steps that are appropriate may vary from setting to setting, but they generally follow five phases.

Problem recognition.   Most managers recognize the need for change via data gathered for routine organizational purposes. Declines in productivity and increases in turnover, absenteeism, and grievances may all trigger change. Information from environmental agents and/or boundary spanners may also suggest the need for change. For example, these sources may suggest new technological breakthroughs relevant to the organization.

Diagnosis.   After a manager has recognized that a problem exists, the next task is to ascertain what the context of the situation is. Specifically, things like productivity declines and turnover increases may be symptomatic of broader problems such as a poor organizational climate. New technological processes must also be evaluated from a cost/benefit perspective.

In the former situation, the diagnosis may take the form of personal observation by the manager, interviews, informal discussion, and/or questionnaires. Questionnaires, especially, are used quite often. The Job Diagnostic Survey (Hackman and Oldham, 1975), discussed in Chapter 5, might be used to assess levels of perceived task characteristics, motivation, satisfaction, and so forth. Data obtained from such a survey would provide the manager with information relevant to the decision at hand. Cost/benefit analysis of a technological innovation would simply involve comparing the costs associated with the potential change with the expected benefits to be derived from the change.

Selection of change technique.   This phase of the change process, as the name suggests, involves selecting the appropriate intervention to alleviate the problem. Based on the results of the diagnosis, the manager might choose one or more change strategies with the objective of enhancing individuals, organizational structures and systems, and/or climate and interpersonal processes. Strategies that have been popular in the past, **203**

and that continue to be used by many organizations, include sensitivity training, Management by Objectives, and job enrichment. At the present time, task redesign appears to be one of the more widely considered change techniques.

Implementation.   Once a manager has selected the appropriate change strategy or strategies, the next step is to actually implement the change. There can be no uniform procedure outlined for implementing a change technique, because the appropriate method is a function of the unique characteristics of the manager and the organization. At a general level, however, it can be noted that the implementation process should proceed in a logical fashion and be designed in such a way as to minimize potential problems and disruptions (some of these will be discussed later).

Evaluation.   The fifth phase of a planned change effort is to evaluate the effectiveness of the change relative to its objectives. For example, in the case of task redesign, the objectives of the change are generally to alter the nature of tasks, thereby improving employee reactions. To know whether or not these objectives were met, it is usually necessary to obtain measures of both tasks and employee reactions before and after the change is implemented. This will usually enable the manager to determine the effectiveness of the change. Unfortunately, rigorous evaluation is probably the single most neglected aspect of planned organization change.

Barriers to Success

As indicated earlier, planned change techniques should be implemented so as to overcome obstacles and barriers to their success. One primary barrier to many change attempts is employee resistance to change. Many people resist attempts at change because they fear the unknown, they are afraid the change will hurt them economically, they do not want existing social relationships disrupted, and so forth. At a more general level, organizational factors such as organization structure (recall that in Chapter 7, we suggested that it would be easier to implement task redesign in an organic organization than in a mechanistic organization) and resource limitations may constrain or hinder change processes. Other common reasons that planned change may be less than successful include:

1. An incorrect diagnosis of the nature of the actual problem may occur.
2. The objective(s) of the planned change may not be clearly understood.
3. Management may not be totally committed to the change.
4. Management may have unrealistic expectations as to the potential benefits of the change.

Of course, there is no way to guarantee that all of these problems and barriers can be overcome. By proper planning and diagnosis, however, their incidence may be minimized.

In this section, we have looked at organization change from a broad, general perspective. The next section presents a particular change framework developed for implementing task redesign in organizations. After summarizing and critiquing this framework, we will discuss an alternative viewpoint that includes a wider variety of organizational factors.

HACKMAN AND OLDHAM IMPLEMENTATION FRAMEWORK

Back in Chapter 3, we briefly examined how Hackman and Oldham's (1976, 1980) job characteristics theory was implemented. At this point, we will look at this approach in somewhat more detail. The Hackman and Oldham framework is summarized in Table 10–1. Essentially, the framework suggests that task redesign efforts revolve around five basic choices managers and organizations must make when contemplating a change.

Five Choices in the Hackman and Oldham Framework

The first choice is whether to make the task change at the individual level or the group level. Inherent in this choice are three other decisions that must be made. First, the manager must ascertain the extent to which there is a *need* for task redesign. For example, there may be a problem involving employee motivation, satisfaction, or work effectiveness, and task redesign may be viewed as a viable solution. Second, the manager must determine the extent to which task redesign is feasible. This decision must be made in the context of existing organizational variables such as technology, climate, and so forth. Finally, the choice must then be made as to whether to focus the redesign effort at the individual level or the group level.

The second choice that must be made is whether to adopt theory-based or intuitive change. Theory-based change might be approached from any of several different frameworks, including Herzberg's two-factor

TABLE 10–1 Hackman and Oldham Implementation Framework

Choice One: Individual versus Group Designs for Work
  Step One: Is there a Need for Work Redesign?
  Step Two: Is Work Redesign Feasible?
      —Feasibility of Enriching Individual Jobs
      —Feasibility of Creating Self-Managing Work Groups
  Step Three: Choosing Between Individual and Group Designs
Choice Two: Theory-Based versus Intuitive Changes
Choice Three: Tailored versus Broadside Installation
Choice Four: Participative versus Top-Down Change Processes
Choice Five: Consultation versus Collaboration with Stakeholders

---

Source: Adapted from Hackman/Oldham, *Work Redesign*, © 1980 Addison-Wesley, Reading, Massachusetts, pp. 222–235. Reprinted with permission.

theory or Hackman and Oldham's job characteristics theory (both of these perspectives were discussed in Chapter 3). Hackman and Oldham (1980) suggest that, in general, theory-based change may be less crucial when the organization is using a knowledgeable and experienced change agent. Alternatively, the use of a well-developed theoretical framework will be more useful when the change agent needs more guidance and direction.

Next, the manager must decide whether to use a tailored or broadside installation. A tailored approach would be one in which task changes were developed so as to correspond with characteristics of individual employees, whereas a broadside approach is one in which all employees receive the same degree of redesign. Hackman and Oldham argue that the appropriate choice is a function of the nature of work technology, the homogeneity of the work force in terms of individual differences, and the management philosophy of key decision makers. For example, a highly structured and mechanized technology, a very homogeneous work force, and/or a very conservative management philosophy might indicate a need for a broadside approach to change.

The fourth choice to be made relates to the degree of participation to be allowed in decisions pertaining to the change. Important situational variables for this choice include: (1) who has the information needed for effective task change, (2) the degree of potential acceptance or rejection by job holders of changes imposed by management, and (3) the degree to which employees can be trusted to develop appropriate changes.

Finally, the decision must be made as to whether to use consultation as opposed to collaboration with stakeholders. Stakeholders include first-line supervisors, union officials, and employees in contiguous units such as personnel, departments supplying work to the focal unit, and so forth. A consultative approach would involve limited involvement by such stakeholders, whereas a collaborative approach would include much more stakeholder involvement.

The consultative approach would typically include management designing, implementing, and directing the work change efforts; union officials would simply be informed about project purposes and plans and invited to react (Hackman and Oldham, 1980, p. 236). In contrast, full collaboration would involve management and union officials serving as full partners in the total project.

Beyond these five choices, Hackman and Oldham (1980) also offer a number of general speculations intended to relate to the issue of "doing it right" as opposed to "getting it done." For example, they raise the issues of planning time frames, the use of external consultants, and evaluation. Their conclusions are that, "It usually is better to risk not doing a project for which the tough issues cannot be resolved beforehand than to do one under circumstances that require compromise after compromise to keep the project alive after it has begun" (p. 243).

Hackman and Oldham Framework: A Critique

Richard Hackman, working in collaboration with Greg Oldham, has probably done more than any contemporary writer to focus the attention of managers and researchers on issues of work design in organizations. The implementation framework summarized above is derived from the job characteristics theory (Hackman and Oldham, 1976). The framework has a number of strengths and, unfortunately, also suffers from some weaknesses. First, we will summarize the strengths.

As noted above, the framework is derived from a well-developed theory; hence, it overcomes one of the primary shortcomings of the job enrichment technique. The framework is accompanied by a complete instrumentation package, the JDS. While the JDS may suffer some potential psychometric deficiencies (e.g., Dunham, Aldag, and Brief, 1977), it is still superior to most assessment instruments. Third, the framework suggests a number of reasonable and logical decisions managers must make in implementing task redesign.

However, it is on this last point that the framework also suffers its greatest shortcoming. Hackman and Oldham are careful to point out that contextual factors such as the technological system may constrain potential task changes. However, they don't discuss other important characteristics such as the organization's design or leader behavior processes. Further, they don't specifically explain how or why such constraints operate, nor do they directly acknowledge that the same factors may also *facilitate* task changes in some instances. Finally, the Hackman and Oldham approach doesn't address the possibility of reciprocal interactions. For example, they don't really deal with the potential impact of task changes on other contextual elements.

In summary, the Hackman and Oldham implementation framework is useful from a number of perspectives. At the same time, however, it is also couched in such general and imprecise terms that managers may be at a loss when trying to follow it. In our next section, we will present an alternative approach to implementing task redesign in organizations. While this framework is also not without fault, it does attempt to describe more explicitly expected relationships among task design processes and the primary contextual variables of technology, organization design, leader behavior, and group and social processes.

AN INTEGRATIVE IMPLEMENTATION FRAMEWORK

The previous several chapters of this book have focused on contextual variables and processes that may be associated with basic task design considerations. We now explain how the manager may contend with these and other issues when dealing with task design in organizations. The basic **207**

TABLE 10–2   An Integrative Framework for Implementing Task Redesign in Organizations

Step 1: Recognition of a need for change
Step 2: Selection of task redesign as a potential intervention
Step 3: Diagnosis of the work system and context
  a. Diagnosis of existing jobs
  b. Diagnosis of existing work force
  c. Diagnosis of technology
  d. Diagnosis of organization design
  e. Diagnosis of leader behaviors
  f. Diagnosis of group and social processes
Step 4: Cost/Benefit analysis of proposed changes
Step 5: Go/No-go decision
Step 6: Establishing the strategy for redesign
Step 7: Implementing the task changes
Step 8: Implementing any supplemental changes
Step 9: Evaluation of the task redesign effort

implementation framework proposed here suggests that a well-developed integrative approach to task redesign will follow nine important steps. These steps are summarized in Table 10–2.

Before describing these steps, however, one additional point is in order. At any or all times in the process, the activities and decisions may be carried out by the manager. However, the manager may also rely on external consultants, internal consultants, task forces, committees, and/or informal discussion groups. The extent to which such assistance is appropriate will generally be a function of the manager's expertise, the scope of the situation, expectations of other organizational members, and so forth. We now turn our attention to a discussion of each of the implementation steps presented in Table 10–2.

Recognizing the Need for Change

The first step in the overall process of task redesign should be the recognition that some form of change is necessary. It is not likely, for example, that a manager will simply decide one day that some task design changes are needed. Rather, some work-related factor or set of factors will typically serve as a stimulus for this recognition. Several potential stimuli may be identified. First, the manager may observe measurable changes in outcome variables. Absenteeism and turnover may increase, productivity may begin to decline, and/or there may be more grievances filed.

Second, indirect indicators of outcome variables may also change. For example, supervisors may begin to hear more worker comments and/or complaints about the work being performed, or they may become aware of decreases in employee effort (e.g., motivation).

Third, an organization that competes for the same employees may make significant and positive changes that increase the attractiveness of its jobs. The focal organization may have to make corresponding changes in order to continue to attract and retain a quality group of employees.

Fourth, the organization may be forced to make changes because of changes in the nature of the work force. That is, the values, mores, and expectations of the work force may shift such that organizational changes are mandated. For example, during the early 1980s, the United States economy was plagued by high inflation and high unemployment (especially in the northern industrial states). During times like these, workers may focus most attention on increasing their salaries to keep pace with the cost of living, while also recognizing their limited employment alternatives. Hence, they may accept jobs that are not particularly well designed. When (and if) the economic picture changes, however, these same workers may demand jobs that are designed to be more satisfying and fulfilling. Further, organizations may be forced to enhance job quality in order to compete for better employees.

Another cause of change might be a technological breakthrough (e.g., the availability of new machines and/or more efficient production processes) that necessitates the introduction of new work methods. To remain competitive, the firm may have to acquire these new work methods. Other changes, in turn, may then be dictated.

A final reason for change may be a general concern for the quality of work life in the organization. Granted, the organization may expect to receive some benefits in return for a better quality of work life for its employees (i.e., avoiding unionization, increasing motivation and/or performance, etc.). Overall, however, the manager may simply decide that the work environment needs to be changed in order to develop a better work experience for employees.

Selection of the Intervention

After the manager has recognized that some sort of change is needed, she or he must then determine the appropriate intervention. The selection of the intervention will be a function of a number of different factors, including the manager's values and preferences, the nature of the problem, and so forth. In addition to task redesign, other change interventions frequently utilized in organizations include Management by Objectives, training and development, survey feedback, organization design, career planning, and the Managerial Grid.

For some change situations, task redesign may be the only alternative. For example, if the change is prompted by the development of new work methods, the use of such methods may dictate certain task changes. In other situations, task redesign may be the "most logical" intervention. If employees are complaining about monotonous and boring jobs, for example, task redesign efforts would seem to be the most appropriate strategy (to the extent that such complaints are not merely symptomatic of larger problems). In some situations, task redesign may be only one of several "equally" reasonable interventions. If motivational problems have

209

arisen, task redesign may be one solution; however, MBO or survey feedback may be equally successful (or unsuccessful) in improving conditions. Finally, some problems will clearly call for interventions other than task redesign. If work force values, for example, are centering on economic and job security factors, then improvements in the reward system and/or benefit package may be the obvious solution. In summary, the manager's expertise, experience, and insights will be crucial at this stage of the process. He or she must assess the situation, bringing to bear all relevant information, and determine the most appropriate intervention strategy.

Diagnosis of the Work System and Context

If the manager decides that task redesign is the most appropriate strategy, the next step will be an in-depth diagnosis of the work system and work context. It is at this point that many of the topics discussed in the previous chapters become particularly important. The crucial questions to be answered at this stage are: (1) will task redesign mesh with the existing work system and context and (2) will the existing work system and context constrain or facilitate task redesign? An adequate diagnosis of the primary elements of the work system and context should provide answers to these questions.

Diagnosis of existing jobs.   As a preliminary step, an assessment should be made of jobs within the organization as they are currently designed. That is, the manager should develop an understanding of what it is that is going to be changed. Several strategies for this diagnosis could be developed. Three specific approaches, however, seem most reasonable.

First, employees may be asked to complete a questionnaire designed to measure perceived task characteristics. Instruments discussed in Chapter 5, such as the Job Diagnostic Survey (Hackman and Oldham, 1975) and/or the Job Characteristics Inventory (Sims, Szilagyi, and Keller, 1976), might be appropriate. The advantages to this technique are: (1) the manager gathers information from employees whose jobs are at issue, (2) the data that is obtained may be used for statistical analysis purposes, and (3) results may be compared to existing normative data (e.g., Hackman and Oldham, 1980). However, disadvantages also exist: (1) questions designed to measure task characteristics may artificially prompt distorted answers (e.g., Salancik and Pfeffer, 1977) and (2) any paper-and-pencil technique is subject to psychometric deficiencies.

A second technique for diagnosing jobs would involve the manager (perhaps with the assistance of other managers and/or supervisors) developing the assessment from personal observation and experience. Specifically, the manager (working alone or with other managers) would study the jobs and ascertain their form or type of design. The advantages of this technique are that it would be relatively efficient and would also make use of the manager's expertise. The disadvantages include the possibility that bias on the part of the manager might be problematic and that this method does not involve the employees whose jobs are subject to change.

The final primary task diagnostic tool would focus on a committee composed of the manager(s) and representatives from the labor force. The group would use interviews, discussions, personal experience, observation, job analysis and evaluation, and work measurement to formulate the task assessment. The advantages to this approach would include the following: (1) the technique utilizes the workers themselves, (2) the manager's expertise is also brought to bear on the issue, and (3) psychometric problems are avoided. On the other hand, the following disadvantages may arise: (1) the group process will probably take longer than either of the first two techniques discussed and (2) quantifiable data may not be obtained.

In summary, three primary techniques are suggested for diagnosing existing tasks in the organization. These techniques are worker responses to a questionnaire, the manager's personal assessment, and a management-worker committee. The appropriate technique for a given setting should be determined by the manager and selected as a function of the manager's skills and preferences, past practices in the organization, and so forth.

Diagnosis of existing work force. Diagnosing existing jobs is probably the most important phase of this process; however, diagnosing existing employees is also very important. The primary objective at this point is to determine those aspects of the individual-task interface that need improving. One aspect of interest would relate to affective factors. Specifically, the manager tries to determine how motivated and satisfied employees currently are, how motivated and satisfied they want to be, and what task elements are most likely to bring about this improvement.

The other factors would involve cognitive and behavioral processes such as skill levels and current performance. For example, the assumption may be that employees can't take full advantage of their skills and abilities in their current jobs (i.e., they are not being challenged). This assessment, then, would involve determining the extent to which relevant skills are currently being used, the extent to which they should be used, and appropriate task elements for facilitating an improved match.

The techniques for assessing individuals would be the same as for assessing tasks. Questionnaires could provide insights into current and desired levels of satisfaction and motivation, managers could assess task-skill congruence, and/or worker-manager groups could provide assessments of all relevant variables. Again, the appropriate technique would be a function of situational variables.

At this point, the manager should have an "ideal" framework for the **211** projected task redesign effort. However, tasks and individuals do not co-exist in a vacuum. Other contextual elements must also be considered. Hence, the manager must also diagnose these factors before proceeding.

Diagnosis of technology.   Technology, as defined back in Chapter 6, is the conversion processes utilized by an organization in the transformation of inputs into outputs. As also indicated earlier, technology may constrain or facilitate task redesign efforts. If the primary inputs into the conversion process are material in nature, task redesign efforts may be more difficult (i.e., technology may be a constraint due to investments in machinery and equipment). At the other extreme, information inputs may result in an easier task redesign effort (that is, technology may facilitate the intervention). Finally, if human and/or monetary inputs dominate, task redesign efforts may have an intermediate level of difficulty.

After establishing a general idea of what to expect, the manager may next look at more specific linkages in terms of one or more of the technology typologies. Using the integrative view of technology presented in Figure 6–7, several considerations are apparent. For example, the manager might categorize the technology in his or her organization along the number of exceptional cases and nature of the search process dimensions (Perrow, 1967). The technology might also be described as being small batch or unit production, mass production, or continuous process production (Woodward, 1958, 1965), or else as being long-linked, mediating, or intensive in nature. A logical classification would result in the manager having more insights into how technology may influence (and be influenced by) the proposed task redesign intervention.

Next, the manager can assess the relevant technological subsystems of operations, materials, and knowledge technologies and relate each to work flow uncertainty, task uncertainty, and task interdependence. The results of this analysis should provide insights into three related areas. First, the manager should be able to develop general profiles of existing tasks based on characteristics of the technology. These profiles could serve as a basis for comparison (i.e., a "check") against the results of the original diagnosis of existing jobs in the organization. Second, the technology diagnosis should identify important elements of the technological systems relevant to the redesign intervention. More specifically, results will indicate which aspects of the technological systems will need to be changed in order to bring about the desired task changes. Finally, the manager should also have a feel for the relative difficulty to be encountered in actually making those changes.

In conducting the technology diagnosis, the manager should probably rely quite heavily on technical specialists familiar with the work-flow system. Examples of such individuals would include the plant manager, first-line supervisors, industrial engineers, and others involved in the various aspects of production and operations management. This diagnosis may be relatively simple or extremely complex in nature. For example, the larger the *number* of technologies utilized by the organization, the more difficult will be the diagnosis. By drawing upon the knowledge of relevant experts, however, the manager should be able to derive useful information about how the organization's technology will mesh with a task redesign intervention.

Diagnosis of organization design. Having assessed the organization's technology, the next step in the process should be a diagnosis of the organization's design. If the focus of the task redesign intervention will be on operating employees, then implications from the perspective of organization design will be relatively minor. If, however, the focus is managerial roles, organization design becomes more critical. First, we will address the relevant factors of importance in dealing with jobs of operating employees.

By analyzing the existing span of control at the operating level, the manager may gain insights into current levels of task autonomy while also getting a feel for potential changes in the span that might be necessary later. At a more general level, the categorization of the organization as being either mechanistic or organic in design will also be useful. If the design is mechanistic, tasks may be in more critical need of redesign; however, the mechanistic framework may also constrain redesign alternatives. On the other hand, an organic design might facilitate change, but existing jobs may already be relatively higher in scope. Finally, a consideration of the status subsystem might be in order. If the proposed redesign effort is aimed at the lowest status jobs in the organization, for example, the manager should recognize that the potential increase in status following the redesign might meet with resistance by higher status employees, and that employees whose jobs are being changed may expect higher salaries to reflect their improved status.

As indicated earlier, the diagnosis of the organization design is most important for changes in managerial roles. Relevant spans of control, for example, might require modification. Desirable aspects of the formalization dimension may be eliminated by redesigning tasks. An especially significant consideration could be the task autonomy–decentralization link. If the proposed change is to increase managerial autonomy, for example, top management must recognize in advance that power and control will be channeled downward in the organization. That is, management must be willing to allow at least a certain amount of decentralization.

Considerations derived from the mechanistic-organic distinction would again be important for redesigning managerial tasks. The Mintzberg (1979) framework would also be very useful for diagnostic purposes. A full-scale redesign program, for example, might involve actually changing the structural configuration of the organization, say from a divisionalized form to an adhocracy. Management must anticipate such a shift in advance. **213**

An analysis of the organization's climate might also be in order. The prevailing climate might facilitate (i.e., if people are optimistic and enthusiastic about their situation) or hamper (i.e., if people are pessimistic and unenthusiastic) the redesign intervention. Status would again be an important aspect to consider. Finally, the communication subsystem should also be diagnosed. Two-way communication, for example, may be especially crucial for an effective redesign intervention focusing on managerial roles.

The organization design diagnosis will probably be conducted by the manager working in concert with his or her peers, supervisors, and immediate subordinates. Questionnaires exist that could be used to measure most of the relevant dimensions of organization design (cf., Hage and Aiken, 1967; Van de Ven and Delbecq, 1974). The manager might also develop profiles based on his or her own observations and experiences, augmented with inputs from others familiar with the organization.

Diagnosis of leader behavior. Analysis of leader behavior processes in the organization may be of extreme importance. On the one hand, the cooperation of supervisors may be crucial to the success of the task redesign intervention. At the same time, however, supervisors may have the greatest potential to be an impedance to the intervention.

At least three different aspects of leader behavior that can facilitate task redesign efforts can be identified. First, supervisors can be a primary source of information in other diagnostic assessments of existing tasks, employees, technology, organization design, and group processes. Second, supervisors will probably be very actively involved in the actual task changes to be made. Finally, they will also be important for clarifying roles and providing additional training after the task redesign intervention.

A primary reason why supervisors may be problematic, however, is that the task changes may involve taking away part of their own job-related activities, power, and control in order to provide more autonomy for subordinates whose jobs are being redesigned. Recall the Lawler, Hackman, and Kaufman (1973) study summarized in Chapter 8. In that organization, supervisors whose jobs were "narrowed" so that subordinates could have more things to do reacted quite negatively.

What could a disenchanted supervisor do to disrupt a task redesign intervention? Just in terms of the three positive roles described earlier, the supervisor could, to varying degrees, provide incomplete or inaccurate information during other diagnostic assessments, be less than totally committed to implementing the changes, and/or fail to provide relevant training after the change. She or he could also grow frustrated and develop an antagonistic attitude toward employees.

The diagnosis of leader behavior, then, should be done with the utmost care. The most logical technique for handling the diagnosis would be to conduct one or more informal discussions with the supervisors to be affected by the change. The manager might also draw upon his or her own observations and insights. Finally, individual meetings might also be appropriate for supervisors who may be particularly opposed to or supportive of the intervention. Of course, the manager must take care not to be perceived as playing favorites, doing things behind someone's back, and so forth.

The primary objective of the meetings would be to gather and, to a certain extent, provide information. Specifically, attempts should be made to find out whether or not supervisory opposition to the intervention actually exists, the severity of the opposition, and what, if anything, can be done to overcome the opposition. At the same time, the manager might also offer reassurance that the supervisors' roles are not being downgraded, etc. (Questionnaires might also be considered as a potential diagnostic tool. However, if supervisors are already aware of the impending intervention, they may be suspicious and provide distorted information. Therefore, the use of questionnaires is not recommended for this phase of the diagnosis.)

Diagnosis of group and social processes. The remaining contextual element, group and social processes, also warrants careful diagnosis. This is particularly true if the task redesign intervention is to include the development of autonomous work groups or similar group-focused characteristics.

The manager should attempt to ascertain the degree of cohesiveness that exists among the workers whose jobs are going to be changed, the level of relevant norms, and the nature of existing and potential role dynamics. In the situation where cohesion is high and performance norms are low, for example, employees may react quite negatively to any change by management that can be viewed as threatening.

The manager should also investigate the extent to which task changes might disrupt existing norm patterns in a negative way. For example, existing norms might facilitate a great deal of interpersonal cooperation and assistance. Elements of the task changes, however, might be expected to increase competition and thereby decrease cooperation. Finally, assessment of role dynamics might indicate expected levels of role ambiguity, conflict, and/or overload that could arise either temporarily or permanently after the intervention; it might also suggest ways to overcome or at least minimize their disruptive consequences.

Using the SIP framework, the manager might also attempt to get a feel for the nature of interpersonal exchanges occurring in the organization. If employees are making relatively favorable assessments of their work situations and are likely to continue to do so, the SIP approach might suggest that these favorable evaluations will be diffused through the work system, thereby enhancing the potential for success of the intervention. The reverse situation could also be present.

Again, a variety of techniques could be used to carry out this diagnosis. **215**

A number of questionnaires, for example, are available for measuring role variables (e.g., House and Rizzo, 1972). Of course, the normal strengths and weaknesses of perceptual measurement would exist. In cases of employee distrust, extreme dissatisfaction, and so forth, questionnaires should probably be avoided.

The manager's insights and observations might also be an important diagnostic tool. This information, combined with results of group discussions with relevant parties, could provide very important and useful profiles of the various group and social processes that might influence and be influenced by the task design intervention.

At this stage of the process, the manager will have completed the diagnosis of the work system and work context. The next step is to assess the potential benefits of the task redesign intervention relative to their expected costs.

Cost/Benefit Analysis of Proposed Changes

The exact nature of the cost/benefit analysis will vary between organizations. Moreover, the specific costs and benefits may be different for each organization. The starting point in the analysis should be the specification of the goals of the intervention. The expectations of the organization should not be excessive; recall from Chapter 4, for example, that the task design–performance relationship is not well established. The goals, then, should be realistic and feasible. The firm should also recognize the costs it will incur in achieving these goals. A list of possible costs and benefits of a task redesign intervention is presented in Table 10–3.

TABLE 10–3   Possible Costs and Benefits of a Task Redesign Intervention

COSTS	BENEFITS
Direct/Quantifiable	Direct/Quantifiable
1. Purchase of new technology 2. Down-time 3. Increased wages	1. Enhanced performance via improvements in the work system
Indirect/Nonquantifiable	Indirect/Nonquantifiable
1. Short-term role ambiguity, conflict, and/or overload following change 2. Alienation of some employees who oppose change	1. Improved employee satisfaction 2. Improved employee motivation 3. Improved quality of work life 4. Improved group performance norms
Potential/Unexpected	Potential/Unexpected
1. Unplanned snags and delays 2. Unplanned supplemental changes 3. Unplanned changes in organizational design 4. Unplanned morale problems with supervisors	1. Enhanced performance via improvements in employee effort 2. Improved employee commitment

A number of direct and quantifiable costs may arise. First, the intervention may require the purchase of new technology (e.g., new machinery, etc.), as discussed in Chapter 6. It is likely that the organization will also incur some down-time (i.e., employees being unable to perform their tasks) during the transition between existing and redesigned tasks. Finally, wage increases may be necessary due to increased task importance.

Several indirect or nonquantifiable costs will also likely follow the change. For example, workers will probably experience a certain degree of role ambiguity, conflict, and/or overload due to their initial lack of familiarity with new task-related procedures (see Chapter 9). Second, some employees may become alienated because of a preference for the original task, suspicion of management's motives, and so forth. In either case, turnover may result.

Finally, several unexpected costs may arise. In a general sense, potential snags and delays may interrupt the intervention, prolong down-time, etc. Unplanned supplemental changes may also be necessary. Contiguous organizational units may be affected in unexpected ways, thereby necessitating other organization design changes (see Chapter 7). Finally, unplanned morale problems with supervisors may arise (see Chapter 8). Of course, not all of these costs may be encountered in any given organization; on the other hand, additional costs may be incurred in some settings. These examples are simply intended to be illustrative.

On the positive side, the organization can also expect to reap some benefits from the task redesign intervention. A direct, quantifiable benefit that may accrue to the organization is enhanced productivity due to improvements and refinements in the work system. Work measurement techniques discussed in Chapter 5 could help the manager project what these improvements could be.

Several nonquantifiable benefits may also be gained. Although some measurement techniques have been developed for assessing some of these variables (e.g., Mirvis and Lawler, 1977), they are still relatively crude. Hence, managers should not place too much credence in numbers obtained from such analyses. One possible outcome variable in this category would be improved employee satisfaction. Satisfaction, in turn, could have a positive affect on turnover and/or absenteeism (see Chapter 4). Other nonquantifiable outcome variables that may follow a task redesign intervention could be improved employee motivation (Chapter 4), improved quality of work life (Chapter 1), and/or improved group performance norms (Chapter 9).

Finally, some unexpected benefits may also arise. The improved employee motivation described above may result in performance increases. Improved commitment (see Chapter 4) may also follow the intervention. Again, not all of these benefits may be applicable and, in other situations, additional benefits may accrue. The exact combination of potential and actual benefits and costs will vary from one organization to another. **217**

The Go/No-Go Decision

At this point, the manager should be in a position to make a decision about whether to proceed with the task redesign intervention or to consider other alternatives. The diagnosis of existing jobs, employees, technology, organization design, leader behavior, and group and social processes will give the manager insights into how these various organizational factors may constrain and/or facilitate task design alternatives. The cost/benefit analysis will then provide additional information relative to the viability of task redesign.

Unfortunately, the results of the diagnoses and cost/benefit analyses will generally *not* provide information in a form amenable to quantitative analysis. That is, the manager will typically not be able to "add up" all of the potential benefits and then "subtract" the costs to yield a positive or negative dollar price tag associated with the intervention. This stems from the nonquantifiable nature of many of the expected costs (i.e., alienation, unexpected snags, etc.) and benefits (i.e., improved employee satisfaction, motivation, and quality of work life) that may relate to the change.

Therefore, the manager must place greater reliance on his or her own intuition and expert opinion, and must be willing to gamble "hard" expenses in the form of new technology, down-time, and so forth in exchange for "soft" benefits such as improved quality of work life. The manager must also expect to wait for perhaps an extended time before these benefits offset the initial costs. In the situations where the manager cannot justify the costs, she or he may back up and consider an alternative intervention or else decide to maintain the status quo. When task redesign does emerge as an acceptable strategy, the manager must now begin to develop the strategy for implementation.

Development of the Implementation Strategy

The implementation strategy will consist of four basic components or steps. First, the manager must make decisions regarding *who* will plan the task redesign implementation. Aldag and Brief (1979) suggest that a job redesign task force composed of representatives from management and labor, as well as ad hoc technical specialists, should be designated. Hackman and Oldham (1980) take a less definitive stance by arguing that some situations will call for a participatory approach, while others will call for a top-down process. The latter suggestion appears to be the most realistic.

The decision regarding the appropriate degree of participation will probably be a function of the extent to which subordinates have needed information, the extent to which employees will require participation in order to accept the change, the extent to which employees can be trusted to make substantive contributions, and the values of the managers involved. In any event, some form of group effort will likely be appropriate. If management decides to minimize participation, the planning group should consist of several managers. Input should be requested from concerned and relevant members of the personnel group, the industrial engineering group, labor officials, and others potentially influenced by the intervention. The management group, however, will retain control over the process. If participation is utilized, then some of these outside individuals, as well as members of the target employee group, should be made formal group members.

Once the group has been formed, it will undertake the second phase of planning: outlining and detailing the actual job changes to be made. Information from the earlier work system and context diagnosis and the cost/benefit analysis will typically be useful at this point. Work measurement data (Chapter 5) will also likely be appropriate to consider. Of extreme importance will be information gathered from current job holders. This information could be obtained from perceptual data gathered during the diagnosis of existing jobs and/or supplemental interviews conducted specifically for this purpose. In most cases, the planned changes should be detailed in writing and supplemented with projections of positive task changes, expected outcome changes (i.e., new standards of productivity), and approximate costs of the changes.

As part of this effort, decisions must also be made regarding whether to use individual- or group-based task changes. Hackman and Oldham (1980) provide useful suggestions for making this decision. Specifically, they suggest that autonomous work groups should be created only when this alternative offers significant advantages over individually-based tasks. The rationale for this suggestion is based on the following points: (1) group designs involve not only the design of tasks but also the design of teams, (2) group decisions will involve more complex interpersonal relationships, and (3) group decisions may dictate more extreme changes in other organizational components such as the reward system (p. 224).

Once the redesign intervention has been mapped out, the planning group should then outline a time frame for implementing the changes. This time frame should allow for job-specific planning, purchasing new equipment, installing the task changes, integrating the new system with contiguous units, working out the "bugs," and, finally, returning to normal operations. An ideal technique for this step would be PERT (Program Evaluation and Review Technique). A hypothetical illustration will be instructive (it is assumed that the reader has some familiarity with PERT: if not, several excellent resources are available; cf., Wiest and Levy, 1977).

Assume the task redesign involves the claims department of an insurance company. Field agents file the claims; the claims clerks take them through a series of steps and then pass them on to the disbursements department for payment. A PERT diagram for the change is presented in Figure 10–1. Prior to the change, each clerk may have performed one of four basic steps and then passed the claim to another clerk for Step 2 (note that this is sequential technology, as described in Chapter 6). Under the **219**

FIGURE 10–1   Hypothetical PERT Diagram of Task Redesign in an Insurance Claims
Department

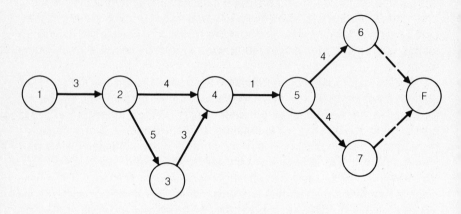

Description of Relevant Activities and Events

Activity	Activity Description	Event	Event Description	Expected Time
1-2	Job Specific Planning	2	Job-Specific Planning Completed	3 Days
2-3	New equipment ordered and installed	3	Equipment in place and ready for use	5 Days
2-4	Training group members in new work processes	4	Process training completed	4 Days
3-4	Training group members in use of new equipment	4	Technical training completed	3 Days
4-5	Begin use of new task procedures	5	New tasks being performed	1 Day
5-6	Smooth interface between claims and field agents	6	Interface adjustments completed	4 Days
5-7	Smooth interface between claims and disbursements	7	Interface adjustments completed	4 Days
6-F 7-F	New work system fully operational			

new task arrangement, each clerk will perform all four steps (perhaps illustrative of a mediating technology) and then send them directly to disbursements.

The various steps in the interventions may include planning the new job activities, training clerks in all four operations, ordering new equipment (i.e., perhaps each clerk will now need a computer terminal), training clerks in how to use the new equipment, and changing the work-flow interfaces between in-coming work from agents and out-going work to the disbursement department. The PERT diagram, then, outlines the overall project for the manager and can be a major tool for managing the time frame for task changes.

Another aspect of the timing issue could pertain to seasonal demands on the organization. For example, the task redesign intervention should probably *not* be introduced during a time of peak demand on the organization. Toy manufacturers gearing up for Christmas, clothing manufacturers changing from summer to winter clothing lines, and tax firms preparing for April 15, for example, should all probably consider planning a task redesign intervention for a less demanding time. This issue, of course, will be more important in some organizations than in others, and it is assumed that the planning committee will have appropriate information to consider.

The final step in the strategy development process would be the specification of needed and/or potentially needed supplements for the task redesign intervention. By supplements, we refer to needed changes, adjustments, and/or modifications to other organizational processes such as, but not limited to, the contextual elements described in previous chapters.

An obvious supplement might be training and/or task redesign for supervisors of the employees whose jobs are changed. As discussed in Chapter 8, task redesign may give the employee power and control previously held by the supervisor; a potential outcome of this change, in turn, could be hostility and/or frustration on the part of the supervisors. As a supplement to the primary task redesign intervention, then, supervisors could receive training to help them cope with and accept the new situation, or their own jobs could be redesigned to compensate for the possible reduction in power and control. Other important supplements may include modifications to the reward system (job analysis and/or evaluation procedures described in Chapter 5 would be useful for this purpose) to reflect the essentially "new" jobs following the redesign and the establishment of new productivity standards by industrial engineers (again, using the work measurement techniques discussed in Chapter 5).

Implementation

In theory, if proper diagnostic activities, cost/benefit analyses, and implementation strategies have been utilized, then the actual implementation of the task changes should go quite smoothly. Of course, as most managers know, theory and practice seldom mesh precisely. We can say very little here about implementation, because the exact mechanics of a task redesign intervention will be unique for each situation. We can, however, offer one very important observation for the manager: expect unexpected difficulties to arise.

Regardless of how complete the diagnosis or how well-developed the strategy, in all likelihood some unforeseen circumstance or problem will appear. This should not be perceived as a significant argument against the **221** use of task redesign (or any other change intervention, for that matter), of course, because to expect any change involving individuals to be 100% predictable would be quite unrealistic. By conducting a careful diagnosis and developing a detailed strategy, the manager can, however, minimize the potentially disruptive and/or costly problems that can arise.

Supplements to the Intervention

As indicated earlier, the task redesign intervention may also dictate supplemental changes in other organizational processes in order to achieve a better integration. These supplements should be identified and planned during the development of the intervention strategy.

One area of supplemental changes may relate to the contextual elements of task design. New work flow technological processes may be appropriate. Changes in the organization's design may be required. Supplements directed at leader behavior and/or group and social processes may also be needed.

Other supplemental changes may be needed in areas such as selection criteria, the reward system, appropriate performance appraisal methods, the organization's work schedules, the actual work environment, and so forth. It is also useful to note that some supplemental changes may precede the task redesign intervention, others may take place during the intervention, and still others may follow the intervention.

As with the implementation process, the exact number and nature of task redesign supplements will vary from one organization to the next. Further, unplanned supplements may also become necessary after the intervention is in progress and/or completed. A careful and systematic diagnosis and strategy, however, will again help to minimize potential problems.

Evaluation of the Intervention

The final step in our integrative implementation framework is an evaluation of the effectiveness of the intervention. Recall that in Step 4 (the cost/benefit analysis), desired outcomes were specified. At this point, it is worthwhile to ascertain whether or not the outcomes have actually been achieved. Unfortunately, this is one aspect of organizational change that is neglected by many managers. The evaluation framework we will suggest is one that meets basic, minimum scientific requirements. (The reader wanting information on other evaluation strategies should consult Campbell and Stanley, 1963).

First, employee perceptions of their jobs and measures of the relevant outcome variables should be obtained prior to the change. This data could be collected as part of the diagnostic activities carried out in Step 3. Data could be gathered by questionnaire (i.e., the JDS or JCI) or by interviews. Simultaneously, data should also be collected from another group of employees whose jobs are not being changed. Measures of all variables should again be taken from both groups after the change.

It is important to measure task perceptions, because in some instances employees have not perceived changes that management has supposedly introduced. Outcomes should obviously be measured in order to assess the degree of change. The importance of collecting data from a comparison group is based on the fact that changes could occur as a result of other, uncontrolled factors. By comparing changes in the group whose jobs are changed against any changes in the group whose jobs are not changed, this possibility can be evaluated. A final point relates to the timing of the measures after the change. Research has shown that employee perceptions and reactions to a task change may not become apparent for an extended period of time. As a general guideline, measures should be taken approximately three to four months after the change and again after one year.

If perceptions have not been altered, further task changes may be necessary. If perceptions have been altered but reactions have not, this fact must be weighed against the original expectations of the intervention. Depending upon the goals, nature, and values of the manager and the organization, a task change which has not fulfilled expectations may call for more extensive task changes, maintenance of the status quo, or abandonment of the intervention. Of course, if the goals of the intervention have been achieved, then the effort can be termed a success. It is to be hoped that both employees and the organization will realize an improved situation.

SUMMARY

This chapter has focused on task redesign processes in organizations. First, we discussed a general organizational change perspective. Next, we summarized the Hackman and Oldham implementation strategy. Finally, we presented a more complete integrative framework for installing task changes in organizations.

The integrative framework is not offered as being the ideal approach to task redesign. A criticism directed at the Hackman and Oldham approach, for example, was that it was too general. We attempted to partially overcome this problem by being more specific. Yet, at a number of places we were still forced to suggest that the appropriate way to do something would "vary from organization to organization," etc. The reason for this is obvious: the more precise and specific guidelines and recommendations become, the less generalizable they are to other organizational settings. Our framework is offered as a step toward a more complete and precise balance between specificity and generality. Certainly, further improvements can be made.

Finally, it is useful to point out the completion of a cycle. Back in Chapter 1, we presented an integrative model of task design (Figure 1–1). **223**

This model included a number of organizational elements we came to refer to as contextual variables. Subsequent chapters explored these variables in detail. In this chapter, we described how and why the context of task design processes relates to task redesign interventions; we hope to have provided managers with some useful guidelines for managing task design and task redesign in organizations.

CONCLUDING COMMENTS AND OBSERVATIONS

This book has dealt with the design of work in organizations. We began our discussion by analyzing the work-related situations of two manufacturing employees, Bill Thomas and Hal Williamson. Bill Thomas works in an automobile assembly plant, while Hal Williamson is employed by a machine shop. The two men described their jobs in dramatically different terms. In retrospect, we could now analyze Bill's job in the automobile plant and characterize it as being very routine, simple, and boring. We could better understand why Bill is dissatisfied and unmotivated by his work. Finally, we could recognize how his job and immediate work environment are at least partially shaped by the organization's technology and design, by leader and supervisory behaviors, and by group and social processes. We could also now describe Hal's job as being nonroutine, challenging, and complex, and better understand why he seems more satisfied and motivated. Finally, the effects of technology, organization design, leader behavior, and group and social processes could also be more clearly identified in Hal's job. The remainder of Chapter 1 was devoted to justifying the study of task design. It was demonstrated that an understanding of task design processes may be important for employees, organizations, society, and to the individual reader.

Chapter 2 provided an historical overview of a number of early task design approaches, including scientific management, job rotation, and job enlargement. Contemporary strategies such as job environment and the job characteristics theory were discussed in Chapter 3. Variables that might be affected by task design, such as satisfaction, motivation, and performance, were the topic of Chapter 4. Chapter 5 focused on task design measurement issues. Chapters 6 through 9 described the primary contextual variables of technology, organization design, leader behavior, and group and social processes. Finally, an integrative implementation framework for installing task redesign in organizations was presented in this final chapter. At this point, we will briefly summarize the current state of and possible future directions for both task design research and practice.

Current State of Task Design

Throughout this book, we have attempted to focus on task design from dual perspectives: scientific research and managerial practice. We will now briefly summarize the current state of task design from both points of view.

Current state of task design research.   For the last several years, and continuing on through the present time, task design research has dominated the pages of scholarly journals and the programs of academic meetings. The initial impetus for this research was the job characteristics theory (Hackman and Lawler, 1971; Hackman and Oldham, 1976). This theory provided a well-developed framework that focused on a topic of obvious importance and that was generally supported by preliminary research findings. Since social science in general and organizational behavior and theory in particular are seldom provided with such frameworks, it was inevitable that a substantive body of derivative literature would emerge. Unfortunately, these findings have generally been frustratingly inconclusive: encouraging enough to stimulate additional research but also inconsistent enough so as to provide few meaningful insights.

The Salancik and Pfeffer (1977, 1978) social information processing approach (discussed in Chapter 9) has recently emerged as a "competing" framework for understanding task design processes in organizations. To date, the research findings developed from this framework have been generally consistent and supportive. However, different methodological approaches, and more information from field settings in particular, are needed to better understand this perspective.

At this time, task design research seems to be at a critical stage in its development. The SIP framework has raised serious questions about the "popular" approach (i.e., the job characteristics theory), but has not yet supplanted it as the dominant view. Apparently, one of three possibilities exists for the near future: the SIP framework will become the generally accepted view, the job characteristics approach will re-emerge as the accepted view, or some new perspective will be developed and accepted by researchers.

Current state of task design practice.   Obviously, all organizations practice task design by defining and structuring jobs that their employees are to perform. The critical issue, of course, is the extent to which the tasks that organizations design are actually compatible with the employees that perform them. No reliable information exists to document the extent to which organizations are attempting to optimize the individual-task interface. For a variety of reasons, a few efforts such as the General Foods experiment (discussed in Chapter 9) are widely referenced in the media. The exact number of such instances, however, is relatively small. There are probably many other such efforts that go unreported. In comparison to the total number of jobs and organizations, however, serious attempts to enhance task quality are still a relative minority.

On a more optimistic note, there probably is increased awareness on the part of many managers about task design issues. A number of factors have evidently led to this increased awareness: (1) media attention on factors such as quality of working life, alienation, and "blue-collar blues," (2) the search by managers for solutions to the productivity declines re-   **225** ferenced in Chapter 1, and (3) the increasing prominence of task design as a topic in management development programs and management courses in colleges and universities. Of course, the extent to which this increased awareness gets translated into practice remains to be seen. This aspect of future directions is the topic of our next section.

Future Directions in Task Design

As in our description of the current situation in task design, we will briefly discuss future directions from the point of view of both research and practice.

Future directions in task design research. The nature of future directions for task design research is, of course, dependent upon the predominant theoretical frameworks in the area. Further, the formulation and refinement of such frameworks could be one particularly important avenue for increased understanding of task design processes. Two topics of immediate importance can be identified. First, Salancik and Pfeffer (1978) note that their SIP framework is incomplete and tentative. Hence, one area for theoretical work would be a more complete explication of this viewpoint. An even more important area of concern could be on the development of a complementary view of the "competing" frameworks. That is, rather than attempting to support one of the frameworks (the job characteristics view or the SIP view) or refute the other, perhaps a more constructive mode would be to attempt to integrate the two.

In terms of empirical work, research is needed in a variety of areas. First, the task design–performance relationship needs clarification. Second, more experimental studies are needed to better assess causality among crucial variables. These studies, of course, should be related to dominant theoretical frameworks. Finally, more research is needed to assess many of the potential task design relationships discussed in this book: how task design processes affect and are affected by contextual variables such as technology, organization design, leader behavior, and group and social processes.

Future directions in task design practice. As indicated earlier, managers are probably becoming more and more aware of crucial task design issues. Whether this awareness gets translated into practice, of course, remains to be seen. There are indications, however, that a variety of factors may stimulate more attention to appropriate task design in organizational settings.

First of all, changes in the physical task environment are occurring at an accelerated pace. Many firms now offer modular work stations for secretarial and clerical employees. For employees who work while sitting down, Norwegian designers have developed a new style of desk chair called the Balans chair. By forcing weight onto the individual's knees, the chair decreases back strain and facilitates improved breathing. Even for operating employees, new physical breakthroughs are available. For example, an inventor has recently patented a revolutionary improvement in a centuries-old tool, the hammer. By placing two slight curves, or bends, in the handle of the hammer, elbow strain is reduced, the need for a tight grip is eliminated, and striking accuracy improves.

Another catalyst for change may be more employee involvement in company ownership. Federal legislation, for example, may require organizations to give employees a bigger voice in management. Stock ownership programs are already fairly common. Romac Industries in Seattle currently allows employees to vote on pay raises for all other employees. It follows that as employees gain more and more control over these kinds of decisions, they may well decide they also want some control over their work activities.

A continuing concern for quality of work life should also serve to increase managerial interest in task design processes. Regardless of the physical surroundings and other considerations, the fact remains that the job the individual performs is the most critical contact point the person has with the organization. Hence, almost by definition, any attempt to improve the employee's work-related experiences must, of necessity, include changes in the task the employee performs.

In the years ahead, many innovative and enlightened approaches to designing work for organizational members will likely be attempted. Regardless of the extent of automation, or work improvement, we are still likely to need human beings to work on our assembly lines, to make our clothing, to sweep our floors, and to do many of the routine but necessary tasks our society has created. It is hoped that organizations and managers will initiate, maintain, and/or increase their efforts at making work more dignified, personally rewarding, and individually fulfilling. All of us stand to gain.

REFERENCES

Aldag, R. J., Barr, S. H., & Brief, A. P. Measurement of perceived task characteristics. Working paper 78–14, College of Business Administration, University of Iowa, 1978.

Aldag, R. J., & Brief, A. P. Impact of individual differences on employee affective responses to task characteristics. *Journal of Business Research*, 1975, *3*, 311–22. (a)

Aldag, R. J., & Brief, A. P. Age and reactions to task characteristics. *Industrial Gerontology*, 1975, *2*, 223–29. (b)

Aldag, R. J. & Brief, A. P. *Task design and employee motivation*. Glenview, Ill.: Scott, Foresman, 1979.

Babbage, C. *On the economy of machinery and manufactures*. London: Charles Knight, 1832.

Bertalanffy, L. von, Hempel, C. G., Bass, R. E., & Jonas, H. General systems theory: A new approach to unity of science. *Human Biology*, 1951, *23*, 302–61.

Bishop, R. C. & Hill, J. W. Effects of job enlargement and job change on contiguous but nonmanipulated jobs as a function of worker's status. *Journal of Applied Psychology*, 1971, *55*, 175–81.

Blood, M. R., & Hulin, C. L. Alienation, environmental characteristics, and worker responses. *Journal of Applied Psychology*, 1967, *51*, 284–90.

Burns, T., & Stalker, G. M. *The management of innovation*. London: Tavistock, 1961.

Campbell, J. P. & Beatty, E. E. Organizational climate: Its measurement and relationship to work group performance. Paper presented at the annual meeting of the American Psychological Association, Washington, D.C., 1971.

Campbell, J. P. & Pritchard, R. D. Motivation theory in industrial and organizational psychology. In M. D. Dunnette (ed.), *Handbook of industrial and organizational psychology*. Boston: Houghton-Mifflin, 1976.

Campbell, D. T. & Stanley, J. C. *Experimental and quasi-experimental designs for research*. Boston: Houghton-Mifflin, 1963.

Chandler, A. *Strategy and structure*, Cambridge, Mass.: The M.I.T. Press, 1962.

Chruden, H. G., & Sherman, A. W. *Personnel management*. Cincinnati, Ohio: Southwestern Publishing Co., 1976.

Cohen, A. R. & Gadon, H. *Alternative work schedules: Integrating individual and organizational needs*. Reading, Mass.: Addison-Wesley, 1978.

Conant, E. H. & Kilbridge, M. An interdisciplinary analysis of job enlargement: technology, cost, behavioral implications. *Industrial and Labor Relations Review*, 1965, *18*, 377–95.

Connolly, T. Information processing and decision making in organizations. In B. Staw and G. R. Salancik (eds.), *New directions in organizational behavior*. Chicago: St. Clair Publishing Co., 1977.

Davis, S. M. & Lawrence, P. R. *Matrix*. Reading, Mass.: Addison-Wesley, 1977.

Dawis, R. V., England, G. W., & Lofquist, L. H. A theory of work adjustment: A revision, *Minnesota Studies in Vocational Rehabilitation Bulletin*, *47*, Minneapolis, 1968.

Dowling, W. F., Jr. Job redesign on the assembly line. *Organizational Dynamics*, Winter, 1973, Spring, 51–67.

Downey, H. K., Sheridan, J. E., & Slocum, J. W. The path-goal theory of leadership: A longitudinal analysis. *Organizational Behavior and Human Performance*, 1976, *16*, 156–76.

Dunham, R. B. The measurement and dimensionality of job characteristics. *Journal of Applied Psychology*, 1976, *61*, 404–409.

Dunham, R. B. Relationships of perceived job design characteristics to job ability requirements and job value. *Journal of Applied Psychology*, 1977, *62*, 760–63. (a)

Dunham, R. B. Reactions to job characteristics: Moderating effects of the organization. *Academy of Management Journal*, 1977, *20*, 42–65. (b)

Dunham, R., Aldag, R., & Brief, A. Dimensionality of task design as measured by the Job Diagnostic Survey. *Academy of Management Journal*, 1977, *20*, 209–23.

Dunham, R. B., Pierce, J. L., & Kolenko, T. Multiple approaches to job design measurement and affective and behavioral responses to job design. Paper presented at the National Meeting of the Academy of Management, Atlanta, Georgia, 1979.

Dunn, J. D., & Rachel, F. M. *Wage and salary administration*. New York: McGraw-Hill, Inc., 1971.

Etzioni, A. Work in the American future: Reindustrialization or quality of life. In C. Kerr & J. M. Rosow (eds.), *Work in America—the decade ahead*. New York: Van Nostrand Reinhold, 1979.

Evans, M. G. The effects of supervisory behavior on the path-goal relationship. *Organizational Behavior and Human Performance*, 1970, *5*, 277–98.

Evans, M. G. Extensions of a path goal theory of motivation. *Journal of Applied Psychology*, 1974, *59*, 172–78.

Evans, M. G. Leadership. In S. Kerr (ed.), *Organizational behavior*. Columbus, Ohio: Grid Publishing Co., 1979.

Evans, M. G., Kiggundu, M. N. & House, R. J. A partial test and extension of the job characteristic model of motivation. *Organizational Behavior and Human Performance*, 1979, *24*, 354–81.

Famularo, J. *Handbook of modern personnel administration*. New York: McGraw-Hill, 1972.

Farris, G. E. Organizational factors and individual performance: A longitudinal study, *Journal of Applied Psychology*, 1969, *53*, 87–92.

Fein, M. Job enrichment: A reevaluation. *Sloan Management Review*, 1974, Winter, 69–88.

Fiedler, F. E. A theory of leadership effectiveness. New York: McGraw-Hill, 1967.

Filley, A. C., House, R. J., & Kerr, S. *Managerial process and organizational behavior*. Dallas, Texas: Scott, Foresman and Company, 1976.

Ford, R. N. Job enrichment lessons from AT&T. *Harvard Business Review*, 1973, Jan.-Feb., 96–106.

Foy, N. & Gadon, H. Worker participation: Contrasts in three countries. *Harvard Business Review*, 1976, May–June, 71–83.

Friedman, G. *The anatomy of work*. Glencoe, Illinois: Free Press, 1961.

Galbraith, J. R. Matrix organization designs. *Business Horizons*, 1971, February, 29–40.

Galbraith, J. R. *Organization design*. Reading, Mass.: Addison-Wesley, 1977.

Gallup, G. H. The Gallup poll. New York: Random House, 1972.

Gibson, C. H. Volvo increases productivity through job enrichment. *California Management Review*, 1973, Summer, 64–66.

Gibson, J. L., Ivancevich, J. M., & Donnelly, J. H. *Organizations: Behavior, structure, processes*. 3rd ed. Dallas, Texas: Business Publications, 1979.

Graen, G. Instrumentality theory of work motivation: Some experimental results and suggested modifications. *Journal of Applied Psychology Monograph*, 1969, *53*, 1–25.

Graen, G. Role-making processes within complex organizations. In M. D. Dunnette (ed.), *Handbook of industrial and organizational psychology*. Boston: Houghton-Mifflin, 1976.

Graen, G., Alvares, K., Orris, J. B., & Martella, J. A. Contingency model of leadership effectiveness: Antecedent and evidential results. *Psychological Bulletin*, 1970, *74*, 285–95.

Griffin, R. W. Task design determinants of effective leader behavior. *Academy of Management Review*, 1979, *4*, 215–24.

Griffin, R. W. Relationships among individual, task design, and leader behavior variables. *Academy of Management Journal*, 1980, *65*, 665–83.

Griffin, R. W. Supervisory behavior as a source of perceived task scope. *Journal of Occupational Psychology*, 1981, *54*, (in press). (a)

Griffin, R. W. Technological and social processes in task redesign: A field experiment. Unpublished manuscript, Texas A&M University, 1981. (b)

Griffin, R. W. A longitudinal investigation of task characteristics relationships. *The Academy of Management Journal*, 1981, *24*, 99–113. (c)

Griffin, R. W. Task attributes and long-term employee productivity. *Human Relations*, 1981, *34*, (in press) (d)

Griffin R. W., Moorhead, G., Johnson, B. H., & Chonko, L. B. The empirical dimensionality of the Job Characteristic Inventory. *Academy of Management Journal*. 1980, *23*, 772–77.

Griffin, R. W., Welsh, A. & Moorhead, G. Perceived task characteristics and employee performance: A literature review. *Academy of Management Review*, 1981, *6*.

Guest, R. H. Job enlargement: A revolution in job design. *Personnel Administration*, 1957, *2*, 9–16.

Gyllenhammar, P. G. *People at work*. Reading, Mass.: Addison-Wesley, 1977.

Hackman, J. R. On the coming demise of job enrichment. In E. L. Cass and F. G. Zimmer (eds.), *Man and work in society*. New York: Van Nostrand Reinhold, 1975.

Hackman, J. R. Work design. In J. R. Hackman and J. L. Suttle (eds.), *Improving life at work: Behavioral science approaches to organizational change*. Santa Monica, Ca.: Goodyear, 1977.

Hackman, J. R. & Lawler, E. Employee reactions to job characteristics. *Journal of Applied Psychology*, 1971, *55*, 259–86.

Hackman, J. R. and Oldham, G. R. *The Job Diagnostic Survey: An instrument for the diagnosis of jobs and the evaluation of job redesign projects*. New Haven, Conn.: Yale University Department of Administrative Sciences, 1974.

Hackman, J. R. & Oldham, G. Development of the Job Diagnostic Survey. *Journal of Applied Psychology*, 1975, *60*, 159–70.

Hackman, J. R., & Oldham, G. R. Motivation through the design of work: Test of a theory. *Organizational Behavior and Human Performance*, 1976, *16*, 250–79.

Hackman, J. R. & Oldham, G. R. *Work redesign*. Reading, Mass.: Addison-Wesley Publishing Company, 1980.

Hackman, J. R., Oldham, G. R., Janson, R., & Purdy, K. A new strategy for job enrichment. *California Management Review*, 1975, Summer, 57–71.

Hackman, J. R., Pearce, J. L., & Wolfe, J. C., Effects of changes in job characteristics on work attitudes and behaviors: A naturally occurring quasi-experiment. *Organizational Behavior and Human Performance*, 1978, *21*, 289–304.

Hage, J. & Aiken, M. Relationship of centralization to other structural properties. *Administrative Science Quarterly*, 1967, *12*, 72–92.

Hamner, W. C. & Organ, D. W. *Organizational behavior: An applied psychological approach.* Dallas, Texas: Business Publications, Inc., 1978.

Heneman, H. G., III. Schwab, D. P., Fossum, J. A., & Dyer, L. D. *Personnel/human resource management,* Homewood, Illinois: Richard D. Irwin, Inc., 1980.

Herbert, T. T. *Dimensions of organizational behavior.* New York: MacMillan Publishing Co., Inc., 1976.

Herzberg, F. *Work and the nature of man.* Cleveland: World, 1966.

Herzberg, F. One more time: How do you motivate employees? *Harvard Business Review*, 1968, Jan.-Feb., 53–62.

Herzberg, F. The wise old Turk. *Harvard Business Review*, 1974, Sept.-Oct., 70–80.

Herzberg, F., Mausner, B., & Snyderman, B. *The motivation to work.* New York: John Wiley and Sons, Inc., 1959.

Hickson, D. J., Pugh, D. S., & Pheysey, D. C. Operations technology and organizational structure: An empirical reappraisal. *Administrative Science Quarterly*, 1969, *14*, 378–97.

House, R. J. A path-goal theory of leader effectiveness. *Administrative Science Quarterly*, 1971, *16*, 321–38.

House, R. J. & Dessler, G. The path-goal theory of leadership: Some post hoc and a priori tests. In J. G. Hunt and L. L. Larson (eds.), *Contingency approaches to leadership.* Carbondale, Ill.: Southern Illinois University Press, 1974.

House, R. J. & Mitchell, T. R. Path-goal theory of leadership. *Journal of Contemporary Business*, 1974, *3*, 81–97.

House, R. J. & Rizzo, J. R. Toward the measurement of organizational practices: Scale development and validation. *Journal of Applied Psychology*, 1972, *56*, 388–96.

House, R. J. & Wigdor, L. Herzberg's dual-factor theory of job satisfaction and motivation: A review of the evidence and a criticism. *Personnel Psychology*, 1967, *20*, 369–89.

Hulin, C. L. Individual differences and job enrichment. In J. R. Maher (ed.), *New perspectives in job enrichment.* New York: Van Nostrand Reinhold Company, 1971.

Hulin, C. L. & Blood, M. R. Job enlargement, individual differences, and worker responses. *Psychological Bulletin*, 1968, *69*, 41–55.

Ivancevich, J. M. & Lyon, H. C. The shortened workweek: A field experiment, *Journal of Applied Psychology*, 1977, *62*, 34–37.

Ivancevich, J. M. & Matteson, M. T. Managing for a healthier heart, *Management Review*, 1978, October, 14–19.

Ivancevich, J. M. & Matteson, M. T. *Stress and work: a managerial perspective.* Glenview, Illinois: Scott, Foresman, 1980.

Johns, G. Task moderators of the relationship between leadership styles and subordinate responses. *Academy of Management Journal*, 1978, *21*, 319–25.

Johnson, R. A., Kast, F. E. & Rosenzweig, J. E. *The theory and management of systems.* New York: McGraw-Hill, 1973.

Kahn, R., Wolfe, D., Quinn, R., Snoeck, J., & Rosenthal, R. *Organizational stress: Studies in role conflict and ambiguity.* New York: Wiley, 1964.

Kanovsky, E. *The economy of the Israeli Kibbutz.* Cambridge: Harvard University Press, 1965.

Karger, D. W. & Bayha, F. H. *Engineered work measurement.* New York: Industrial Press, 1977.

Kennedy, E. M. *Worker alienation,* 1972. (Subcommittee on Employment, Manpower, and Poverty of the United States Senate), Washington, D.C.: U.S. Government Printing Office, 1972.

Kerr, S. Substitutes for leadership. Paper presented at the annual meeting of the American Institute for Design Sciences, San Francisco, 1976.

Kerr, S. & Jermier, J. Substitutes for leadership: Their meaning and measurement. *Organizational Behavior and Human Performance*, 1978, *22*, 375–404.

Kilbridge, M. D. Reduced costs through job enrichment: A Case. *The Journal of Business*, 1960, *33*, 357–62.

Kornhauser, A. *Mental health of the industrial worker*. New York: Wiley, 1965.

Kreman, B. Search for a better way of work: Lordstown, Ohio. *The New York Times*. September 9, 1973, Section 3, pp. 1–4.

Lawler, E. E., Hackman, J. R., & Kaufman, S. Effects of job redesign: A field experiment. *Journal of Applied Social Psychology*, 1973, *3*, 49–62.

Lawrence, P. R. & Lorsch, J. W. *Organization and environment*. Boston: Harvard University, Division of Research, Graduate School of Business Administration, 1967.

Lewin, K., Lippitt, R., & White, R. K. Patterns of aggressive behavior in experimentally created social climates. *Journal of Social Psychology*, 1939, *10*, 271–99.

Likert, R. *The human organization*. New York: McGraw-Hill, 1967.

Maher, J. R. Job enrichment, performance, and morale in a simulated factory. In J. R. Maher (ed.), *New perspectives in job enrichment*. New York: Van Nostrand Reinhold Company, 1971.

March, J. G. & Simon, H. A. *Organizations*. New York: John Wiley and Sons, 1958.

Mayo, E. *The human problems of an industrial civilization*. New York: MacMillan, 1933.

McClelland, D. C. Toward a theory of motive acquisition. *American Psychologist*, 1965, *20*, 321–33.

McCormick, E. J. *Human factors in engineering design*. New York: McGraw-Hill, 1976.

McCormick, E. J., Jeanneret, P. R., & Mecham, R. C. A study of job characteristics and job dimensions as based on the Position Analysis Questionnaire (PAQ). *Journal of Applied Psychology Monograph*, 1972, *56*, 347–68.

McGregor, D., *The human side of enterprise*. New York: McGraw-Hill Book Co., 1960.

McMahon, J. T. The contingency theory: Logic and method revisited. *Personnel Psychology*, 1972, *25*, 697–711.

Merrens, M. R. & Garrett, J. B. The Protestant ethic scale as a predictor of repetitive work performance, *Journal of Applied Psychology*, 1975, *60*, 125–37.

Miles, R. H., *Macro organizational behavior*. Santa Monica, California: Goodyear Publishing Company, 1980.

Miller, E. J. & Rice, A. K., *Systems of organizations*. London: Tavistock Publications, 1967.

Miller, F. G., Dhaliwal, T. S., & Magas, L. J. Job rotation raises productivity. *Industrial Engineering*, 1973, *5*, 24–36.

Mintzberg, H. *The structuring of organizations*. Englewood Cliffs, N.J.: Prentice-Hall, 1979.

Mirvis, P. H. & Lawler, E. E., III. Measuring the financial impact of employee attitudes. *Journal of Applied Psychology*, 1977, *62*, 1–8.

Mitchell, T. R. Motivation and participation: An integration. *Academy of Management Journal*, 1973, *16*, 160–79.

Moller, T. The people's television factory: Workers' ownership in practice, *Scandinavian Review*, 1977, *2*, 52–55.

Moorhead, G. Organizational analysis: An integration of the macro and micro approaches. *Journal of Management Studies*, 1981, *18*, 191–218.

Nash, A. N. & Carroll, S. J. *The management of compensation*. Monterey, California: Brooks/Cole Publishing Co., 1975.

Nemiroff, P. M. & Ford, D. L. Task effectiveness and human fulfillment in organizations: A review and development of a conceptual contingency model, *Academy of Management Review*, 1976, *1*, 69–82. (a)

Nemiroff, P. M. & Ford, D. L. A contingency approach to human fulfillment in organizations: A limited test of a conceptual model. *Organization and Administrative Sciences*, 1976, *7*, 101–123. (b)

Oldham, G. & Hackman, J. Work design in the organizational context. In B. M. Staw & L. L. Cummings (eds.), *Research in organizational behavior*, (Vol. 2), Greenwich, Conn.: Jai Press, Inc., 1980.

Oldham, G., Hackman, J., & Pearce, J. Conditions under which employees respond positively to enriched work. *Journal of Applied Psychology*, 1976, *61*, 395–403.

Oldham, G. R. & Miller, H. E. The effect of significant other's job complexity on employee reactions to work. *Human Relations*, 1979, *32*, 247–260.

O'Reilly, C. Personality-job fit: Implications for individual attitudes and performance. *Organizational Behavior and Human Performance*, 1977, *18*, 36–46.

O'Reilly, C. A. & Caldwell, D. F. Informational influence as a determinant of perceived task characteristics and job satisfaction. *Journal of Applied Psychology*, 1979, *64*, 157–65.

O'Reilly, C., Parlette, G., & Bloom, J. Perceptual measures of task characteristics: The biasing effects of differing frames of reference and job attitudes. *Academy of Management Journal*, 1980, *23*, 118–31.

Orpen, C. The effects of job enrichment on employee satisfaction, motivation, involvement, and performance: A field experiment. *Human Relations*, 1979, *32*, 189–217.

Osborn, R. N. & Hunt, J. G. Environment and organizational effectiveness, *Administrative Science Quarterly*, 1974, *19*, 231–46.

Paul, Jr., W. J., Robertson, K. B., & Herzberg, F. Job enrichment pays off. *Harvard Business Review*, 1969, March-April, 61–78.

Perrow, C. A framework for the comparative analysis of organizations, *American Sociological Review*, 1967, *32*, 194–208.

Pierce, J. L. Technology and job design: An exploratory examination of employee absenteeism, performance and work satisfaction. Working paper, University of Minnesota-Duluth, 1979.

Pierce, J. & Dunham, R. Task design: A literature review. *Academy of Management Review*, 1976, *1*, 83–97.

Pierce, J. L. & Dunham, R. B. The measurement of perceived job characteristics: The Job Diagnostic Survey versus the Job Characteristics Inventory. *Academy of Management Journal*, 1978, *21*, 123–28. (a)

Pierce, J. L. & Dunham, R. B. An empirical demonstration of the convergence of common macro- and micro-organization measures. *Academy of Management Journal*, 1978, *21*, 410–18. (b)

Pierce, J. L., Dunham, R. B., & Blackburn, R. S. Social systems structure, job design, and growth need strength: A test of a congruency model, *Academy of Management Journal*, 1979, *22*, 223–40.

Porter, L. W. & Lawler, E. E., III. *Managerial attitudes and behavior*. Homewood, Ill.: Richard D. Irwin, Inc., 1968.

Porter, L. W., Lawler, E. E., III, & Hackman, J. R. *Behavior in organizations*. New York: McGraw-Hill Book Company, 1975.

Porter, L. W., Steers, R. M., Mowday, R. T. & Boulian, P. V. Organizational commitment, job satisfaction, and turnover among psychiatric technicians. *Journal of Applied Psychology*, 1974, *69*, 603–609.

Productivity—an elusive essential. *Chicago Tribune*, Sept. 16, 1979, p. 18.

Quick, J. C. & Griffin, R. W. Situational determinants of goal setting behavior and evaluation: Task variability. Paper presented at the annual meeting of the Southwest Division of the Academy of Management, San Antonio, 1980.

Read, W. H. Upward communication in industrial hierarchies. *Human Relations*, 1962, *15*, 3–15.

Rice, A. K. *Productivity and social organization: The Ahmedabad experiment*. London: Tavistock, 1958.

Robey, D. Task design, work values, and worker response: An experimental test. *Organizational Behavior and Human Performance*, 1974, *12*, 264–273.

Roethlisberger, F. G. & Dickson, W. J. *Management and the worker*. Cambridge, Mass.: Harvard University Press, 1939.

Rousseau, D. M. Technological differences in job characteristics, employee satisfaction, and motivation: A synthesis of job design research and sociotechnical systems theory. *Organizational Behavior and Human Performance*, 1977, *19*, 18–42.

Salancik, G. & Pfeffer, J. An examination of need-satisfaction models of job attitudes. *Administrative Science Quarterly*, 1977, *22*, 427–56.

Salancik, G. & Pfeffer, J. A social information processing approach to job attitudes and task design. *Administrative Science Quarterly*, 1978, *23*, 224–53.

Schein, V. E., Maurer, E. H., & Novak, J. F. Impact of flexible working hours on productivity. *Journal of Applied Psychology*, 1977, *62*, 463–65.

Schrank, R. On ending worker alienation: The Gaines pet food plant. In R. P. Fairfield (ed.) *Humanizing the Workplace*. Buffalo, New York: Prometheus Books, 1974.

Schriesheim, C. A. & Kerr, S. Theories and measures of leadership: A critical appraisal of current and future directions. In J. G. Hunt and L. L. Larson (eds.), *Leadership: The cutting edge*. Carbondale, Ill.: Southern Illinois University Press, 1977.

Schuler, R. S. Role conflict and ambiguity as a function of the task-structure-technology interaction. *Organizational Behavior and Human Performance*, 1977, *20*, 60–74.

Schwab, D. P. & Cummings, L. L. A theoretical analysis of the impact of task scope on employee performance. *Academy of Management Review*, 1976, *1*, 23–35.

Scott, W. E. Activation theory and task design. *Organizational Behavior and Human Performance*, 1966, *1*, 3–30.

Shaw, M. E. *Group dynamics* (2nd ed.). New York: McGraw-Hill,1976.

Sims, H. P. & Szilagyi, A. D. Job characteristic relationships: Individual and structural moderators. *Organizational Behavior and Human Performance*, 1976, *17*, 211–30.

Sims, H. P., Szilagyi, A. D., & Keller, R. T. The measurement of job characteristics. *Academy of Management Journal*, 1976, *19*, 195–212.

Skinner, W. The impact of changing technology in the working environment. In C. Kerr and J. M. Rosow (eds.), *Work in America: The decade ahead*. New York: Van Nostrand Reinhold Company, 1979.

Slocum, Jr., J. W. & Sims, Jr., H. P. A typology for integrating technology, organization and job design, *Human Relations*, 1980, *33*, 193–211.

Smith, A. *An inquiry into the nature and causes of the wealth of nations*. New York: Modern Library, 1937. Originally published in 1776.

Smith, G. L. *Work Measurement*. Columbus, Ohio: Grid, 1978.

Starbuck, W. H. Organizational growth and development. In J. G. March (ed.) *Handbook of organizations*. New York: Rand-McNally, 1965.

Steers, R. M. Problems in the measurement of organizational effectiveness. *Administrative Science Quarterly*, 1975, *20*, 546–58.

Steers, R. M. Antecedents and outcomes of organizational commitment, *Administrative Science Quarterly*, 1977, *22*, 46–56. (a)

Steers, R. M. *Organizational effectiveness*. Santa Monica, California: Goodyear Publishing Company, 1977. (b)

Steers, R. & Spencer, D. The role of achievement motivation in job design. *Journal of Applied Psychology*, 1977, *62*, 472–79.

Stogdill, R. *Handbook of leadership*. New York: The Free Press, 1974.

Stogdill, R. M. & Coons, A. E. (eds.). *Leader behavior and its description and measurement.* Columbus, Ohio: Bureau of Business Research, Ohio State University, 1957.

Stone, E. F. Job scope, job satisfaction, and the Protestant ethic: A study of enlisted men in the U.S. Navy. *Journal of Vocational Behavior*, 1975, *7*, 215–24.

Stone, E. F. The moderating effect of work-related values on the job scope-job satisfaction relationship. *Organizational Behavior and Human Performance*, 1976, *15*, 145–67.

Stone, E. F., Mowday, R. T., & Porter, L. W. Higher-order need strengths as moderators of the job scope-job satisfaction relationship. *Journal of Applied Psychology*, 1977, *62*, 466–71.

Svetlik, B., Prien, E. & Barrett, G. Relationships between job difficulty, employee's attitude toward his job, and supervisory ratings of employee effectiveness. *Journal of Applied Psychology*, 1964, *48*, 320–24.

Szilagyi, A. D. & Wallace, M. J. *Organizational behavior and performance*, (2nd ed.). Santa Monica, California: Goodyear Publishing Co., 1980.

Taylor, Frederick W. *The principles of scientific managment*, New York: Harper and Row, 1911.

Thompson, J. D. *Organizations in action.* New York: McGraw-Hill Book Company, 1967.

Thorsrud, E. From ship deck to shop floor, *Scandinavian Review*, 1977, *2*, 21–26.

Trist, E. L. & Bamforth, K. W. Some social and psychological consequences of the long-wall method of coal-getting. *Human Relations*, 1951, *4*, 3–38.

Turner, A. N. & Lawrence, P. R. *Industrial jobs and the worker.* Boston: Harvard Graduate School of Business Administration, 1965.

Umstot, D. D., Bell, Jr., C. H., & Mitchell, T. R. Effects of job enrichment and task goals on satisfaction and productivity: Implications for job design. *Journal of Applied Psychology*, 1976, *61*, 379–94.

Van de Ven, A. H. & Delbecq, A. L. A task contingent model of work unit structure. *Administrative Science Quarterly*, 1974, *19*, 183–97.

Van Fleet, D. D. & Bedeian, A. G. A history of the span of management. *Academy of Management Review*, 1977, *2*, 356–72.

Vroom, V. H. *Work and motivation.* New York: John Wiley & Sons, Inc., 1964.

Walker, C. R. The problem of the repetitive job. *Harvard Business Review*, 1950, *28*, 54–58.

Walker, C. R. & Guest, R. *The man on the assembly line.* Cambridge, Mass.: Harvard University Press, 1952.

Walsh, E. Garbage collecting: Stigmatized work and self-esteem. In R. P. Fairfield (ed.), *Humanizing the workplace.* Buffalo, N.Y.: Prometheus Books, 1974.

Walton, R. E. How to counter alienation in the plant. *Harvard Business Review*, 1972, *50*, 70–81.

Walton, R. E. Improving the quality of work life. *Harvard Business Review*, 1974, *52*, 12ff. Reprinted by permission of the Harvard Business Review. Excerpt from "Improving the quality of work life" by Richard E. Walton (May–June 1974). Copyright © 1974 by the President and Fellows of Harvard College; all rights reserved.

Walton, R. E. The diffusion of new work structures: Explaining why success didn't take. *Organizational Dynamics*, 1975, *3*, 3–32.

Walton, R. E. The Topeka story: Teaching an old dog food new tricks. *The Wharton Magazine*, 1978, Spring, 38–46.

Wanous, J. Individual differences and reactions to job characteristics. *Journal of Applied Psychology*, 1974, *59*, 616–22.

Weed, E. D. Job enrichment "cleans up" at Texas Instruments. In J. R. Maher (ed.), *New perspectives in job enrichment.* New York: Van Nostrand Reinhold Company, 1971.

Weick, K. *The social psychology of organizing.* Reading, Mass.: Addison-Wesley Publishing Co., 1969.

235

Weick, K. E. Enactment processes in organizations. In B. M. Staw and G. R. Salancik (eds.), *New directions in organizational behavior*. Chicago: St. Clair Press, 1977.

Weiss, H. M. & Shaw, J. B. Social influences on judgements about tasks. *Organizational Behavior and Human Performance*, 1979, *24*, 126–40.

White, J. K. Individual differences and the job quality-worker response relationship: Review, integration, and comments. *Academy of Management Review,* 1978, *3*, 267–80.

White, S. E. & Mitchell, T. R. Job enrichment versus social cues: A comparison and competitive test. *Journal of Applied Psychology*, 1979, *64*, 1–9.

Whyte, W. F. *Money and motivation*. New York: Harper and Brothers, 1955.

Wiest, J. D. & Levy, F. K. *A management guide to PERT/CPM*. Englewood Cliffs, N.J.: Prentice-Hall, 1977.

Winpisinger, W. W. Job enrichment: A union view. *Monthly Labor Review*, 1973, April, 54–56.

Woodward, J. *Management and technology*. London: Her Majesty's Stationary Office, 1958.

Woodward, J. *Industrial organization: Theory and practice*. London: Oxford University Press, 1965.

Work in America. Cambridge, Mass.: The MIT Press, 1973.

Wren, D. A. *The evolution of management thought*. New York: John Wiley & Sons, 1979.

NAME INDEX

SUBJECT INDEX

Continuous process, 106–107, 117–121, 148, 212
Definition of, 102
Exceptional cases, number of, 110–112, 117–121, 212
Future, 121–122
Intensive, 108–109, 117–121, 212
Knowledge, 110, 117–121, 212
Long-linked, 107–109, 117–121, 212
Mass production, 106–107, 117–121, 148, 212
Materials, 110, 117–121, 212
Mediating, 107–109, 117–121, 212
Operations, 110, 117–121, 212
Search process, 110–112, 117–121, 212
Small batch, 106–107, 117–121, 148, 212
Task interdependence, 108–109, 112–114, 117–121; Pooled, 108–109; Reciprocal, 108–109; Sequential, 108–109; Task uncertainty, 112–114, 117–121; Workflow uncertainty, 112–114, 117–121
Texas Instruments, 7, 32
Time study, 94
Topeka (see General Foods)
Turnover, 7–8, 39–41, 46, 49, 192–198, 201–203, 208–212
Two-factor theory, 27–31, 50, 205–206

Unions, 8–9, 33, 174, 201, 206, 218–219

Volvo, 46, 192–194, 198

Work effectiveness (see Performance)
Work measurement, 94–98, 219
Work redesign (see Task redesign)
Work sampling, 94–95

Yale Job Inventory, 66–69, 79